A Chance for Change

THE JOHN HOPE FRANKLIN SERIES IN AFRICAN AMERICAN
HISTORY AND CULTURE

Waldo E. Martin Jr. and Patricia Sullivan, *editors*

CRYSTAL R. SANDERS

A Chance for Change

Head Start and Mississippi's Black
Freedom Struggle

The University of North Carolina Press *Chapel Hill*

This book was published with the assistance of the John Hope Franklin Fund of the University of North Carolina Press.

Set in Arno by Westchester Publishing Services
Manufactured in the United States of America

The paper in this book meets the guidelines for permanence
and durability of the Committee on Production Guidelines for
Book Longevity of the Council on Library Resources.

The University of North Carolina Press has been a member of the
Green Press Initiative since 2003.

Cover illustrations: "Two Girls on a Swing facing Mileston (Mississippi)
Head Start Center" and "Ms. Winson Hudson, of the Harmony Community
Head Start Center, leading three youth down a dirt path, on a nature hike,"
© 1968, 2015 by Bob Fletcher

Library of Congress Cataloging-in-Publication Data
Sanders, Crystal R., author.
A chance for change : Head Start and Mississippi's Black freedom struggle /
Crystal R. Sanders.
pages cm — (The John Hope Franklin series in African American history
and culture)
Includes bibliographical references and index.
ISBN 978-1-4696-2780-9 (pbk : alk. paper)—ISBN 978-1-4696-2781-6 (ebook)
1. African Americans—Social conditions—1964–1975. 2. African American
women—Mississippi—Social conditions. 3. African American teachers
and the community—Mississippi. 4. African Americans—Civil rights—
Mississippi—History—20th century. 5. Child Development Group of
Mississippi—History. 6. Head Start programs—Mississippi. I. Title.
II. Series: John Hope Franklin series in African American history and culture.
E185.86.S257 2016
323.1196'0730762—dc23
2015028001

To my parents, Velvaline and Nathaniel L. Sanders, Jr.

Contents

Illustrations

Acknowledgments

When the Reverend Doctor Martin Luther King Jr. accepted the Nobel Peace Prize in 1964, he remarked, "Every time I take a flight, I am always mindful of the many people who make a successful journey possible—the known pilots and the unknown ground crew." This book came to fruition because of a host of people and institutions who invested in my well-being through their time, talent, and treasure. I am indebted to everyone mentioned below—my known pilots and unknown ground crew—and I do not take your unwavering support of me lightly. Thank you!

First, I would be remiss if I did not acknowledge the individuals who shared their stories and experiences with me. Thank you for returning my phone calls and inviting me into your homes. We talked for hours, laughing and crying, reminiscing about the most radical Head Start program in the nation. We became friends in the process. I am thankful for every interview, every piece of memorabilia shared, and every friendship cultivated. A few people I must call by name are Polly Greenberg, Marilyn Lowen, Marvin Hoffman, John Mudd, Lucia Clapps Mudd, Paul Murray, Doris Derby, Lillie Ayers, Alice Giles, and Mable Giles Whitaker. Many of my interviewees passed away before I completed the project. My sincere hope is that I have done justice to the Child Development Group of Mississippi story.

I am also grateful to the institutions that provided financial support, including Northwestern University, the Ford Foundation, the Spencer Foundation, and the American Academy of Arts and Sciences. Pennsylvania State University provided funding and support in myriad ways. I am especially indebted to Bill Blair and the George and Ann Richards Civil War Era Center and Lovalerie King and the Africana Research Center. My colleagues in the Departments of History and African American Studies never hesitated to offer an encouraging word and smile. In particular, I thank Nan Woodruff and Lori Ginzberg for their close reading of the manuscript. Michael Kulikowski and Dan Letwin also provided unparalleled support.

I have had the good fortune of being mentored by first-rate scholars. Without their mentorship and training, I could not have crossed the finish line. Thank you from the bottom of my heart: Nancy MacLean, Martha

Biondi, Darlene Clark Hine, Charles Payne, Ray Gavins, Peter Wood, Katherine Charron, David Cecelski, Dylan Penningroth, Felecia Kornbluh, Annelise Orleck, and John Dittmer. Thank you for reading drafts of my work and pushing me to be a better historian.

Historians are only able to do what we do because of archivists. I am indebted to the archivists who mailed me documents I realized I needed *after* completing an archival visit, who fulfilled my numerous photocopy requests, and who pointed me in the direction of collections I needed to be aware of. In particular, I owe a debt to Joellen ElBashir of the Moorland-Spingarn Research Center at Howard University; Lisa Jacobson of the Presbyterian Historical Society; Jennifer Ford of the University of Mississippi Archives and Special Collections; Mattie Sink Abraham of the Mississippi State University Special Collections; and Minnie Watson of the Tougaloo College Archives.

A larger community of friends and scholars made the project a labor of love. Thank you for reading drafts, sharing meals, and cheering me on: Nickie Burney, Martina Bryant, Kellie Carter-Jackson, Brandon Dorsey, Jessie Dunbar, Mary Maples Dunn, Reginald Ellis, Brett Gadsden, Reena Goldthree, Cynthia Greenlee, Dominic Harris, Ade Hassan, Brandi Hinnant-Crawford, Marva Hinton Gibson, Jason Morgan Ward, Cynthia Pierre, Michelle Purdy, Leah Wright Riguer, Carmen Scott, LaKisha Simmons, Patricia Meyer Spacks, William Sturkey, Elizabeth Todd-Breland, and Debbie Wahl.

Finally, I must thank my family for their love, encouragement, and support. My first history lessons came from my elders who kept alive our family stories of faith, perseverance, and education. I will forever be thankful for the love, support, and precepts of my late grandparents, Jesse and Victoria Shepherd and Nathaniel and Ida Sanders. Thinking of extended family, I give special thanks to my uncle and aunt, Bill Lawson and Renee Sanders-Lawson, who showed early interest in the project and cheered me on. My sister, Natalie Sanders, read and edited several drafts and believed in me when I doubted myself. Last, but certainly not least, I thank my parents, Nathaniel L. Sanders Jr. and Velvaline Sanders, who have been by my side my entire life. Thank you for the prayers and limitless support in varied forms. You two made conferences and archival trips more enjoyable. You helped me get to the finish line. This book is dedicated to you both.

Abbreviations and Acronyms Used in the Text

ACBC   Associated Communities of Bolivar County
ACSC   Associated Communities of Sunflower County
ASCS   Agricultural Stabilization and Conservation Service
CCAP   Citizens Crusade Against Poverty
CDGM   Child Development Group of Mississippi
CIC   Catholic Interracial Council
COFO   Council of Federated Organizations
CORE   Congress of Racial Equality
FBI   Federal Bureau of Investigation
FCM   Friends of the Children of Mississippi
MAEP   Mississippi Adequate Education Program
MAP   Mississippi Action for Progress
NAACP   National Association for the Advancement of Colored People
OEO   Office of Economic Opportunity
SCI   Sunflower County Progress Incorporated
SCLC   Southern Christian Leadership Conference
SNCC   Student Nonviolent Coordinating Committee

A Chance for Change

Introduction

Taking Rights

The sixty-eight Mississippi Freedom Democratic Party delegates who made the long bus ride home from Atlantic City, New Jersey, to Mississippi after the 1964 Democratic National Convention had every reason to be tired, frustrated, and weary of community organizing. The interracial group, despite the justness of their cause, had come up short in their effort to unseat Mississippi's segregationist Democratic Party delegation at the convention. Yet, many of the activists returned to the Magnolia State and continued their earlier civil rights work. Fannie Lou Hamer, a former sharecropper and Mississippi Freedom Democratic Party delegate, declared, "We have to build our own power. The question for black people is not, when is the white man going to give us our rights, or when he is going to give us good education for our children. We have to take [rights] for ourselves."[1]

African Americans in Mississippi understood that their long quest for full freedom was far from over. President Lyndon Johnson had signed into law the 1964 Civil Rights Act weeks before the Democratic National Convention, but enforcement was a different matter. For example, segregationists in Mississippi closed facilities rather than comply with the ban on racial discrimination in public accommodations. After President Johnson signed the Voting Rights Act of 1965, over a year passed before federal voter registrars arrived in Hamer's Sunflower County, an area with one of the worst records of black disfranchisement.[2] For Mississippi's black residents, full freedom included enforcement of civil rights legislation, the chance to earn a decent wage, the opportunity to participate in community governance, and access to quality education.[3]

This book examines the Child Development Group of Mississippi's (CDGM) Head Start program in order to explore exactly how black Mississippians followed Hamer's lead and took rights for themselves in pursuit of full freedom after 1964. Individuals such as Unita Blackwell, Mary Lane, and Robert Miles, who had joined Hamer as Mississippi Freedom Democratic Party delegates at the 1964 Democratic National Convention, cast their lot with the preschool program. These activists, many of them sharecroppers and domestics, possessed a sophisticated understanding of the limitations of civil rights legislation and sought to address the shortcomings through the federally sponsored Head Start program. They translated a grassroots educational endeavor into an opportunity to better themselves, their communities, and their children's futures.

Head Start was a component of President Johnson's War on Poverty authorized by the Economic Opportunity Act of 1964 and administered by the Office of Economic Opportunity (OEO). OEO aimed to provide poor Americans with the skills, training, and political power to help ameliorate their poverty. The Economic Opportunity Act contained seven titles that expanded opportunity for the nation's poorest citizens. Funded programs included Job Corps, work-study, and Volunteers in Service to America. Title II of the Economic Opportunity Act created the Community Action Program to be operated with the "maximum feasible participation" of the poor. Including the poor in the administration of programs established for their benefit upset the status quo where "institutions did things *to* the poor rather than *with* the poor."[4] The Community Action Program proved to be the most controversial title of the Economic Opportunity Act because it allowed OEO to bypass local governments and fund nonprofit agencies. This meant that in some parts of the South, the federal government worked directly with African Americans without local white oversight.[5]

OEO created Head Start as a Community Action Program whose purpose was to improve the lives of economically disadvantaged children and their families. The early childhood initiative was not a part of the original Economic Opportunity Act. OEO officials, searching for a highly visible program that would lead Congress to refund the antipoverty effort, added it in 1965 after learning that 50 percent of all the poor in the United States were children. The program offered young children from low-income families educational and developmental services to prepare them for school. While conceived in early 1965 as an eight-week summer program to prepare disadvantaged youth for the first grade, Head Start became a year-round program that fall. As a Community Action Program rather than merely an early childhood education intervention, Head Start provided opportunities for parents and other members of poor communities to create institutional change at the local level through their "maximum feasible participation" in Head Start employment and decision making. Black parents in Mississippi wielded authority in the education of their children, an opportunity denied to them in the public school system that was under white supervision. Moreover, Head Start gave these citizens the financial freedom to send their children to the best schools without the threat of job termination and the authority to refuse to enter into food contracts with racist merchants. To make clear the program's twofold mission, an official OEO publication stated that Head Start was "not a kindergarten, but a 'communigarten.'"[6] Many OEO employees, politicians, and private citizens, however, debated the merits of combining community action with preschool education and questioned whether social revolution would take precedence over early childhood education.[7]

Working-class black Mississippians, taking the position that they had no permanent allies or enemies, only permanent interests, championed the CDGM "communigarten" program as an important educational, political, and employment opportunity. For them, early childhood education was social revolution. Their state had no public kindergartens, and well-paying jobs were hard to come by for African Americans. Despite holding population majorities in several towns, they found themselves at the mercy of elected officials, who benefited from their poverty and disfranchisement. In supporting the federal program, local black people broke ranks with some of the Student Nonviolent Coordinating Committee's (SNCC) most prominent members, who had organized in Mississippi for several years prior. According to SNCC field secretary Charles Cobb, many civil rights organizations "dissolved" their alliance with the Democratic Party after the 1964 Democratic National Convention because the party had turned a blind eye to the widespread racialized voter registration irregularities in the South.[8] Stokely Carmichael, another SNCC official, called for independent black political power after Atlantic City.[9] Yet, grassroots people with long histories of challenging white supremacy through SNCC and the National Association for the Advancement of Colored People (NAACP) backed a program sponsored by a Democratic administration and became some of CDGM's most ardent supporters. Local NAACP leaders Amzie Moore and Winson Hudson played significant roles in CDGM's program, as did Victoria Jackson Gray and Mary Lane, individuals who had been active in SNCC's earlier voting rights campaign. These activists took a different post-1964 path from Carmichael by partnering with OEO officials and liberal whites with movement ties. They secured $15 million in federal assistance and provided early childhood education, health screenings, and nutritious meals to more than 6,000 black children over a three-year period. Unlike nonnative SNCC workers, local people could not easily leave the state, because of family ties and work obligations. CDGM became their best option and a path for survival.

Black women greatly outnumbered black men in program personnel throughout CDGM's existence, although men held top administrative and board positions. The women's presence and the authority they wielded as center directors, teachers, cooks, and secretaries was especially important since Labor Department employee Daniel Patrick Moynihan called into question the value of black women's leadership at the very time that CDGM got off the ground.[10] Head Start programs nationwide became a vehicle for women-led activism, although it is not clear that OEO officials anticipated or supported such activism. Official documents refer only to the gender-neutral word "parent" when discussing parental involvement in the pre-school program.[11] One thing that is certain is that Head Start attracted large numbers of women in part because normative gender roles prescribed child-rearing and teaching as women's work. With respect to CDGM, more black women than men readily saw the program as an extension of their earlier civil rights work. Just as they had canvassed more than men, showed up more often at mass meetings, and more frequently attempted to register to vote, black women in Mississippi took to early childhood education in larger numbers than men, as a way to further movement goals.[12]

Head Start in its initial years did not require teachers to have formal licenses, dismissing the idea that only credentialed educators had something to offer children.[13] While CDGM women might not have had high school diplomas, they did have histories of acting in the face of fear and discouragement. They imparted this militancy to their impressionable pupils. Head Start jobs provided over 2,000 working-class black women in Mississippi with higher wages than other employment options while insulating them from white economic reprisals. For example, Lillie Ayers, a Head Start teacher in Glen Allan, became her family's main breadwinner after civil rights work cost her husband his job. Even women who did not teach found CDGM to be a financial resource. Roxie Meredith worked as a cafeteria worker in a CDGM center. She had lost her public school cafeteria job in 1962 after her son James desegregated the University of Mississippi.[14]

The tactical turn to education at the grassroots suggests that black women's commitment to the freedom struggle was about much more than securing the ballot or having their children enrolled in a white school. They perceived Head Start, with its access to social services and its stated commitment to their maximum participation, as the logical way to continue their struggle for political and socioeconomic justice. Whether making personnel decisions on a local CDGM committee or negotiating food vendor contracts with white merchants, women were empowered by the Head Start program to take rights for themselves and address Mississippi's intertwined racial and economic problems.

The opportunity to offer black children quality early childhood education also attracted many women. Since slavery, African Americans had championed education as a path to advancement and considered it a central part of their freedom struggle. During Reconstruction, black Mississippians created one of the most radical public systems of education in the nation. While Virginia, Tennessee, and Georgia mandated segregated public schools from the outset, Mississippi did not erect a color line in the 1870 state constitution that created a statewide public school system and guaranteed every student an education with "equal advantages" without regard to race. The absence of mandatory segregation, however, did not translate into equitable educational opportunities for black students. Black schools faced inadequate funding, shorter academic terms, no bus transportation, and white hostility. After Democrats overthrew the Magnolia State's Republican government in a violent coup, they codified racial segregation in public education in 1878. From the 1870s until well into the post–World War II period, spending disparities existed between black and white education. Many areas did not even offer high school education for black students. African Americans remained powerless to address the inequity since they lacked access to the ballot box.[15]

Black women supported CDGM because the 1964 freedom schools had shown them a new approach to teaching and learning that fostered racial pride and civic engagement. Curricula in black public schools usually neglected black history and discouraged intellectual curiosity. Textbooks stereotyped African Americans as "buffoons" or "faithful darkies."[16] During the 1964 summer, SNCC activists tackled the educational deficiencies through freedom schools that they offered to black children and adults.[17] The freedom schools celebrated black history and equipped students with the skills to be social-change agents in their communities. CDGM women intended to make the Head Start program another transformative educational experience.

Teachers in CDGM classrooms prepared black youngsters to live in what they hoped was a post-segregated society. The limits of freedom for African Americans had been defined since emancipation. Generation after generation of black Mississippians learned from their elders how to respect the laws and customs that governed race relations. Ignorance of or blatant disregard for Jim Crow etiquette could be downright fatal for African Americans in the segregated South. Civil rights activist and CDGM employee Unita Blackwell, born in 1933, recalled that she "learned how to 'act right' around white people" before she knew that fear governed her actions. Her parents taught her to address all white people—adults and children—with courtesy titles such as "ma'am" and "sir." She learned not to look a white person in the eye and to step on the grass if a white person walked toward her on the sidewalk.[18] The civil rights movement and the experiences individuals gained from participating in it upended these traditional social habits. CDGM readied black children to live in an equal and integrated society rather than teaching them to survive white supremacy.

Segregationists understood CDGM's revolutionary potential. After the grassroots Head Start program received a $1.5 million grant from OEO for the 1965 summer, but before a single preschool center opened its doors, many white political leaders in Mississippi opposed it. The editors of the largest circulating newspaper in the state released an editorial on Head Start that said, "on the face of this undertaking . . . it appears to be the most wholesome and humane." But, its editors warned, "here is one of the most subtle mediums for instilling the acceptance of racial integration and ultimate mongrelization ever perpetrated in this country."[19] The opposition was not always sensational; sometimes it was tangible and far-reaching. For example, not one school superintendent rented out public school buildings or school buses to CDGM.

CDGM's opponents worked to undercut a program that placed federal dollars and control of an educational enterprise directly into the hands of black activists, upsetting a tradition where federal largesse propped up white supremacy in the Magnolia State. For example, the New Deal's Agricultural Adjustment Act paid millions to white planters in Mississippi in a voluntary program of acreage reduction without ensuring that funds trickled down to black sharecroppers and tenant farmers.[20] CDGM disrupted the tradition of black exclusion from government money. United States Senator John Stennis (D-Miss.) led the charge to retain white domination of federal government assistance in Mississippi. Instead of race-baiting the program that threatened the undemocratic status quo, Stennis charged CDGM with fiscal mismanagement and corruption to weaken and ultimately end the program in 1968. He thus established a technique that is still in play today of undermining community organizations run by the poor with charges of incompetence or economic malfeasance.

The segregationist senator so badly wanted to wrest control from working-class black activists that he agreed to support Mississippi Action for Progress (MAP), a rival Head Start program affiliated with the NAACP—a largely middle-class organization increasingly viewed by pragmatic whites as a moderate alternative to other civil rights organizations in the state. This new, biracial Head Start program brought old-guard leadership from black and white communities together in an unprecedented manner and demonstrated just how deep the fissures had become in civil rights alliances after Atlantic City. Aaron Henry, president of the Mississippi State Conference of NAACP Branches, supported MAP rather than CDGM in part out of concern for his organization's declining state dominance.

The battle over Head Start in Mississippi demonstrates the complexity of civil rights organizations' constituencies. Many CDGM women had been loyal members and even officers in their local NAACP chapters. Several of these women had housed SNCC workers. Their loyalty to CDGM, an organization that developed a new black leadership, put them at odds with both those SNCC workers who were suspicious of the federal program and with Aaron Henry who was concerned about the vitality of the state NAACP. Intra-racial and intra-organizational tensions surrounding Head Start suggest that local people were not wedded to a particular organization's priorities. They moved fluidly between organizations and opportunities to meet their community's goals.[21]

Finally, CDGM's story illuminates the achievements and limitations of the War on Poverty. For far too long, critics on both the left and the right have assailed the antipoverty effort either for doing too little or for fostering dependency.[22] These assessments fail to consider how the War on Poverty played out on the ground in an area with abject poverty and deplorable race relations. Through CDGM, southern black women restructured civic life under the banner of preschool education. By giving black sharecroppers the opportunity to allocate multimillion dollar grants and vote on the locations of Head Start centers, OEO ushered in a redistribution of power. Moreover, CDGM developed a new cadre of independent black leaders and helped to increase the state's black middle class. CDGM's successes fueled its demise. The grassroots Head Start program attempted to eradicate both the poverty of want and the sin of white supremacy. White supremacists used their political influence to fight back. OEO officials in Washington, D.C., buckling under the pressure from powerful political interests, withdrew their support. Thus, the commitment of antipoverty warriors wavered in the face of political pressure, while those who stood to lose from an empowered black working class remained steadfast in their opposition. White supremacy had, once again, "remodeled itself to meet any challenge."[23] This book's bottom-up view of the War on Poverty in a southern locale joins other recent scholarship that has recognized the transformative aspects of antipoverty programs.[24]

Many former SNCC activists and perhaps a few civil rights historians will be surprised that this book considers a federally funded Head Start program an integral part of the Mississippi freedom struggle. Careful not to confuse a change in tactics with the disappearance of activism, this work demonstrates that rather than claim premature victory with work left undone, African Americans in the Magnolia State moved from protest to program.[25] First-class citizenship remained elusive despite direct action campaigns, voter registration operations, and the legislation that these organizing activities produced. Thus, black Mississippians championed a federal anti-poverty Head Start program in order to achieve full freedom, including the financial ability to eat at the lunch counter; the chance to vote without the threat of job termination; and the opportunity to secure quality education for one's children without physical or financial reprisal. In doing so, these resourceful individuals created one of the most impressive examples of participatory democracy in the country.

For certain, there were limitations to seeking full freedom through Head Start. Both a federal agency that was not completely committed to institutional change and a local white power structure that stood to lose from an empowered and engaged black polity did in fact limit CDGM's reach. Black Mississippians understood very well the challenges of government-funded social change. Yet, these local people perceived the chance of securing full freedom to be worth the risk of betrayal and disappointment. Working within the establishment rather than completely outside of it, they balanced principle with political realities and brought about some meaningful changes in their everyday lives.

The following pages detail how working-class black Mississippians sought full freedom for themselves through a Head Start program after the civil rights movement's peak. Black women are at the center of this story, although, as evidenced in several chapters their voices were often muted during CDGM's many funding battles. Their absence from key political fights highlights the gendered aspects of negotiations and demonstrates the complexity of antipoverty initiatives that were simultaneously bottom-up, top-down, and lateral. Events and individuals in locations near and far from the Mississippi towns where the women worked had a profound influence on their CDGM experiences.

A Chance for Change begins with an overview of black Mississippians' long quest for education. Since the antebellum period, African Americans in the state sought education as a way to secure their freedom. Chapter 1 shows that long before CDGM's establishment black Mississippians championed, financed, and mobilized for their schooling. The Head Start program was simply the next educational battle.

Chapter 2 details exactly how black Mississippians took rights and education for themselves as they leveraged Head Start curriculum and employment as an opportunity to change their communities from the ground up. Many black civil rights activists in the state partnered with northern white liberals and OEO officials to exploit the possibilities of War on Poverty programs and fight state racism. Their efforts challenge the argument that antipoverty programs co-opted movement activism.

Chapter 3 considers how CDGM provided working-class black women with unprecedented leadership and educational opportunities. These women seized the normative female role of child caretaker as their mantle to become educators who used the classroom to instill pride in youngsters and model courage to parents. Their newfound occupation not only provided educational opportunities and higher incomes but also elevated their status to that of "activist mothers," a designation conferred on women who engaged in community work on behalf of their children and families.[26]

Chapter 4 maintains that Mississippi's white political establishment developed interest in the antipoverty program as CDGM's transformative potential became more apparent. Alarmed by the greater financial independence and self-determination that CDGM provided black Mississippians, segregationists worked to end the program. When their attempts to defund CDGM failed, these civil rights opponents worked to take control of antipoverty funds by setting up rival programs.

Chapter 5 chronicles how segregationists' political pressure led OEO to back away from CDGM and instead support one such competing group, MAP. In funding the rival Head Start program, OEO preserved both preschool education in the Magnolia State and key congressional support for the entire War on Poverty. The chapter also considers working-class black

Mississippians' response to MAP. CDGM parents and staff refused to accept the new program as their only option for Head Start and chose to run their own centers on a voluntary basis. They also mobilized supporters nationwide to pressure OEO to re-fund their program.

CDGM demonstrated the links between education and full freedom. Today, access to quality education continues to be a challenge in Mississippi as the state consistently ranks last in national educational rankings. This book demonstrates that the fight for education is a long one and that all community members have a role to play in the education of succeeding generations.

CHAPTER ONE

Reading Is Power

Sometimes we don't have any bread for a whole week, but I mean to educate my children if I have to work my hands off.
—Mississippi freedman, 1869

The overall theme of the school would be the student as a force for social change in their own state [Mississippi].
—Charles E. Cobb Jr., 1963 Prospectus for a Summer Freedom School Program

Education has always been political in Mississippi. Access to it, or rather the lack thereof, undergirded the state's racial caste system from the antebellum era until well into the twentieth century and provided white planters with an endless supply of cheap black labor for cotton production. Both slave masters and the enslaved recognized literacy as a key to humanness, a larger world, and freedom itself. An 1823 Mississippi statute stipulated that any slaves, free black people, or mulattoes found to be assembling for the purpose of teaching slaves to read or write should receive corporal punishment "not exceeding thirty-nine lashes." Some enslaved people learned to read secretly despite the barriers white slave owners implemented to limit black literacy.[1]

Black Mississippians' enthusiasm for education intensified with the outbreak of the Civil War. Even before a Freedmen's Bureau existed, African Americans tried to shape their own destinies by using their meager resources to set up schools. In some parts of Mississippi, the formerly enslaved acquired Bibles or primers and transformed parts of the "big house" into classrooms with semiliterate teachers.[2] After the war, Freedmen's Bureau agents reported that "colored men have paid their own money to prepare and furnish a room for a school."[3] Such initiative demonstrated the priority freed people placed on education and their desire to control their own schools.

African American state legislators during Reconstruction understood firsthand the links between education, freedom, and citizenship. The ability to read and write offered African Americans some measure of protection from exploitative labor contracts and created greater distance from their enslaved past. Southern black politicians led the charge to institutionalize universal public education. By 1870, every state in the former Confederacy had a constitution that made provision for a state-funded public school system.[4] Mississippi's 1870 school law called for tax-supported public schools with "equal advantages" for all children. The lack of a provision explicitly mandating racially separate schools differentiated Mississippi from other southern states such as Virginia. While the Magnolia State's school law did not mandate racially separate schools, very few mixed race schools opened. Black parents focused not on the idea of their children sitting in classrooms with white students, but rather on their children's right to an equal education.[5]

Black Mississippians seeking educational opportunities faced white resistance. In Chickasaw County, arson destroyed two black schools in the spring of 1871. Around the same time, in Lowndes County Klansmen intimidated black and white teachers working in black schools and vandalized such schools in Holmes County. One of the most flagrant offenses occurred in Winston County, where a group of white men visited the home of a black teacher to demand that he leave town. The teacher was not home, so the men whipped his female roommate, who died the next day from her injuries.[6] Opposition also manifested itself in nonviolent forms, such as underfunding. White taxpayers begrudged having to support black education, believing that black children belonged in cotton fields rather than in classrooms.[7]

Black education suffered even more when the former slaveholding class regained voting rights in 1875 and overturned the Republican state government that had authorized universal public schools. Democratic political leaders prevented black men from voting and regained power through fraud, intimidation, and violence. Mississippi's Republican governor requested federal troops to stop the lawlessness, but President Ulysses S. Grant refused to intervene. Unchecked violence and Democratic control spelled disaster for black schooling. Legislators in 1876 mandated that state and county funds could be used only for the salaries of teachers and county superintendents. They appropriated no money for the building of schoolhouses. Since emancipation, black churches had doubled as schools. Without public funding, the majority of black children continued to receive their lessons in places of worship that were poorly lit, outfitted with homemade benches, prone to winter drafts, and little conducive to academic purposes. Moreover, debates over whether white tax dollars should fund black schools at all became more common with each successive academic term. The Civil War had devastated Mississippi economically, so financing schools for white children was difficult. Providing similar accommodations for black children was out of the question.[8]

Reconstruction's end in 1877 not only removed federal troops from the South but also ushered in white supremacists' full-fledged assault on black rights, including education. In 1878, Democratic legislators reversed the 1870 statute that left the racial status of public schools up to local option and prohibited white and black children from learning in the same school. The Democratic legislature gave county superintendents the sole authority to evaluate teachers. These evaluations served as the basis for teacher salaries, allowing a superintendent to evaluate black teachers based on how much or how little the superintendent wanted to pay them rather than on their strengths and qualifications. White Mississippi public school teachers, taking cues from state lawmakers, banned their black counterparts from the Mississippi State Teachers Association.[9]

Gross inequity existed between white and black education. The 1890s student-to-faculty ratio in white schools in Bolivar County was 17:1 as compared to 43:1 in black schools. White teachers in the county received an average of fifty-two dollars monthly, while their black counterparts received twenty-eight dollars.[10] The differentials occurred in every region of the state.

Southern Democrats codified their undemocratic rule in 1890 and thus kept black parents from unseating elected officials who denied their children quality education. Lawmakers approved a new state constitution that mandated racial segregation in education and allowed for seemingly race-neutral voting requirements that were in fact designed to circumvent the Fifteenth Amendment and disfranchise black voters. The 1890 constitution required voter applicants to be able to read a section of the state constitution or to give a reasonable interpretation of a section read to them by a registrar. Since the state did not provide voter registrars with standards to ensure uniform examinations and since 60 percent of Mississippi's black population was illiterate, compared to 10 percent of the white population, the allegedly color-blind literacy test disqualified a large proportion of black applicants as intended. Moreover, the new constitution required citizens to pay a poll tax every year in order to vote. Other states soon followed Mississippi's lead and "legally" disfranchised black citizens, outlining in new state constitutions voter requirements that did not technically violate the Fifteenth Amendment.[11] The United States Supreme Court upheld these laws in *Plessy v. Ferguson* (1896), which sustained segregation, and *Williams v. Mississippi* (1898), which supported black disfranchisement.

Mississippi's 1890 constitution limited black political participation for the next seventy-five years. Even after black literacy rates improved, the understanding clause allowed registrars to subjectively fail black applicants.[12] Registrars ensured that even in black-majority counties, white voters, including illiterate ones, outnumbered black voters.[13] The 67 percent of eligible black voters registered in Mississippi in 1867 decreased to 6 percent in 1892.[14]

White antipathy to black education had economic as well as political roots. White supremacists sought to limit black educational opportunities to maintain a large supply of cheap black labor. After the Civil War, cotton remained king in the Magnolia State, and 400,000 landless African Americans entered a "free labor" system. To restrain black Mississippians' ability to do something other than work the land they had cultivated during slavery, the state's political leaders limited their access to education. James K. Vardaman, a Mississippi politician who served in the state house, the governor's mansion, and the United States Senate between 1890 and 1919, opposed funding black schools because, in his opinion, the effect of educating African Americans "is to spoil a good field hand and make an insolent cook."[15]

Vardaman coupled his hostility to black education with a commitment to improving white education. As governor, he unsuccessfully proposed tax segregation: black tax dollars for black schools and white tax dollars for white schools. He took aim at the planter aristocracy in Mississippi's black-majority counties, where state funds designated for black schools were diverted to their white counterparts. This arrangement gave white Mississippians in black-majority counties a funding advantage over white Mississippians in white-majority counties who did not have access to large amounts of black tax dollars to divert for white schools. Vardaman, a champion of poor white men and women, hoped to curb the tradition of white schools in black-majority counties being superior to white schools in white-majority counties. He believed that the status quo arrangement benefited the white ruling class.[16]

Remarkably, tax segregation would have benefited black education. Black Mississippians comprised 60 percent of the school population in 1899, but they received less than 20 percent of the state's school expenditures. Black Mississippians paid city, state, and poll taxes. Their children would have fared better had black tax dollars been spent on black schools.[17] This pattern of racial discrimination in Mississippi public schools where politicians redirected public school funds for black children to use for the education of

A school building for black children in Camden, Mississippi (Madison County), in 1921. The 1896 United States Supreme Court ruling in *Plessy v. Ferguson* upheld racial segregation under the doctrine of "separate but equal." Facilities for black students were separate but never equal. (NAACP Visual Materials, Library of Congress, Prints and Photographs Division)

white children lasted well into the twentieth century. In 1915, Mississippi spent five times more per capita on its white students than it did on its black students. By 1943, the gap had widened, and the state spent eight times as much on white education.[18] Black disfranchisement ensured the continuity of funding disparities.

Educational disparities were most extreme in the Delta, a region that African Americans dominated in population for much of the twentieth century. Historian David Cohn once quipped that "the Mississippi Delta begins in the lobby of the Peabody Hotel in Memphis and ends on Catfish

Row in Vicksburg."[19] The folksy description failed to capture the region's racialized political economy that was underpinned by peonage, murder, and disfranchisement. The Delta contained the richest soil in the country, enabling Mississippi to produce a significant percentage of cotton for the nation. Most African Americans sharecropped on plantations owned by wealthy white planters. Sharecropping was a labor arrangement where a planter or company furnished everything but the labor. At harvest time, the sharecropper and landowner split the crop. After repaying the landowner for feed, seed, fertilizer, housing, and food, many sharecroppers remained in debt. Planters often prohibited sharecroppers from moving off the plantation until they had settled their debts.[20]

In addition to sharecropping, some white landowners used poor-quality black schools to foster the physical and occupational immobility of their black employees. If denied decent education, black Mississippians had very few employment prospects other than farming.[21] Washington County provided an excellent example of how planters' need for labor shaped the Delta's public schools. Although black pupils in Washington County outnumbered their white counterparts eight-to-one in 1915, the local school district spent eight times as much per capita on white education as on black education. Thirty years later, the district spent twice as much on white education, even though three times more black children than white children enrolled in Washington County schools.[22] The gross disparity remained until the 1950s when state leaders embarked on an effort to make separate education truly equal in the face of legal challenges about segregation.

Violence and terror kept most black Mississippians from challenging the status quo, but some did fight back openly. As early as 1890, black property owners in the Magnolia State dared to seek legal redress for the underfunding of black schools. The lawsuit they brought in the town of Brookhaven was especially brave given the racial climate. Between 1889 and 1945, Mississippi had 476 of the nation's 3,786 lynchings. That number only accounted for the reported acts, and it is likely that the actual number was much higher. Even worse, not one white man was ever convicted for killing a black person in the state.[23] Simply the threat of lynching was enough to maintain the color line. Author Richard Wright wrote in *Black Boy*, "the things that influenced my conduct as a Negro did not have to happen to me directly; I needed but to hear of them to feel their full effects in the deepest layers of my consciousness." The Mississippi native went on to say, "indeed, the white brutality that I had not seen was a more effective control of my behavior than that which I knew."[24] The ever-present threat of bodily harm governed black actions.

Such conditions shaped the life course of Lillie Short Ayers, one of several hundred black Mississippi women who turned to CDGM's Head Start program in 1965 to improve her living conditions and ensure that black youngsters received a quality educational foundation. Born in 1927 to sharecropper parents Jim and Lillie Short on a Delta plantation outside of Glen Allan in Washington County, Ayers learned early that the state's system of disfranchisement and black economic dependence limited her possibilities. She attended the Strangers Home Church School on the Jordan Plantation until the eighth grade, the highest educational level available in a society where planters feared that education would upset the region's social order. "As long as there was work in the fields," noted Ayers, "we had to do that. We had a very short period of time that we went to school. We'd go to school after we harvested all the cotton. We would go about three months out of a six-month school term. We couldn't go until we picked all the cotton."[25] The planter rather than black parents controlled if, when, and for how long black students attended school. He successfully limited the opportunities available to black children like Ayers.

One hundred and twenty miles north of Glen Allan, future CDGM district organizer Unita Brown Blackwell also experienced a white landowner defining the limits of freedom for her family. Born in Lula, a Delta town in Coahoma County, Mississippi, Blackwell recalled Willie Brown, her sharecropping father, arguing with the white landowner, who had disrespected her mother. Blackwell remembered that the landowner "was enraged over daddy's behavior and my daddy feared for his life." Brown had good reason to be scared. His own father had been killed in a sugar cane field for standing up to a white man. Under the cover of darkness, Blackwell's father left Mississippi the very same day as the confrontation with the landowner. Blackwell and her mother soon followed him to Memphis.[26] Blackwell's family was fortunate to be able to move without violent repercussions. Often, a tenant who challenged his boss proved unable to find a new farm.

The Delta was not the only region curtailing the rights of black citizens. Areas of the state with white majorities were statistically more dangerous places for African Americans to live. Because more black Mississippians owned small parcels of land outside of the Delta, white residents in those areas used force to combat black autonomy. Thus, measured in terms of population density, the risk of lynching was lower in the Delta even if African

Americans in that region experienced higher degrees of other forms of oppression.[27] Such differences did not go unnoticed. One black Mississippi native recalled that, during the age of Jim Crow, moving from the white-majority hills to the black-majority Delta was the equivalent of black southerners going North.[28]

Anger Winson Gates Hudson, a CDGM teacher and administrator born in 1916, lived and worked outside of the Delta. She was the tenth of thirteen children born to farmers John Wesley Gates and Emma Kirkland in the hills of predominately white Leake County, the geographic center of Mississippi. Hudson came of age in a proud black family that owned land in the rural and isolated all-black community of Harmony. In the years after the Civil War, former slaves in Harmony purchased land from former slaveowners. Black landownership provided the Gates family with pride, self-reliance, and greater financial freedom from white economic reprisals.[29] It also meant enduring the intimidation and violence of those set on reminding African Americans of their place in the racial social order. Hudson grew up hearing stories of white supremacists who lynched black men for offenses such as "riding a too fine saddle horse." Hudson herself lost an uncle to lynching.[30]

Hudson's family demanded that she always stand up for herself despite racial oppression and the violence that undergirded it. She was named after her paternal grandmother Angeline "Ange" Gates Turner who, as an enslaved woman, had been raped by her owner and bore him children. Sexual violence did not quench Grandma Ange's determination to assert her humanity. Gates family stories abounded about the ways in which Grandma Ange had stood up to white people, both during and after slavery. Such courage made an indelible impression on Hudson and her siblings. As she would later recall, "There's not a one of us in the family that's afraid of anything. We would stand up and say whatever we wanted to."[31]

The independence that came along with landownership allowed Hudson to attend school longer than most black Mississippians. She attended the Harmony School, established in 1922 by local black people who were determined to educate their youth. Harmony residents pooled their resources, purchased land, and erected a school building. Hudson's aunt, for example, used part of the survivor's benefit she received from her son's death in World War I to make a cash donation toward the school's construction costs. The Harmony community received assistance from the Rosenwald Fund, a philanthropic program sponsored by Julius Rosenwald, president of

Sears Roebuck and Company, that provided funds for the construction of black schoolhouses in the rural South. Between 1919 and 1931, the Rosenwald Fund contributed to the construction of over 633 schools and school-related facilities for black Mississippians. Since money from the Rosenwald Fund had to be matched with funds from the local school system and with funds from the communities served, African Americans in Harmony and other places double-taxed themselves to secure educational opportunities. For the 123 Rosenwald schools built in Mississippi between 1920 and 1922 at a cost of $689,235, African Americans contributed 49 percent of the funds, the Rosenwald Fund gave 18 percent, white residents contributed 16 percent, and county funds amounted to 16 percent. Black citizens' contributions to black education were substantial.[32]

The fact that the Harmony School was nickeled and dimed into existence did not lessen residents' belief in its importance and benefits. Grandma Ange encouraged Hudson to make the most of her education. She told her young granddaughter, "one day you will be able to write with your fingers [type] and you'll be able to ride on an airship just like a bird."[33] The acquisition of knowledge according to Grandma Ange, was the avenue to raise one's social and economic status and expand one's horizons. Black parents all across the state shared this belief even though state expenditures for black schooling fell far short of what was needed for adequate education.

Once she came of age, Winson Hudson found ways to express her discontent with the inequality in Mississippi's public education system. In 1937, she tried to register to vote, the first of her many failed attempts at the hands of racist registrars. She wrote letters to United States congressmen Adam Clayton Powell (D-N.Y.) and Charles Diggs (D-Miss.), but disguised the letters to make sure white Mississippians did not intercept them. "I had to wrap 'em in a socks box and send them to my husband's brother in Chicago like it was a gift. I sent two or three letters by my brother-in-law to different places." She concealed the true recipient of the letters because local Klansmen sorted through her mail to follow her activities.[34]

Segregationists recognized the threat in black people's political activity. Black teachers in 1941 pressed white lawmakers to lengthen the short school terms for black schools and equalize teacher salaries. Black teachers and administrators received smaller salaries than white teachers and administrators with similar education and experience. In 1948, Gladys Noel Bates, a public school teacher in Jackson, filed a suit in the U.S. District Court to challenge the racial inequity in teachers' pay. Black activist educators in the state had secretly raised funds for the state NAACP to file a pay-equalization suit, and Bates agreed to be the plaintiff. Beginning in 1936, black teachers in the South had gone to court seeking the same salaries as their white counter-parts. While these educators had made segregation much more expensive for their states with rulings in their favor, black teachers did not prevail in Mississippi. The Jackson school board quickly fired Bates and her teacher husband. The board then argued that Bates's lawsuit was without merit since she no longer worked for the district. To ensure that the case contin-ued, R. Jess Brown, a teacher at Jackson's all-black Lanier High School, be-came an intervening plaintiff. He, too, lost his job for daring to challenge the unequal salaries. The presiding judge ruled against Bates and Brown, find-ing that they had not pursued the proper channels before filing suit.[35] Swift punitive action against Gladys Bates and R. Jess Brown kept other black edu-cators in the state from openly supporting civil rights.

Organized resistance to black educational advancement increased in the wake of the 1954 *Brown v. Board of Education* decision that declared segrega-tion in public schools unconstitutional. Fearing miscegenation if black and white children attended school together, Mississippi's state legislators did away with compulsory school attendance laws. Leading white citizens closed ranks in a new organization called the Citizens' Council, which employed economic reprisals rather than violence to preserve segregation. Residents—black or white—who did not respect the racial order often had their mort-gages foreclosed, lost their jobs, or lost the ability to purchase goods on credit. By the end of the 1954 summer, 25,000 dues-paying Citizens' Council members existed throughout the state. The Council itself disavowed vio-lence, but its aggressive stance fostered violent actions.[36]

Citizens' Councils moved swiftly to enact reprisals. In Yazoo City, fifty-three black parents petitioned in 1955 for school desegregation plans. The local Citizens' Council placed an advertisement in the town newspaper list-ing the names and address of the petitioners. Most of the individuals listed lost their jobs despite offering to remove their names from the petition. Banks in the town refused to do business with the petitioners. At least four-teen signers moved to different towns for their safety, and membership in the local NAACP chapter declined from 200 to sixty-five members.[37]

The Citizens' Councils worked closely with the Mississippi State Sover-eignty Commission, a state agency created in 1956 to resist civil rights and preserve segregation.[38] Funded by tax dollars, the Sovereignty Commission acted as Mississippi's public relations firm, disseminating direct mail to northern media outlets and sponsoring tours for northern newspaper editors to favorably shape the state's image throughout the country and "give the South's side" in the national debate about segregation. The Commission also had an investigations unit that spied on individuals and organizations suspected of civil rights activities. Paid investigators worked with local police chiefs and county sheriffs, as well as local opponents, to collect information on suspected activists. The Commission was "complicit" in the 1964 murders of civil rights workers James Chaney, Andrew Goodman, and Mickey Schwerner.[39]

Mississippi had created an elaborate system of white supremacy that SNCC and other civil rights organizations worked to dismantle. The student sit-in movement that began on 1 February 1960, in Greensboro, North Carolina, led to SNCC's birth. The organization operated as a decentralized, student-run entity that promoted nonviolent direct action and the development of grassroots leaders. SNCC workers helped local people in Mississippi discover the untapped potential for leadership and action within themselves. Bob Moses, a black Harvard-trained New Yorker with a passion for social justice and action, put down SNCC's roots in the Magnolia State when he traveled to Cleveland, Mississippi, in the summer of 1960 and met with Amzie Moore, a local NAACP leader. Moore told Moses that he preferred voter registration campaigns in the black-majority Delta rather than efforts to secure black access to public accommodations since most black Mississippians were too poor to eat at a lunch counter or frequent a movie theater. Black participation in electoral politics, however, could lead to better schools and more impartial enforcement of the law. Moses agreed to return to Mississippi the following summer and work with Moore.[40]

Moses returned to Mississippi in July of 1961, but not to the Delta as originally planned. Amzie Moore was unable to secure a black church for a voter registration project. Curtis Conway "C. C." Bryant, an NAACP leader in Pike County, however, had read about Moses's proposed voter registration campaign in *Jet* magazine and wrote to him suggesting that McComb was a place ripe for voter registration. Located in southwest Pike County rather than the black-majority Delta region, McComb had a black population that made up 42 percent of the town's 12,000 residents. Only 200 out of 8,000 eligible black voters in all of Pike County were registered. African Americans had the potential to affect the outcome of an election. Moses relocated to McComb in August and began building local support for SNCC workers' living arrangements and expenses.[41]

Educational and political rights were inextricably linked. Increased black electoral participation in McComb meant that black parents could participate in local board of education elections and in the statewide election of the superintendent of public education.[42] Two SNCC field secretaries soon joined Moses in McComb, and voter registration classes began in early August in the black Masonic Temple. Since many of their students were semiliterate, they borrowed pedagogical techniques from the Citizenship Schools, an adult education program began in 1957 by the Highlander Folk School and taken over by the Southern Christian Leadership Conference (SCLC) in 1961. Veteran public school teacher Septima Clark developed the Citizenship Schools' student-centered curriculum, which taught adults how to read and made clear how the electoral process influenced everything from school funding to old-age pensions.[43] In McComb, SNCC workers introduced potential registrants to the twenty-one questions on Mississippi's application form and went over the 285 sections of the Mississippi constitution that potential voters were required to know. After attending the class, sixteen people traveled to the courthouse to register. Six passed the test.[44]

Word of SNCC's efforts in McComb traveled. By the end of August, student workers led voter registration drives throughout southwest Mississippi at the invitation of local residents. In Amite County, only one registered voter existed out of over 3,500 eligible black voters. The fact that black Mississippians began inviting young activists into their communities to organize was a sign of a changing tide. Local officials in turn quickly moved to curtail organizing activity. Law enforcement officials arrested Moses when he accompanied people to register to vote in Amite County. A week later, he endured a beating at the hands of the local sheriff's cousin. In September, E. H. Hurst, a member of the Mississippi state legislature, shot and killed Herbert Lee, an Amite County NAACP member who had agreed to introduce Moses to potential voter registrants. Lee's murder suppressed the nascent voter registration campaign and underscored the certain harassment and violence that came along with black assertion.[45]

SNCC's efforts in Southwest Mississippi may not have yielded large numbers of successful registrants, but registering to vote was a public act—it took courage for someone to walk into a courthouse and tell a voter registrar that he or she wanted to register to vote. In Mississippi, such an exercise of one's constitutional right was a direct action protest that often had swift and violent consequences. In May of 1962, the Mississippi legislature enacted a law requiring the names of voter applicants to be published in the newspaper once a week for two weeks.[46] Such a measure gave employers and landlords time to demand that workers or tenants withdraw their application.

SNCC made inroads in Mississippi because organizational staff tapped into the state's old-guard black leadership. An older generation of activists had already risked their lives and livelihoods to challenge black subjugation before SNCC entered Mississippi. Individuals such as C. C. Bryant, T. R. M. Howard, Vernon Dahmer, Medgar Evers, Aaron Henry, and Amzie Moore had earlier laid the foundation for SNCC's work in the Magnolia State. World War II veterans Moore, Henry, and Evers had returned home determined to experience the democracy they had fought for overseas. All three men participated in the Regional Council of Negro Leadership that black physician and activist T. R. M. Howard of Mound Bayou had created in 1951 to build black economic and political power in the state. Additionally, all the men including Bryant participated in the NAACP, with Evers serving as the state's first field secretary from 1954 until his murder in 1963 and Henry serving as the state president from 1959 until 1993. While Moore led the Cleveland chapter, Dahmer headed the Forrest County chapter in Hattiesburg, and Bryant oversaw the local chapter in McComb.[47] These men associated more openly with the NAACP because they owned their own businesses or worked at jobs—like the United States Post Office Department—independent of the local white power structure.[48]

Another reason for SNCC's success was the organization's ability to make personal connections with the local people they set out to assist. SNCC staff accomplished this by visiting local churches, pool halls, and juke joints. They played with small children in rural communities and established meaningful relationships with residents. In time, they won the confidence of a range of residents including domestics, cab drivers, beauticians, barbers, bootleggers, and agricultural workers. SNCC, with its group-centered leadership and bottom-up organizing strategies that asserted local people's right and ability to identify and solve their own problems, differed from other organizations. Unita Blackwell summed up the difference between SNCC and the NAACP when she explained, "I found out later they [the NAACP] had been in the state for forty years, but we sure hadn't seen 'em."[49] SNCC, unlike the NAACP, was locally based and developed issues and strategies alongside indigenous activists rather than in a faraway national office. Moreover, SNCC disdained hierarchy in favor of group-centered leadership.

The fight to secure the ballot and equal educational opportunities required a concerted effort among civil rights groups. By 1962, SNCC had partnered with the state NAACP, the Congress of Racial Equality (CORE), and the SCLC under the aegis of the Council of Federated Organizations (COFO). Collectively, these groups established black voter registration operations in all four corners of Mississippi. SNCC had the largest number of field workers and thus dominated COFO.[50]

Increased black political participation was the key to improved educational resources for black Mississippians. In the mid-sixties, only 6.7 percent of the state's adult black population was registered to vote. White supremacists often employed fear tactics to prevent the few registered black citizens from voting. COFO decided to show the nation that black Mississippians would vote if allowed to register without intimidation. On 2 November 1963, activists staged a freedom vote or mock election with NAACP leader Aaron Henry as a candidate for governor and the Reverend Edwin "Ed" King, white chaplain of the black Tougaloo College, as a candidate for lieutenant governor. COFO's freedom vote was open to all adult citizens whether or not they were registered to vote, using the rally cry of "one man, one vote." White college students from Stanford and Yale helped with the campaign. Over 80,000 black Mississippians—four times the number of black voters actually registered—participated in the freedom vote. Black churches and businesses served as polling places. The freedom vote had no bearing on official election outcomes, but it accomplished two important goals. First, the mock election demonstrated to federal officials that black Mississippians would vote in much greater numbers if not impeded by terror. Second, the freedom vote challenged the legitimacy of one's voting right hinging on academic achievement or some other qualification.[51]

The 1963 freedom vote laid the foundation for COFO's 1964 Freedom Summer, a statewide campaign to end black disfranchisement and cultivate the leadership skills of local people. Two months after the mock election, white supremacists killed Louis Allen, a World War II veteran and logger, outside of his home, ironically in a town named Liberty. Allen's "crime" had been witnessing a white state legislator murder Herbert Lee in 1961 and reporting that ambush to federal officials.[52] The violence led Bob Moses to wager the lives of white college students as collateral for the federal government's protection during the 1964 summer. Moses envisioned a summer project where hundreds of white college students from across the country came into the state to help African Americans register to vote. Their presence would focus national attention on the dire situation in Mississippi.[53]

Moses's plan did not go unchallenged. Many SNCC and CORE staff members initially voted down the idea of inviting white college students, fearing that the students might dominate leadership positions and undo the progress that had been made in getting black Mississippians to take control over their own lives. In the end, several COFO activists decided that the influx of white students, and the national media that followed them, might prick the conscience of a nation unmoved by extralegal violence against African Americans.[54]

Moses and others understood that bringing in 1,000 young people required multiple levels of support. Thus COFO arranged for legal and medical assistance. The Law Students Project, the Lawyers' Constitutional Defense Committee, and the National Lawyers Guild sent 150 lawyers and law students to represent volunteers who were arrested because of their summer work. Physical violence was also expected. To treat the wounded, Tom Levin, a Jewish psychoanalyst from New York, cofounded the Medical Committee for Human Rights, an organization of physicians, nurses, and dentists. While the Medical Committee was Levin's first foray in Mississippi, it would not be his last. He returned to the state the following summer to cofound and lead CDGM.[55]

Freedom Summer began in bloodshed. In June, while hundreds of volunteers trained in Ohio, three civil rights workers lost their lives in Mississippi. Klansmen and Neshoba County law enforcement killed James Chaney, a native black Mississippian, and Michael Schwerner and Andrew Goodman, Jewish young men from New York. Chaney had stayed with Winson Hudson in the weeks leading up to his murder, and Schwerner had boarded with Hudson's sister, Dovie. The murders of Schwerner and Goodman proved Moses's point: the deaths of two northern white men drew national attention and brought in the Federal Bureau of Investigation (FBI). Three other young black men's bodies—Henry Dee, Charles Moore, and a never-identified black teenager—were found during the dragging of the river bottoms in the search for the three missing civil rights workers. These three black men might still be missing had there not been a massive manhunt for the two white men. Despite the unprecedented number of federal agents and media outlets that descended upon Mississippi, white supremacists did not let up. Over the course of the ten-week summer project, white Mississippians bombed or burned thirty-seven churches and thirty black homes. They also beat eighty workers and arrested over a thousand people on trumped-up charges.[56]

Freedom Summer included an educational component that offered students a creative learning environment that encompassed traditional academics and strategies of resistance. Charlie Cobb, a SNCC worker who had organized in Mississippi since 1962, recognized that black education in the state was "inadequate and inferior." Moreover, he was troubled by the state's public school curriculum, which stressed conformity, glorified the Old South, and prohibited discussion of civil rights. For example, a black teacher in Centreville, Mississippi, lost her job for mentioning fourteen-year-old Emmett Till's murder in the classroom. Such white oversight even limited the actions of activist educators and meant that the state's public schools lacked intellectual freedom and accurate and inclusive history. To combat this problem, Cobb conceived of freedom schools to teach black history and encourage critical thinking.[57]

There had been an earlier experimentation with freedom schools prior to Freedom Summer. In 1961, SNCC organizers set up "Nonviolent High," a freedom school forerunner in McComb, where over one hundred black high school students walked out of school after the principal demanded that they not participate in civil rights demonstrations. Bob Moses taught math, while other SNCC staff taught history and science to prevent the students from falling behind in their studies.[58] The fact that an alternative school was necessary demonstrated that the public schools maintained the political and racial status quo.

COFO staff used freedom schools in 1964 to reach both those too young to vote and those who were afraid to take part in voter registration. Many black parents revered even inadequate schools because they believed that education was the pathway to a better life. Some may have feared signing a voter roll, but would attend a freedom school class. COFO seized black citizens' enthusiasm for education, using freedom schools as a way to "fill an intellectual and creative vacuum" in black communities.[59] The schools offered their students remedial education in traditional subjects such as math, reading, and history and introduced French and typing. The makeshift institutions also celebrated black culture and history and equipped pupils with the tools to be effective leaders who had the know-how to change their communities.[60]

Forty-one freedom schools operated during Freedom Summer and served over 2,000 students. While the average student was fifteen years of age, preschool-aged children and the elderly attended as well. Freedom school classes met in churches, basements, homes, and under trees. Student attendance was voluntary in the freedom schools. In several Delta locales, the freedom schools competed with many public schools that were in session during the summer, because the academic calendar for black school children revolved around cotton season.[61]

Approximately 280 white student volunteers who were not engaged in voter registration staffed the freedom schools. Most of the teacher volunteers—affluent, white liberals from the North—had no prior experience teaching and very little knowledge of black history. They received training during one of two week-long orientations at Western College for Women in Oxford, Ohio, before relocating to various towns in Mississippi, where they stayed with local people. Scholar and activist Howard Zinn described the training the teachers received:

> You'll arrive in Ruleville, in the Delta. It will be 100 degrees, and you'll be sweaty and dirty. You won't be able to bathe often or sleep well or eat good food. The first day of school, there may be four teachers and three students. And the local Negro minister will phone to say you can't use his church basement after all, because his life has been threatened. And the curriculum we've drawn up—Negro history and American government—may be something you know only a little about yourself. Well, you'll knock on doors all day in the hot sun to find students. You'll meet on someone's lawn under a tree. You'll tear up the curriculum and teach what you know.[62]

The freedom schools functioned explicitly as agents of social change. In addition to remedial reading and math classes, volunteers offered their students exposure to black history, drama, art, and music. Since one of the main goals of the summer project was to help local people resist passivity and see themselves as change agents, both visual and performing arts became ways to foster creativity. Students created stories and art that included black people and discussed the possibility of a society inclusive of all. Ruleville freedom school students wrote and performed a puppet show where a knight named Bob Moses fought a wicked witch named Segregation. In Holly Springs the students created a play about the life and death of Medgar

Evers. Roleplaying not only fostered ingenuity but also groomed students for direct action protests.[63]

Activities varied by locale, but the objective of empowering students was the same. A volunteer reported that in the Greenwood freedom school students began with the goal of leaving Mississippi as soon as they were legally able to do so. After discussions about the myth of the "good life" that supposedly existed in Chicago and New York, students changed their minds and looked for ways to improve their own community.[64] A teacher from a Vicksburg freedom school read to her students from Thomas Wolfe's *Look Homeward, Angel* and from Dr. Martin Luther King's "I Have a Dream" speech, and then had them write speeches as if they were senators urging passage of the civil rights bill. She encouraged them to extend the idea of oppression beyond race. Writing speeches was a form of expression. Other forms of expression used throughout the summer included poetry and songs. Long silenced by fear or custom, students freely shared their feelings and goals in freedom schools.[65]

Twelve freedom schools published newspapers that demonstrated the students' political awakening and increasing confidence. The newspapers provided coverage of civil rights events that mainstream media outlets in the state ignored and they gave students a platform to voice their own opinions. Students as young as six, seven, and eight years old used typewriters and paper donated by northern organizations to demand parks and other municipal services. In a newspaper published by a Hattiesburg freedom school, students lamented a public school education that neglected to mention black abolitionists. They also drafted a declaration of independence that declared their freedom from unjust Mississippi laws. In a Greenwood freedom school newspaper, a student drawing on the language of American independence wrote, "give us freedom or give us death."[66]

The radical nature of these makeshift educational institutions made them ripe for white backlash. Two days before a freedom school in Leake County opened, the white county school superintendent announced a special school session for black students only. School officials also refused to allow the abandoned Harmony School building to serve as a freedom school site, even though African Americans had provided a significant proportion of the funds for its construction. In Canton, whites who opposed Freedom Summer broke into the local freedom school's library and urinated on the books. Resistance sometimes took violent turns. White supremacists firebombed the freedom school facilities in McComb and Gluckstadt, just as

A 1964 Freedom Summer volunteer and local resident keep guard at a Holmes County community center that doubled as a freedom school. Vandalism of black churches, freedom schools, and community centers was common that summer. (Matt Herron/ Take Stock/The Image Works)

Klansmen had firebombed black schoolhouses during the Reconstruction period. In the latter location, a sixteen-year-old female who attended the freedom school there maintained that "burning down churches and society hall is not going to stop us from having our freedom." Undaunted students vowed to attend classes held under trees rather than quit. In the face of widespread violence and fear, freedom schools did indeed survive and thrive.[67]

By summer's end, freedom schools had helped to "loosen the hard knot of fear" that governed black actions.[68] Even with challenges such as competition with the black public schools' summer session and classrooms with pupils whose ages spanned five decades, the freedom schools succeeded at helping many black Mississippians realize that they could take charge of the institutions and policies controlling their lives. In the statewide convention of freedom school students held in August, there were calls for decent and affordable housing, an end to public support of private schools, economic sanctions against South Africa, and the appointment of black police officers to local police forces. In the penultimate week of freedom schools, six students from one of the Hattiesburg freedom schools ventured to the local library and requested library cards. The librarian closed the library rather than issue the students cards.[69] Liberatory education had given black students a more expansive vision of what was possible. Their hopes for a more democratic society would not be stifled.

Just as the freedom schools operated as an empowering antidote to a public school system that sought to promote black docility, the Mississippi Freedom Democratic Party acted as a parallel institution to the all-white state Democratic Party in Mississippi. COFO's boldest move came with the creation of an interracial political party that challenged both the state and national Democratic parties. Black Mississippians had attempted to participate in Democratic Party precinct meetings held across the state throughout the summer. The precinct meeting was the first step in the selection of delegates to the national convention. As expected, the majority of black citizens were turned away at the door of precinct meetings because of their race or found that white organizers had changed the meeting site or time so that they could not participate. Racial exclusion led black Mississippians and their white allies to set about creating their own political party by holding Mississippi Freedom Democratic Party county and district conventions. Winson Hudson and her husband attended party meetings in Leake County, while Lillie Ayers and her husband followed suit in Washington County. At these gatherings, delegates passed resolutions supporting racial justice in Mississippi and pledging loyalty to the national Democratic Party, something members of the all-white state Democratic Party refused to do. On 6 August 1964, the Mississippi Freedom Democratic Party held its state convention in Jackson. Following Democratic Party rules, the convention elected sixty-eight delegates, including four whites, to represent the party at the national convention in Atlantic City, New Jersey. Fannie Lou Hamer and Unita Blackwell served as delegates. Party members had also selected Winson Hudson as a delegate, but she did not make the trip to New Jersey because she was knee-deep in school desegregation plans and could not leave town.[70]

In Atlantic City, members of the Mississippi Freedom Democratic Party delegation asserted that they, and not the all-white Mississippi Democratic delegation, were the bona fide representatives of the state, since they had held open and fair elections and did not exclude anyone from participating in the selection of delegates to the national convention. National Democratic Party officials disagreed and offered the interracial grassroots political party delegation two at-large seats—a proposition that the group refused. In addition to the offer of two seats, the convention pledged to ban, beginning in 1968, racial discrimination in the selection of future delegations. Many white liberals, including United States Senator Hubert Humphrey (D-Minn.) and United Automobile Workers President Walter Reuther, individuals who had professed a commitment to justice and equality, chastised the Mississippi Freedom Democratic Party delegation for refusing the proposal.[71] Although the pledge said nothing about voter registration and only a few thousand black Mississippians could vote, it did mean that sharecroppers and domestics had taken on the country's political elite and forever changed the face of presidential electors.

Long-term political promises, however, were little consolation to a group of people who experienced racial terror and discrimination on a constant basis. Working-class black Mississippians, holding fast to memories of the freedom schools, decided in 1965 to once again turn to education as an avenue for liberation. Exposure to black authors and to the idea of participatory democracy had opened up a whole new world for the state's most marginalized residents. Head Start became their next vehicle for full freedom.

CHAPTER TWO

A Revolution in Expectations

These people will never come. They don't care that much about education.
—White superintendent in the Mississippi Delta speaking about
African American interest in Head Start, 1965

The program [CDGM] is something that our children have never had before.
We are a race of people who never had anything for our children except
standing around at the end of the cotton fields.
—Anonymous CDGM mother

In April of 1965, Winson Hudson and Minnie Lewis traveled more than 120 miles from Harmony, Mississippi, to Edwards, outside of Jackson, to learn about a new federal program called Head Start. The women's activist backgrounds signaled the connection between the early childhood education program and the black freedom struggle in Mississippi. Four years earlier, Winson Hudson had led the fight to save the Harmony School, an institution built with Rosenwald Funds and donations from black residents. Leake County school officials planned to close the institution and bus students to a new black school built to defy the *Brown* decision with the appearance of separate but equal. School officials failed to realize that the Harmony School was more than brick and mortar. The institution represented the black community's independence and resiliency. Harmony residents resolved that if they could not keep their school, then they would demand integration of the white school. Hudson herself started a local chapter of the NAACP in 1961 to oversee the desegregation challenge. By the time of Head Start's founding in 1965, Hudson and Lewis had spent the past several years embroiled in the effort to desegregate public schools in Leake County. Their legal challenge was the first suit against a rural school system in Mississippi.[1]

The Fifth Circuit Court of Appeals ordered Leake County to desegregate its schools in the fall of 1964. The Leake County school board, in a clever tactic to delay desegregation, presented a staggered plan that desegregated one grade per year beginning with the first grade.[2] Initially, nine black families announced their intentions to enroll their rising first-graders in the all-white Carthage Attendance Center. Intense economic pressure from local whites, however, left only the Lewis family willing to put their jobs and child on the line. Thus, the burden of putting a court ruling into practice fell on the shoulders of six-year-old Debra Lewis, Minnie's daughter. One day in early September 1964, Army veteran A. J. Lewis and his wife Minnie sent Debra into a previously all-white elementary school in search of the quality education that black parents had sought for their children since Reconstruction. Debra's entrance cost her father his job at a local sawmill, caused the family's home to be shot into twice, and resulted in their landlord evicting them. White resistance dragged on for months. An assailant struck and beat Debra's father from behind while he was Christmas shopping. Mississippi's legal system not only failed to arrest the perpetrator but also chose to arrest A. J. Lewis for assault and battery, even though he was the aggrieved party.[3]

Winson Hudson and Minnie Lewis traveled to Edwards because if school boards, law enforcement agencies, and ordinary citizens across the state continued to thwart African Americans' efforts to provide black children with quality education, then the women hoped that Head Start would give black parents another way to have control over their children's educational careers. Edwards was home to the Mount Beulah Conference Center, a site leased by the National Council of Churches. The ecumenical group had played a significant role in Mississippi's black freedom struggle through its civil rights arm, the Delta Ministry.[4] Mount Beulah, one of the few places other than black churches where integrated groups could meet outside of the purview of segregationists, was just the place to promote black control of black education. The property was a hotbed of civil rights movement activity in the state. SCLC voter registration workshops took place there, as did Mississippi Freedom Democratic Party meetings and state conventions.[5]

At Mount Beulah, Winson Hudson and Minnie Lewis were joined by black freedom fighters from several rural hamlets and towns in Mississippi. Annie Seaton Smith, Alice Beard, and Valentine Blue came from the Tougaloo community. Beard, a public school teacher, had been fired for her civil rights work.[6] Lavaree Jones, a community activist and Mississippi Freedom Democratic Party leader from Hollandale, also attended the informational meeting. Jones recalled, "organizers announced, 'I have some good news for you. Money has been appropriated for Head Start and this means that if you find a building, [and] get some children [to sign up], you can keep and teach your own children and get paid.' Well, that was the answer to a prayer."[7] Head Start appeared promising for Jones and others who had witnessed

firsthand the slow pace of change and deliberate noncompliance with desegregation orders. The forty-two-year-old mother desired improved educational opportunities for her children. She also sought a well-paying job
for herself that allowed her to continue political work without economic
reprisals. Jones had worked as an unlicensed cosmetologist for several years.
Licensed beauticians, threatened by her successful business, constantly
reported her to state authorities, who were all too eager to sanction her
because of her connection to the civil rights movement. Jones had housed
volunteers during the 1964 Freedom Summer and had made her home
available for strategizing meetings.[8] She and other likeminded black Mississippians left Mount Beulah excited about the possibilities of a black-run,
grassroots Head Start program.

One month before the Mount Beulah meeting, six northern white liberals met in New York City and discussed the potential of a preschool program for black children and their parents in Mississippi. The Head Start
program had not been on the agenda at the New York meeting. Tom Levin,
a psychoanalyst who had worked in Freedom Summer and who convened
the March meeting, proposed establishing five to ten day care centers. Mississippi did not offer public kindergartens, and the minimum school age was
six years, so working-class black children raised in environments that were
void of stimulation and that did not encourage language development at
home were often unprepared for the first grade.[9] Levin wanted to replicate
freedom schools at the preschool level, but with the crucial difference of
having parents replace the northern white teachers, so that black children
saw their parents as role models in positions of authority. He explained:
"when a Negro kid in Mississippi enters the school system, he enters into
the hands of the white power structure. It could be a Negro school; it doesn't
make any difference. It is still into the hands of the white power structure.
And, I think, at this point, the child turns to the parents and says 'look, help
me.' So the kid turns to his parents, and, I think, receives the first major rebuff of his life when, essentially, the parents say, 'You know I can't help you.
That system beat me and I can't help you with it.'"[10]

An early childhood education program that built up children's self-
esteem and included their parents in the educational process would serve as
an antidote to the debilitating racism that black children encountered once
in school. Levin sought to develop confident, inquisitive students who would
later populate the public schools and produce meaningful changes from the
inside.[11] He invited four white people to New York to discuss his idea:

Jeannine Herron, a young educator, activist, mother, and the wife of SNCC photojournalist Matt Herron; Art Thomas, director of the Delta Ministry; psychologist Sol Gordon; and a National Council of Churches representative.[12]

Levin's personal background and his professional training in childhood psychoanalysis fueled his interest in Mississippi. A native of the Bronx, he came of age during the Great Depression and witnessed firsthand from his Russian Jewish, immigrant, working-class parents the hardships that poverty and illiteracy caused. He recalled how devastating it was to watch his father unable to find work: "He couldn't support his family. It was very painful. That's a molding memory in my life. [When] I was six years old or seven I said to my father, 'Daddy, why don't you tell those government people we need a job?' And he said 'don't you understand? We don't matter.' And that's become the single mission of my life. That no one should feel they don't matter."[13] Levin's personal experience of knowing what it felt like to be disregarded and swept to the side allowed him to bring a sense of inclusion and respect for the poor to his preschool endeavors.

He worked odd jobs without finishing school until he enlisted in the Navy and was sent to Japan during World War II. He later recalled, "in Okinawa, at the time of the invasion, I heard American marines and sailors bragging about raping grandmothers, taking prisoners and knocking their teeth out for gold."[14] That experience shaped his psyche and made him uneasy about failing to speak out against human indignities. After the war, Levin attended Long Island University and then New York University, where he earned a Ph.D. in psychology and educational psychology.[15]

Levin watched on television as Commissioner of Public Safety Eugene "Bull" Connor turned hoses and dogs on black activists in 1963 Birmingham, Alabama. He created the Committee of Conscience, an organization of northern academics who came south to participate in demonstrations. The next year, during Freedom Summer, Levin organized teams of physicians to work in Mississippi treating medical ailments and giving public health lectures. The Medical Committee for Human Rights, as the healthcare providers came to be known, helped to expose racist practices within the American Medical Association, as they desegregated southern hospitals and provided emergency care when local doctors refused to treat civil rights workers.[16]

Several of the individuals Levin summoned to New York had similar experience fighting racism. For example, Jeannine Herron and her husband

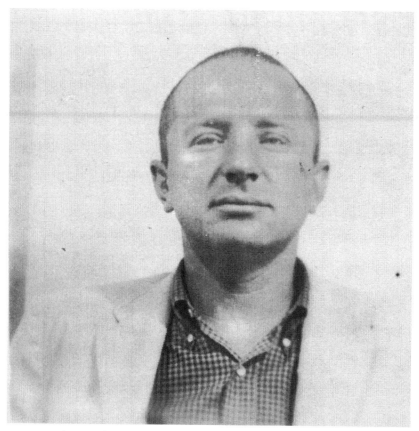

Tom Levin (ca. 1960s), a psychoanalyst and cofounder of the Medical Committee for Human Rights, was one of CDGM's architects. Levin believed that one of the best ways to help poor children was by empowering their parents. As CDGM director, he ensured that black parents who had previously worked as domestics and field workers played integral roles in the Head Start program. (Ronny Diamond Personal Collection)

Matt worked in the Philadelphia, Pennsylvania, CORE chapter in 1962. The next year, they moved to Jackson where they joined SNCC. Photojournalist Matt Herron's 1965 photograph of a Mississippi highway patrolman wrestling an American flag from Anthony Quinn, a five-year-old black boy, garnered him an award from the World Press. Delta Ministry director and Methodist minister Art Thomas also had freedom struggle credentials. In 1960, he organized the first interracial church in Durham, North Carolina. He relocated to Mississippi in 1963 and collaborated with SNCC and CORE workers on numerous projects. Thomas, along with Staughton Lynd and

Septima Clark, among others, wrote the freedom school curriculum. He also ensured that the COFO literacy projects and voter registration campaigns continued through the Delta Ministry after Freedom Summer volunteers left the state.[17]

Polly Greenberg, the senior Head Start program analyst for OEO's Southeast region, was the sixth person present at the New York meeting. She heard about the meeting by chance and made her way north out of frustration with the kinds of Head Start applications from Mississippi that OEO had received. Mississippi applications were generally submitted by public school superintendents who had no intention of complying with the federal government's nondiscrimination policies. Many of these applications showed evidence that the applicants cleverly planned to maintain segregation by hiring black workers for white Head Start centers and employing them in positions where they would not directly work with children. In many of these proposed centers, the only job offered to black women was custodial work. These applications also seemed to prioritize developing obedient first graders who sat quietly and learned by rote memorization.[18]

This is not how Head Start's architects imagined their program. They had conceived of a racially integrated early childhood education/medical/community action program that developed preschoolers' self-confidence and created new careers for the poor, rather than simply a preparation program for the first grade that maintained the racial status quo. Throughout January and February of 1965, a panel of child development experts including Mamie Phipps Clark, Edward Ziegler, and Robert Cooke met and considered ways to increase achievement and opportunities for the children of the poor. They recommended a comprehensive program that improved children's physical well-being; facilitated children's mental, emotional, and social development through spontaneity, curiosity, and self-discipline; and established patterns and expectations of success for the children. Panelists also stressed the importance of parental participation in planning and executing early childhood educational opportunities. The focus on Head Start enrollees' families was twofold. First, parental involvement helped to build trust and respect between children and their families. Second, Head Start employment helped many parents to work their way out of poverty, ensuring that their children had brighter futures. OEO solicited applications from school superintendents, health administrators, welfare administrators, Parent-Teacher Association (PTA) chapter officers, governors, and mayors who would carry out Head Start's vision. Greenberg traveled to

New York seeking individuals to apply for Head Start funding in Mississippi who would reflect the architects' goals and adhere to the spirit of civil rights law.[19]

In doing so, Greenberg remained true to her grassroots upbringing. Born in Milwaukee in 1932, she came of age in a household that supported organizations such as the NAACP, the Southern Tenant Farmers' Union, and the Highlander Folk School. Greenberg's father worked as the editor of Wisconsin's leading newspaper, *The Milwaukee Journal*. Her mother, a 1915 graduate of Barnard College, counted Highlander founders Myles and Zilphia Horton among her friends. Greenberg recalled that her mother constantly spoke out against oppression, injecting herself into matters such as the National Park Service's proposed usurping of Havasupai Indians' grazing lands. The social consciousness that Greenberg saw in her parents left an indelible impression on her. While studying at Sarah Lawrence College, she met and later married Danny Greenberg, the brother of Jack Greenberg who became the NAACP Legal Defense and Education Fund director in 1961. Greenberg's family gatherings included such individuals as civil rights lawyers Thurgood Marshall and Constance Baker Motley, and her own experiences as a daycare center teacher, elementary school teacher, and federal government employee prepared her to seek out individuals who dared to operate untraditional Head Start programs.[20]

The commitment to establishing integrated Head Start programs came not only from Greenberg but also from her superiors. Robert Sargent Shriver, John Kennedy's brother-in-law, the former director of the Peace Corps, and director of the OEO, did not intend for segregationists to disregard nondiscrimination laws in the antipoverty program. Shriver, before running the Peace Corps, ran Chicago's Merchandise Mart and served on many civic boards. He dined in the mid-1950s with Ralph Bunche at the Merchants and Manufacturers Club, the Merchandise Mart's private dining club, breaking the implicit Jim Crow codes of the North. He was also active in the city's Catholic Interracial Council (CIC), whose mission was "to eradicate the sin of racism," and was elected president of the group in 1955. In that position, Shriver worked to integrate Catholic high schools by raising money to send black students to the all-white and quite expensive institutions. Shriver's CIC work led to his appointment to the Chicago Board of Education, a position he used to directly attack segregation in public schools and indirectly address residential segregation throughout the city.[21] Shriver brought this racial consciousness to OEO, where he envisioned the agency creating real

Polly Greenberg, the OEO's senior program analyst for Head Start's Southeast region, was responsible for soliciting Head Start applications in seven southern states. Greenberg believed so strongly in CDGM's program that she resigned from her OEO job in May 1965 and moved to Mississippi with her four young daughters in tow. (Polly Greenberg Personal Collection)

and meaningful changes in the lives of the American people by sidestepping traditional channels of power that favored political machines in the urban North and segregationists in the South.

Yet, Shriver minimized the racial implications of his vision in order to woo Congress and see the Economic Opportunity Act become law.[22] Many members of Congress—both Republicans and Democrats—considered the antipoverty effort simply a way for President Johnson to win votes in an election year. In addition to having to prove the program's necessity, Shriver had to quell opposition from southern representatives still upset about passage of the Civil Rights Act of 1964 and suspicious that the Economic Opportunity Act was yet another civil rights bill. Richard Russell (D-Ga.), the South's leader in the Senate, had already spoken out against the legislation as a violation of states' rights. Shriver sought the advice of Georgia's other senator, Herman Talmadge (D-Ga.), to rebut this accusation. Talmadge suggested that he put a governor's veto into the legislation to make the poverty program "states' rights friendly," with the understanding that he would likely get "very, very few vetoes from governors."[23] The amendment brought more of the southern delegation on board by giving governors a thirty-day window to veto such arrangements as the particular location of Job Corps sites (enabling them to prevent the establishment of integrated sites) and the funding of community action programs through private organizations.[24] The "states' rights friendly" Economic Opportunity Act passed both houses in Congress and was signed into law by President Johnson in August of 1964.

Shriver's vision for the War on Poverty was liberal, despite his public support of the governor's veto. In 1964, Shriver addressed the NAACP national convention. He mentioned Emmett Till, Medgar Evers, and the three recently murdered civil rights workers before remarking that the United States had to tackle not just the poverty of want, but the "poverty of American law, power, and spirit."[25] Months later, while addressing questions before the National Committee for Community Development about the community action component of the Economic Opportunity Act, Shriver remarked, "we face a revolution in expectations—a radical shift in the hopes, demands, and aspirations of the poor themselves. We cannot stem that tide. And we do not wish to do so."[26] There were several departments within OEO, including the Inspection Division and the Civil Rights Division that served as watchdogs for violations of the spirit and law of the Economic Opportunity Act. Shriver's comments suggest that OEO welcomed the participation of poor citizens willing to upset the status quo and create a more equitable society by means of antipoverty programs. In Mississippi, the poor people Shriver alluded to included Unita Blackwell, Lillie Ayers, and Winson Hudson. They all had integral roles in the Head Start program created in 1965. Greenberg facilitated their inclusion when she traveled to New York and carried out the spirit of the OEO director's words.

Tom Levin and Art Thomas, along with Jeannine Herron, hesitated to apply for Head Start funds because they worried that federal money meant regulations that might imperil the earlier work of SNCC and the Mississippi Freedom Democratic Party. Greenberg countered their concerns with the assurance that federal money meant more Head Start centers and more students receiving medical care and hot meals. It also meant new and well-paying jobs for many black sharecroppers and domestics. The group refused to make any immediate commitments despite Greenberg's passionate sell. Levin later contacted Greenberg and declined to participate. He explained that he was not interested in helping the federal government to buy off grassroots black activists.[27]

Unbeknownst to Polly Greenberg, Jule Sugarman, OEO deputy director and chief administrator of Head Start, also worked behind the scenes to diversify the Head Start applications that his office received. Sugarman dispatched 100 contract employees to the poorest counties in the nation to explain the program and help local groups write Head Start grant applications. Dudley Morris, the chief civil rights reporter for *Time* and *Life* magazines, was sent south to seek out liberal individuals and groups to run Head Start centers. Morris, familiar with the Delta Ministry, contacted Art Thomas, not knowing that Greenberg had already spoken with him. Morris impressed Thomas enough to lessen the Delta Ministry director's doubts about the limitations of federal programs. Thomas in turn convinced Tom Levin to bring the news of the Head Start program to Mississippi and let the people decide.[28]

OEO officials sought the involvement of white liberals such as Tom Levin in southern antipoverty programs because of his administrative expertise and to ensure the meaningful inclusion of the black poor. Those with civil rights movement sympathies were more likely to comply with the Community Action Program requirement of "maximum feasible participation" of the poor. Richard "Dick" Boone, a member of the White House Special Projects staff who helped to write the Economic Opportunity Act, had insisted that the stipulation calling for the poor's participation be included in the legislation. Boone had previously established a program to counteract adolescent street gang activity in Chicago, where he observed that the worst gang prevention workers were "highly institutionalized," while the best were local people right off the street. The former group "only had answers," while the latter group "asked questions." A friend implored him, when he joined the War on Poverty, to use the federal government's relationship with Native Americans as a lesson in what not to do in the War on Poverty. His friend told him that "with those you are trying to help, plan with them, don't plan for them. They have their own priorities." Boone took that advice to heart and in the Economic Opportunity Act Title II language advocated for the "maximum feasible participation" of the poor.[29]

Despite the legislative mandate calling for the inclusion of poor citizens in anti-poverty programs, it was not certain that black Mississippians would support Head Start. Bob Moses had left Mississippi, and several SNCC workers had developed a palpable distrust of the Democratic Party and interracial organizing. They maintained that the Johnson Administration's refusal to create a large federal presence in the state had contributed to the deaths of Chaney, Goodman, and Schwerner. Moreover, the president himself had schemed to weaken support for the Mississippi Freedom Democratic Party challenge at the national convention. One SNCC leader, Stokely Carmichael, recalling the period immediately after the 1964 Atlantic City challenge, opined, "African Americans could no longer talk of connection with the Democratic Party. We must go into direct organizing and opposition to the Democratic Party."[30]

Yet, black Mississippians from rural hamlets and backwoods areas listened attentively to details about a national Head Start that a Democratic administration sponsored. They learned that OEO had appropriated federal funds to run an eight-week preschool program and that all communities were eligible to apply for a grant. Those who gathered at Mount Beulah seemed hopeful that this signaled their big break, despite a lingering sense of betrayal over the Mississippi Freedom Democratic Party challenge in Atlantic City. Besides, voting rights legislation had been before Congress for twenty-five days when Levin put the question of early childhood education before sharecroppers and domestics. A program promising the "maximum feasible participation" of the poor appealed to the group since the outcome of the voting bill was far from certain. Those assembled, including Winson Hudson, Minnie Lewis and Lavaree Jones, decided to submit a Head Start application in hopes of creating better futures for themselves and their children.

Local people cared little that white liberals had conceived of the program. They received assurances from Levin, Thomas, and an OEO representative that they would make decisions about staff hiring, the use of buildings, transportation, and center operation. Many of them could not vote for their mayor since Congress had not yet passed the Voting Rights Act of 1965, but they had the chance to become administrators of a federal anti-poverty program.[31] The Head Start program also offered them the educational choice and community control that they still lacked despite years of organizing.

Moreover, Head Start was a matter of economic survival for many African Americans. Mississippi's black-majority Delta region had been the last plantation stronghold in the South, but increased mechanization of agriculture in the 1950s and 1960s made black labor expendable. During this time, the percentage of the Delta's cotton picked by machine rose from 7 to 50 percent, while the number of sharecroppers fell by 70 percent.[32] Compounding the problem was the new food stamp program that Mississippi debuted in 1964. Previously, impoverished families received monthly distributions of flour and canned goods from the federal commodity distribution program. With the food stamps program, poor families had to purchase food stamps that could be spent like cash in grocery stores. A family of six would have to pay twelve dollars per month to receive food stamps for seventy-two dollars worth of groceries.[33] Because many had been forced off the land due to mechanization or political activity, they lacked the cash to purchase the stamps. Head Start and the employment opportunities that it provided meant that some of the most impoverished citizens could feed their families.

Black women like Winson Hudson, Lavaree Jones, and Alice Beard returned from Mount Beulah to their home communities and recruited students. They received help from Delta Ministry volunteers whom Art Thomas dispatched to knock on doors and spread the word about the promising possibilities of Head Start. By late April, when those interested met for a second time at Mount Beulah, 4,200 children had enrolled from sixty-four communities for the first summer. The large number disproved claims that white superintendents had made to Polly Greenberg that black parents did not value education. Thousands of black Mississippians, without the promise of a grant, mobilized to ensure that their children had a chance at nutritious meals, vaccinations, and school preparation just as earlier generations had double-taxed themselves to provide schooling for black youth. Organizers also reached out to poor white people, but their overtures were generally met with slammed doors and gunshots. The slights, however, did not diminish the excitement and determination of the local people interested in early childhood education. At the second meeting of black Mississippians interested in Head Start, those assembled selected Tom Levin as the program director and voted to call their Head Start program the Child Development Group of Mississippi (CDGM), a project of Mississippi Action for Community Education (MACE). Just as a mace is a weapon used to strike, CDGM was to be a weapon used to break down an old order.[34]

The children identified for CDGM's program ranged in age from four to seven years old, with a few even older. OEO guidelines prioritized students who were five or six and preparing to enter kindergarten or first grade (if their school system did not offer kindergarten), but CDGM included children of all ages, because the rural and isolated nature of many black communities meant that some needed several years of intervention to be ready for the first grade. Moreover, some students were older than six, yet they had never attended public school, so Head Start provided compensatory education for them.[35]

In anticipation of a grant from OEO, CDGM supporters sought facilities to serve as Head Start centers. The use of public school buildings was out of the question, even for a summer program, because white superintendents saw CDGM as a civil rights organization. As had been the case during the Reconstruction era, black church buildings, sometimes no more than a one-room, mason-blocked, plank-floored edifice, served as CDGM classrooms. In some areas, it was even hard to secure black churches, because many pastors believed that CDGM, with its stated compliance with civil rights law, posed too great a risk of vandalism. Not one church in Sunflower County opened its doors for Head Start during the 1965 summer. In areas where churches were unavailable or unwilling to host centers, CDGM supporters made plans to turn vacant homes, juke joints, or community centers into makeshift Head Starts classrooms.[36]

Tom Levin had gained the support of local people, but still needed to secure the approval of SNCC, the very organization that had politicized many in the communities that CDGM hoped to serve. He correctly worried that SNCC veterans mistrusted white liberals because of the 1964 Mississippi Freedom Democratic Party challenge and compromise offer. Indeed, John Lewis, SNCC's chairman from 1963 until 1966, had advised fellow

SNCC workers in 1964 not to count on the support of "white liberals and the so called affluent Negro leader. . . . They will sell us down the river for the hundredth time in order to protect themselves."[37] Lewis was undoubtedly referring to Senator Hubert Humphrey (D-Minn.), who had orchestrated the rejected offer at the 1964 Democratic National Convention to shore up his vice presidential nomination. Many black SNCC workers no longer believed white people had a role to play in the movement or that partnership with the federal government was possible. Well aware of those sentiments, Levin nevertheless met with SNCC Executive Secretary James Foreman. While Foreman refused to support the Head Start program, he also promised not to publicly disavow it. He encouraged Levin to attend a regional SNCC meeting and hear from other activists. Hollis Watkins, who was at the meeting, recalled Levin proposing a statewide preschool program and SNCC unequivocally opposing it. "We discussed that thing right and left, up and down, and ultimately said to Tom 'as a short range program we think this is a good idea. Long range, this is going to be bad for our people and therefore, we don't want it.'"[38] Many SNCC staff rightfully wondered if the federal government could be trusted. President Johnson had covertly undercut Mississippi Freedom Democratic Party support in Atlantic City. These veteran organizers feared that the Head Start program might cause local people to become dependent on an unreliable federal government.

Levin's determination to bring Head Start to Mississippi, however, caused SNCC activists to think more deeply. With or without their blessing, millions of dollars were headed to the communities they had organized over the previous four years. Eventually, Levin was able to get a SNCC pledge to neither support nor denounce the preschool program if SNCC workers were included on the payroll. He therefore agreed to hire Frank Smith, one of the first SNCC organizers in Mississippi, as director of community organizing. Smith had experience in cultivating leadership among local people, and his presence strengthened Head Start's legitimacy as a program committed to meaningful social change.[39] Most SNCC workers, however, saw no connection between Head Start and the earlier efforts in the state to forge racial and political change. They had their own reasons for getting involved. Hollis Watkins recalled, "we decided that certain ones of us would work in the program [CDGM] and certain ones of us would continue to do the work of the civil rights movement, and the money that the ones who was working in the program [were making] would be used to finance the ones who were still working in the civil rights movement."[40]

Despite this agreement, many of the state's black SNCC veterans resolved to have nothing to do with Levin's venture. For them, federal jobs for poor black people spelled the end to activism. Watkins argued that no money came without strings attached.[41]

With the elimination of possible SNCC opposition, it appeared that Levin and Thomas were prepared to submit a strong Head Start application on behalf of thousands of working-class black Mississippians. Obstacles remained, however. First, Levin had proposed that a Council of Neighborhood Centers comprised of poor citizens from CDGM communities serve as a governing board, participating in program administration and the allocation of resources. OEO officials in Washington, D.C., however, wanted a more traditional board of directors that included established leaders. The request signaled that despite a pronounced commitment to the maximum participation of the poor, OEO expected experts and professionals to play a leading role in CDGM's operation. Levin and Thomas, then, hastily selected a group of individuals who both satisfied officials in Washington and also sympathized with the grassroots spirit of the proposed Head Start program. Selected members included Art Thomas; Victoria Gray and Adam Daniel Beittel, who had both served as Mississippi Freedom Democratic Party delegates at the 1964 Democratic National Convention; NAACP Legal Defense and Education Fund attorney Marian Wright; and Will Byndum, the working-class black mayor of the all-black town of Winstonville. The Reverend James McRee, a pastor and civil rights activist from Canton who had hosted a freedom school in 1964 and served as an alternate Mississippi Freedom Democratic Party delegate to the 1964 convention, also served on the board. If OEO funded CDGM, then the communities served had the chance to formally elect or replace the selected board members.[42]

Tom Levin also worried about insulating the program from local white oversight. Mississippi governor Paul Johnson, who as lieutenant governor had physically blocked the federal marshals who escorted James Meredith as he desegregated the University of Mississippi in 1962, threatened to veto any grant that CDGM received. Section 209 of the Economic Opportunity Act, though, prohibited state governors from vetoing projects administered by institutions of higher education.[43] This meant that if a university or college served as CDGM's applicant agent, then the governor could not block the flow of Head Start dollars into black communities.

Tougaloo College was the logical choice to administer a civil rights movement–affiliated Head Start program, given its role in the state's freedom struggle. In 1961, nine Tougaloo students walked into the Jackson Municipal Library and began to study even though blacks were not allowed in the building. Their actions set off a series of organized protests in Jackson against Jim Crow. In the following years, the integrated Tougaloo hosted James Baldwin, Dr. Martin Luther King Jr., William Kunstler, and Eudora Welty. The college also served as a refuge for Hattiesburg natives Dorie and Joyce Ladner after they were expelled from state-supported Jackson State for their activism.[44]

Tougaloo had been a bastion of activism under the leadership of President Adam Daniel Beittel. A native of Pennsylvania, Beittel was an ordained United Church of Christ minister who had served as the president of Talladega College before coming to Tougaloo. When Tougaloo students held sit-ins in downtown Jackson, Beittel offered his support by coming to the riot scene and demanding that local police protect the demonstrators. The school's pivotal role in the freedom movement eroded after Brown University and Tougaloo formed a partnership in 1963. Barnaby Keeney, president of the Ivy League institution, did not support Tougaloo's civil rights activity. In 1964, Tougaloo's board forced Beittel to retire at Keeney's urging.[45] Keeney's ability to secure significant financial donations for Tougaloo meant that the college's administrators avoided overt activism to remain in his good graces. George Owens, Beittel's successor at Tougaloo, who had earlier pledged the school's assistance to CDGM, changed his mind twenty-four hours before CDGM's application was due in Washington.[46]

Obtaining the support of publicly funded black colleges in Mississippi was out of the question, so Art Thomas scrambled to find a black private institution of higher education to sponsor CDGM. The pickings were slim. After checking with U.S. Department of Education lawyers, OEO, in an indirect show of support for CDGM, defined an institution of higher learning as a school with at least one alumnus who had been accepted into a graduate program. Mary Holmes Junior College, an unaccredited black institution in the northeast section of the state, met that qualification. It was one of a number of Presbyterian schools in the country, all of which were integrated. Thomas met with Dawson Horn, Mary Holmes's president, who was reluctant to undertake the responsibilities and risks entailed in becoming involved with the Head Start program. He agreed to have his institution serve as the applicant agency only after learning that the college would receive a substantial amount of money for making the project possible. Mary Holmes Junior College served as the applicant agency, while

CDGM administered the program from Mount Beulah nearly 200 miles away.[47]

While antipoverty officials in Washington, D.C., helped to keep CDGM out of the governor's reach, OEO director Sargent Shriver crisscrossed the country extolling his agency's respect for gubernatorial authority. Shriver told the West Virginia legislature that no one from Washington could "force Head Start on West Virginia. Your governor could veto that."[48] Shriver recognized that the South's history of racism allowed a governor's veto to maintain race and class exclusion. He also understood that adherence to state sovereignty perpetuated poverty in Mississippi, so he covertly supported CDGM's program that circumvented such gubernatorial control.

OEO backed up its lofty ideals with generous funding. In May 1965, the agency awarded CDGM a grant for $1,460,748, substantially more than the three-quarters of a million dollars that the program had requested. The Head Start grant—one of the largest made throughout the country that summer and one-half of the Head Start funds appropriated for Mississippi—signaled OEO's intention to enter into partnership with the black poor to support social change. Nationwide, 2,300 Head Start programs served 560,000 disadvantaged children during the first summer. One hundred and sixty five Head Start centers in Mississippi served 10,838 children. In addition to private nonprofits such as CDGM, community action agencies and public school districts also sponsored Head Start programs. Public school districts operated over three-fourths of the Head Start programs in Mississippi. CDGM received funds to operate 84 centers and serve 6,000 children in 24 counties. Fifty of those centers resided in the Delta.[49]

The list of funded communities could have easily been mistaken for a SNCC or Mississippi Freedom Democratic Party roster of sites. Winson Hudson's Harmony became a CDGM location, as did all the black settlements in Forrest County that had strong 1964 freedom schools. Philadelphia, the site of the murders of three civil rights workers, was included along with McComb, a place of intense white resistance to black organizing. OEO funded CDGM centers in Fannie Lou Hamer's Sunflower County as well as in Lillie Ayers's Washington County.[50] Head Start became a major player in the ongoing freedom struggle.

OEO officials anticipated the links between CDGM and civil rights. In May 1965, before a single Head Start center opened, senior Head Start staff circulated a memo declaring that CDGM would be the first time that blacks had any real say "in the direction and management of a program from the very beginning." They predicted that the preschool program would bring "a new era of dignity for some Negroes in Mississippi." Senior staff officials in Washington also warned that the white power structure—including white moderates—would not be pleased with the program. This information did not cause Sargent Shriver to backtrack on the partnership his office had established with the black poor. Rather, the agency took the position that CDGM would become a model for other rural areas in the South.[51]

Segregationists also immediately recognized CDGM's connections to the black freedom struggle. The *Jackson Daily News* labeled CDGM as a vehicle for "mongrelization," and a newspaper in Hattiesburg alleged that CDGM was run "by outside forces, which have no knowledge of local problems and no comprehensive solutions."[52] In reality, women like Winson Hudson had intimate knowledge and understanding of the problems that confronted Mississippi's black poor. They also had the know-how to go about solving those problems, despite the "outside agitators" rhetoric that white supremacists used to deflect attention from the real issues. The newspapers' real issue was CDGM's lack of respect for segregation. Tom Levin had pledged compliance with civil rights laws in a statewide press release. The 1964 Civil Rights Act compelled every Head Start center in the country to operate in a nondiscriminatory manner, but enforcement was a different matter. A representative from a Jackson Head Start program maintained that his program was "not concerned with social revolution."[53] In other words, black and white children did not learn together. Lack of compliance with civil rights law happened across the South. For example, Head Start centers in Ozark, Alabama, and in Worth County, Georgia, practiced blatant segregation. OEO officials in the Civil Rights Division and in the General Counsel's Office tried to root out noncompliant programs, but they were not always successful.[54]

CDGM promoted integrated staffing at all levels. A forty-person Central Staff based at Mount Beulah oversaw the nuts and bolts of program administration, handling tasks such as payroll, teacher training, and social services. Central Staff employees included social services coordinator Jeannette King, who, like her husband, the Reverend Edwin "Ed" King, had been a central figure in the Mississippi freedom struggle. The Kings, native white Mississippians, experienced physical and economic reprisals for being "race traitors." Black SNCC field secretary Frank Smith coordinated the program's organizing activities, and white SNCC workers Jim and Lenore Monsonis oversaw supply and fiscal matters. White Tougaloo College professor

Marvin Hoffman acted as a staff counselor, and Helen Bass Williams, a black professor at the college, coordinated health initiatives. Maria Varela, a Latina activist who had organized SNCC literacy projects in Alabama from 1963 to 1965 coordinated the reading program. Joan Bowman, a white woman from Georgia who had been a SNCC field secretary in Mississippi, served as CDGM historian. Jeanine Herron and Polly Greenberg acted as program coordinators and managed the teacher training program. Greenberg became a CDGM employee in June 1965, after resigning from OEO in protest over a perceived shift in agency commitment from quality to quantity. She decided to join forces with the Head Start program that she believed best embodied "maximum feasible participation of the poor." The Central Staff also had five district coordinators, four from SNCC and one from the Delta Ministry.[55]

The plan called for local people to replace Central Staff members after the summer. As written in CDGM's original grant proposal, the "primary purpose of the summer is to stimulate communities to function autonomously so that the program can continue permanently with or without outside help."[56] Thus, CDGM, like SNCC had done earlier, sought to foster leadership among ordinary citizens and increase the confidence and political know-how of working-class Mississippians. Whether they worked for CDGM or pursued other ventures in the future, the program gave marginalized people the experience and clout to make their voices heard.

In addition to Central Staff, CDGM's workforce during the 1965 summer included 1,100 black individuals who worked as teachers, teachers' aides, social service and health staff, community organizers, janitors, bus drivers, cooks, and administrators in Head Start centers. All these positions paid salaries much higher than most black Mississippians had ever been offered. CDGM teachers were called "teacher trainees" during the first summer, even though they managed the classrooms and taught pupils. Teacher trainees, according to CDGM policy, did not need "COLLEGE DEGREES OR TEACHER'S CERTIFICATES" (caps in original document), but simply needed to read on an eighth-grade level, have lots of energy, and enjoy "the noise young children make when they play."[57] Their pay was sixty dollars per week. Teacher's aides made fifty dollars per week, while cooks and janitors received twenty-five dollars per week—significant salaries for individuals unlikely to have a high school diploma.[58] These jobs offered poor black Mississippians more than a higher standard of living. Federally funded jobs also offered them dignified employment and independence from local white employers, who had often limited their activities with the threat of firing.

CDGM did not seek out Mississippi's black public school teachers for several reasons. First, almost all educators in the state lacked early childhood education training. Mississippi had no public statewide kindergarten. In the spring of 1965, while still an OEO-employed Head Start specialist, Polly Greenberg emphasized to Tom Levin that the antipoverty agency did not consider elementary and high school teachers particularly desirable for Head Start because they had no early childhood education experience and most were not flexible enough to adapt to Head Start's comprehensive program that prioritized parental involvement, healthcare, and social services.[59]

Second, CDGM did not seek out public school teachers because the program was often a liability for individuals who taught in the public school system. School superintendents—both those who received funds to run Head Start centers and those who did not—often prevented public school teachers from their districts from seeking summer employment with CDGM, because they saw the connections between the Head Start program and the civil rights movement. Central Staff learned that black public school teacher Coloniece Gavin retracted her application for CDGM employment as a teacher during the 1965 summer after the superintendent of her county made it clear to her that she would lose her job in the public school system if she worked for CDGM.[60] Some did in fact lose their jobs because of CDGM affiliation. One teacher explained, "I am from the public school. I had a job there till yesterday," when she told her principal that she planned to teach for CDGM.[61] Thus it was unwise for CDGM to ask black teachers to risk their full-time job for a summer opportunity.

Given the lack of early childhood education specialists and the hostility on the part of many superintendents, CDGM filled its classroom with rank-and-file community members. With proper training and assistance, parents, who lacked formal credentials but who had experience dealing with small children, were the best available option for CDGM.[62] Putting parents in the classroom made them leaders in the eyes of young children, increased their involvement in their children's education, and gave them a well-paying job that addressed their material lack. CDGM, as SNCC had done earlier, celebrated the potential of ordinary men and women by not prioritizing licensed educators.

The program's use of teachers who did not have formal credentials was not a Head Start anomaly. There were not enough university-trained teachers who specialized in early childhood education to staff Head Start programs nationwide. For example, Pearlene Reese, a black woman who had quit school in the tenth grade to work in cotton fields, secured a job as an instructional aide in a Westley, California, Head Start center in 1965.[63] Head Start trained its untraditional teaching staff through forty-hour orientation courses and eight-week training programs held at universities. Programs like CDGM supplemented that training with workshops and on-the-job instruction led by early childhood education veterans such as Polly Greenberg. College-trained teachers, however, usually participated in Head Start programs run by public school systems. Head Start centers nationwide were uneven in quality because there were not uniform requirements of teachers.[64]

In Mississippi, not all working-class black citizens enthusiastically applied for CDGM jobs despite the numerous benefits of Head Start employment. Thelma Barnes, a Delta Ministry employee who took leave in 1965 to organize CDGM in Washington County, recalled that she had a hard time finding teachers. Domestics in Washington County's Greenville made an average of twelve dollars and fifty cents per week. CDGM teachers earned more than four times that amount. Barnes explained, "people were not realizing that although they could go and nurse white children, they were made to believe that they were not qualified for their own."[65] Many local black women believed that college-trained educators could lead most effectively in the classroom. District organizers from the Delta Ministry and local people who oversaw hiring had the arduous task of helping local people to realize that they had valuable skills to contribute to the new program.

Even with such hesitation, every center was staffed when the program began on 12 July. Each center had a community governing committee that acted as a pseudo–school board and oversaw hiring and program logistics. The local governing committees ensured that disempowered people had an opportunity to make meaningful decisions. In many communities, civil rights veterans comprised committee membership. This meant that those who had risked their livelihoods to challenge white supremacy now had a chance at the spoils of war. In fact, the CDGM employment application instructed applicants to list previous civil rights activity.[66] For some, Head Start employment served as delayed compensation for civil rights risks taken when they were neither prudent nor lucrative.

Civil rights veterans hired their allies in Mississippi's largest Head Start program. In black-majority Panola County, located in the northwestern part of the state, the go-to man for CDGM was Robert Miles, the county's Mississippi Freedom Democratic Party chairman. Miles was a fearless, fifty-year-old man who had endured cross burnings, house bombings, and nightriders from 1959 until 1964 as he led voter registration drives. He and his wife Mona housed and fed as many as thirteen Freedom Summer volunteers at one time in their bullet-ridden home. He became active in the movement because he was fed up with the racial status quo. From 1890 until 1962, white officials permitted only two African Americans in Panola County to register to vote. Miles' courage and commitment was legendary. His homeowner's insurance was canceled after he first attempted to register to vote, but he kept trying. His resolve earned him a seat on the local CDGM governing committee for the Batesville centers. He used his position to reward those who had worked alongside him during the most dangerous times. Every teacher's aide except one in Panola County's three CDGM centers was a member of the local Mississippi Freedom Democratic Party.[67]

Panola County was not exceptional in this. Amzie Moore, a World War II veteran and one of the earliest leaders of the freedom struggle in the Delta, had served as the point man for SNCC workers coming into Mississippi between 1961 and 1964. He oversaw the Cleveland CDGM centers in Bolivar County, demonstrating that even though SNCC field staff may not have supported the federally funded Head Start program, some local people saw it as the next phase of their organizing efforts. Sixty-five percent of African Americans in Cleveland were unemployed, so those who had established working relationships with Moore stood to do well if in need of a job. In Glen Allan, an unincorporated town of 100 white and 200 black residents, Lillie Ayers was one of the first hired as a CDGM teacher. Her husband Jake had registered to vote in 1958, a move so brazen that whites "tolerated it as a joke." He secured a seat on the CDGM Board of Directors.[68] In Harmony, local NAACP president Winson Hudson ran the CDGM center. The Head Start program became another way for her to invest in the education of young black children just as older residents had once invested in her own education. Pap Hamer, the husband of Mississippi legend Fannie Lou Hamer, found employment as a Head Start bus driver after his wife's civil rights activity cost him his plantation job. Issaquena County legend Henry Sias was also active in the Head Start program. The eighty-four-year-old black landowner had served as a Mississippi Freedom Democratic Party delegate to the 1964 Democratic National Convention. Freedom school founder Charlie Cobb once remarked of Sias's prominence, "Once Henry Sias said it was ok, then everybody in the county was willing to deal with us

[SNCC]."[69] In Humphreys County, Willie Hazelwood, the local NAACP president, directed CDGM operations. Hazelwood and his family had been among the few blacks in the county who dared to challenge white supremacy in the face of ongoing terrorism. The family paid dearly for their political work, losing access to credit and being refused service at local stores. CDGM employment was a welcomed and hard-won benefit.[70]

Awarding CDGM jobs to movement veterans was a form of patronage, but, more importantly, it was a continuation of a much longer freedom struggle that included access to quality educational opportunities, access to well-paying jobs, and access to the ballot. The employment of civil rights veterans in the program ensured that CDGM parents came into contact with employees who encouraged them to register to vote and challenge white supremacy. The Head Start program operated in counties with the highest levels of white violence in the state, so in modeling courage and consistently challenging parents to speak up for themselves and their children, CDGM staff brought new adherents into the fold. There were also some staff members in many CDGM centers who had not been involved with the movement previously, and they too became more willing to risk working for change by providing opportunities for their community's children and perhaps also by registering to vote.

The preference for individuals with movement experience was another reason for the very small number of public school teachers in CDGM's program. Many CDGM supporters who had risked everything to challenge white supremacy did not want credentialed black educators to play any role in the Head Start program, because it appeared that these educators had not supported civil rights earlier. After Gladys Bates and R. Jess Brown lost their jobs for challenging salary differentials between white and black teachers, most black teachers in the state refrained from publicly challenging racial discrimination. In fact, NAACP Mississippi field secretary Medgar Evers had once warned black teachers not to get involved in the civil rights movement. This lack of overt political activity rendered most public school teachers ineligible for CDGM jobs according to local hiring committees, even though many teachers had found ways to secretly support movement activities.[71]

The exclusion of black middle-class teachers appeared contradictory, given the presence of white middle-class employees on the Central Staff. The white personnel, however, had bona fide civil rights experience and understood that their employment was temporary. Each northern white professional worked side by side with a local black trainee who was to take over the job as soon as possible. The arrangement was problematic in that it fed into the stereotype that working-class black residents were dependent upon white people. Yet, the administrative expertise of these Central Staff members was absolutely crucial in getting CDGM off the ground and ensuring that CDGM got funded and remained funded. Their presence gave local people a glimpse of views, values, and experiences other than those of white and black middle-class Mississippians who were constrained by their "closed society," which had no tolerance for dissent.[72] Local trainees' need for assistance from white northerners or middle-class black leaders decreased as they learned to run the program themselves.

Tom Levin recruited one hundred college students from prestigious universities, including Columbia, Duke, Howard, and Northwestern, to work as resource teachers in CDGM centers during the summer.[73] CDGM utilized white resource teachers when available, to achieve integration at the various Head Start centers around the state. To maintain center autonomy, local communities chose "their own whites by meeting with likely candidates" vetted by the Central Staff.[74] Hollandale preschool workers chose Harriet Feinberg, a young white student from New York, as their resource teacher because she talked "slow enough so that the people can understand."[75] Typically, there was one resource teacher per center. Resource teachers provided guidance but did not offer instruction, so as to not dominate classrooms and stymie the leadership that had emerged among local people. In many areas, local black Mississippians and their out-of-state resource teachers developed close and lasting friendships.

Resource teachers helped CDGM to fulfill the federal government's requirement for integration in programs that received federal funds. CDGM sought unsuccessfully to recruit in white communities, with the exception of the Gulf region. The Gulf Coast was one of the most progressive areas in Mississippi, with many of its hotels admitting integrated groups as early as the 1950s. The coastal area's relatively moderate race relations stemmed from its lack of an agricultural tradition.[76] In other parts of the state, poor white parents feared being ostracized for working in the program or for allowing their children to go to school with black children. Even if a center had no white students, there was usually a white resource teacher present who assisted black teachers in the classroom.

At orientation sessions that had the ethos of a civil rights movement mass meeting coupled with the agenda of a pedagogical summit, over 800 former black sharecroppers and domestics received training to lead Head Start classrooms. At one of two five-day orientations held at Mount Beulah in early July, attendees sang freedom songs, listened to inspirational and fiery speeches, and discussed the best teaching practices for preschools. Frank Smith gave an impassioned address stating that CDGM would not raise black children "to be second-class citizens and Uncle Toms," demonstrating that the Head Start program, like the earlier freedom schools, sought to nurture change agents rather than passive children.[77]

In addition to the freedom school parallel, CDGM also modeled the Freedom Summer philosophy of recognizing ordinary people's right and ability to make decisions for themselves. Polly Greenberg recalled, "We didn't develop guidelines and notebooks full of recommended procedures, patterns, recipes, and games ahead of our Head Start teacher orientation. We first formally considered these things at the orientation with the poor people hiring committees and with the poor people who would be there."[78] Many of the resource teachers brought in from out of state had not expected the egalitarian and inclusive lesson-planning sessions. During orientation, they discovered that they were not hired to rescue poverty-stricken Mississippians. Rather, their job was to serve as a catalyst or resource for the poor.[79]

Resource teachers took a back seat, because what grassroots people hired from communities across Mississippi lacked in experience, they made up for through commitment to social change. Few had any knowledge of the most popular pedagogical methods of the day. They did know, however, that their children's unquestioned acceptance of and obedience to the status quo presaged an even more dismal future. Polly Greenberg and other Central Staff used the Socratic method and helped orientation attendees think about the kind of education they planned to offer CDGM youngsters. Questions such as "do children need freedom like adults?" and "should children express their feelings?" stimulated discussion about classroom management and preschool activities. This dialectical exercise forced local people to think about how they wanted to change the lives of their students and how to turn dreams into reality.

During a discussion of student discipline, one black woman asserted, "If we don't teach the children anything else, let's teach them to speak their mind. Never mind obedience. They will fit in as they grow. I don't want anyone shaming my grandchildren in no chair." Commanding obedience from black children had been a form of survival since slavery. In many instances

Women at a CDGM orientation session at Mount Beulah in July 1965. The orientation sessions' underlying premise was that local people had the ability and will to operate programs for themselves. Resources teachers, who were normally white, had not been hired to run or lead classrooms but to offer assistance in the background. (Matt Herron/ Take Stock/The Image Works)

black parents had demanded complete obedience to ensure their children's acquiescence to the rules of a segregated society. Whether it was stepping off the sidewalk when a white person passed or not making eye contact with a white woman, black parents had laid out the rules and meticulously ensured their enforcement.[80]

The civil rights movement had forced segregation's demise, and CDGM women thus created a new and unorthodox vision of child rearing in the South. Fear no longer governed their actions. They taught their children to speak up rather than to remain silent and invisible. They taught their children to challenge the status quo rather than conform to it. These untraditional teachers prepared their pupils to live in a post–civil rights world that heralded a new mentality and new behavior. In doing so, these activist educators carried out a long tradition of racial uplift, transforming education into a vehicle for liberation.[81]

Not everyone present at orientation championed curiosity and structured chaos in the classroom. A white licensed kindergarten teacher stated that the program's goal should be to teach black children to be obedient. This educator believed that school readiness should be Head Start's focus and teaching children discipline would serve them well in the future. This opinion, however, was the minority among CDGM staff. For most, quality education meant raising up a generation of uninhibited children. Local people were slow to challenge the traditional educator during orientation, but spoke up in opposition after being reminded by a discussion facilitator that "you're all teachers starting day after tomorrow, so if you have other ideas, feel free to say them so we can all hear."[82] These types of discussions were important, because poor people had the opportunity to design their own curriculum and policies rather than be handed a set of instructions from experts. This was their opportunity to speak rather than have a minister or expert speak for them. They had a chance to play a role in providing black children with the kind of quality education that black Mississippians had sought since emancipation.

Over the course of orientation, local people received the training needed to run Head Start centers. They toured a classroom exhibit set up by a Montessori teacher. They participated in sample arithmetic workshops where they played with teaching resources such as the colorful, rectangular Cuisenaire rods used for counting exercises. They practiced holding conversations with preschoolers. In short, they learned how to interact with their future pupils. If the newly minted educators remembered nothing else, Greenberg advised them to encourage children to talk and listen to what they had to say. Eye contact and physical activity allowed the youngsters to know that they were important. CDGM teachers also heard from Henry Kirksey, a black printer who planned to partner with CDGM so that students had books that featured people who looked like them. While CDGM teachers undoubtedly had on-the-job training throughout the 1965 summer, orientation ensured that they had a basic grasp of how to set up and run their classrooms.[83]

In addition to academic matters, the Central Staff discussed security and legal issues during orientation, in anticipation of widespread white resistance to CDGM. They reminded those assembled at Mount Beulah that CDGM employees could not engage in political activities during work hours or in work vehicles. They did so because they knew that the strict use of CDGM materials and vehicles for official business was antithetical to the communal civil rights movement spirit that anything available to anyone was available to everyone. CDGM employees had a right to participate in political activities while off duty, but not to use program vehicles, materials, and funds while engaging in partisan activities. If employees were detained, arrested, or fined through no fault of their own while carrying out their CDGM duties, the Central Staff instructed them to immediately contact Gordon Wilcox, whom Tom Levin had retained to deal with white harassment.[84]

In fact, white harassment began before orientation. On 25 June 1965, George Shaw, a white Mississippi attorney, entered the Mount Beulah grounds and fired shots from a .45 pistol at staff members before fleeing. That same day state highway patrol officers stopped Jim Dann, one of CDGM's white district coordinators, in two different traffic stops. After learning that the rental car Dann drove was leased to the preschool program, the officers asked several questions unrelated to the traffic stops. Law enforcement officials were not the only people troubled by CDGM before the program started. Klansmen burned crosses in front of a house that was to serve as a Head Start center, and a white cotton gin manager threatened the husband of the Choctaw CDGM governing committee chairperson.[85]

White resistance to CDGM continued after centers opened on 12 July. Some landowners evicted families from plantations for sending their children to CDGM's program. An unidentified white man ran Tom Levin's vehicle off the road in Sharkey County, and five white men in Bolivar County entered a CDGM center and beat two teachers in late July. Days later, shots were fired from either end of the street where the center was located. In Leake County, nails were placed on the roads CDGM bus drivers used to transport students to and from Head Start centers. On 8 August, Klansmen in Washington County burned down a wooden church that served as a CDGM site. Glen Allan's white community strategized to get the insurance policy on the black church that housed the CDGM center canceled. Soon after, the building inspector deemed the facility unsafe and ordered it closed. Tellingly, the inspector had never voiced concerned about the splintered shacks without water or plumbing that black people in Glen Allan had rented from white planters for years.[86] The unprecedented level of violence that CDGM's Head Start program faced led OEO officials to request assistance from the FBI. FBI officials proved to be little help, going so far as to dismiss a bullet-ridden CDGM vehicle as the product of a "random hunter's shots." Most CDGM centers did not have phones in them. Some centers went so far as to have telephone drills where staff practiced running several miles to the nearest phone in case of emergency.[87]

White supremacists opposed CDGM because the Head Start program allowed rank-and-file black Mississippians to control something other than their churches. They understood that if the poorest of the poor ran Head Start centers, they could also run towns and make decisions for themselves. These segregationists also resisted CDGM because it was an educational institution free of local white control. Since Reconstruction white Mississippians had been able to monitor, limit, and filter what black students learned. The ground had shifted under the white supremacists' feet, and they held on for dear life.

Intimidation and violence, however, did not weaken the resolve of black parents and community leaders who were determined to secure better educational opportunities for black children. Local staff decided to hold classes outside under pecan trees after Klansmen burned one of the Washington County CDGM centers.[88] Meetings outside made them easier targets for white supremacists, yet their commitment to early childhood education meant that instruction had to continue. They did not retreat, because CDGM provided black children with their first educational opportunities void of inferior resources. Black Mississippians had spent nearly a century fighting for fulfillment of a state constitutional right to a quality education. Arson did not move them, for they had the chance through a Head Start program for a better future. CDGM, as the next phase of a long African American freedom struggle in the state, had helped to develop a new attitude among the marginalized.

CDGM's Head Start program, unlike many Mississippi black public schools, openly encouraged black children to think critically. Teachers fostered assertiveness in their students by designing lessons that required student response. For example, teachers at the Asbury center in Madison County led an exercise that encouraged children to expand their minds, speak up, and make suggestions:

TEACHER: How many ways can you find to go from this tree to that one?
CHILD: Walk.
TEACHER: Ok, good. Let's all walk to that tree. How else can we get there?
ANOTHER CHILD: Run!
TEACHER: Let's run. Can anyone think of another way?
CHILD: SKIP (We skipped. I noticed many skip only on one foot).

CHILD: Let's jump (We jumped).

CHILD: Hop (We hopped).

TEACHER: Now let's all hop on the other foot. (This they found more difficult. This should help them learn to skip with both feet).[89]

Such exercises sought to reward initiative and stretch the young pupils' impressionable minds. They were also a direct carryover of the freedom schools' pedagogical style that favored discussion over lecture.[90]

Program leaders saw developing black children's capabilities as a way to change society. CDGM taught its students not just letters and numbers, but how to ask questions and think for themselves—skills that also prepared children to question the status quo. Lessons were hands on and open ended. Science class was often held outdoors where the inquisitive youth marveled over creatures found in a pond and squealed with joy at the sight of a frog. One science lesson plan distributed to all CDGM centers stated that if students were encouraged to be curious, they would not "simply accept every word a white man said later in life."[91] Exploration of nature fostered curiosity. Something as simple as a nature walk and the self-discovery it promoted helped to "build iron egos needed by children growing up to be future leaders of social change in a semifeudal state."[92] Preschoolers who had no concept of asserting themselves were suddenly voting on what color crayon they should use—red or blue.[93] Activities such as finger painting and clay sculpting allowed children to make things, to experiment, and to be creative.[94] Maria Varela and Polly Greenberg went so far as to craft a reading readiness program that avoided standard children's books that did not portray black children. Instead, they instructed center staff to have students bring in materials from home, be it a piece of cotton picked by a parent or an insect caught by an older sibling. Teachers helped the children to make their own storybooks based on the materials collected. The familiar subject matter helped children to like and enjoy books, a necessary first step in inculcating a love of reading in small children.[95]

The storybooks encouraged critical thinking and self-expression among CDGM students. Teachers gave children construction paper and told them to draw what they wanted; they then asked the children for a caption to go along with the drawing. CDGM staff was careful not to think for their young charges. They did not make comments about the drawings such as "houses don't have three legs" or "the tail goes here." In validating how children perceived their surroundings, CDGM encouraged imagination, an ability that would help prepare the youngsters to one day conceive of solutions to the problems plaguing their communities. Printer Henry Kirksey published several CDGM storybooks including *Pond* and *Toad* and distributed them to the various centers.[96]

The use of everyday items such as cotton in CDGM classrooms not only made for relevant reading material but also allowed students to learn about difficult and complex subjects. When the goldfish at the Armstead CDGM center died, teachers used the incident to teach the preschoolers about both fish and death. Rather than discard the fish immediately, a class discussion was held about the fish's color, gills, fins, and scales. These were all new words for the children. Later, the class went outside and dug a hole with spoons, giving the fish a proper burial. After every child held the fish, they lowered it into the ground and covered it with dirt. A preschooler preached a short eulogy and was instructed by the teacher to say "ashes to ashes and dust to dust." After a round of the song "Jesus Loves Me," the funeral concluded and all went inside and washed their hands.[97]

Head Start introduced its students (and in many instances its staff) to their history in order to imbue them with a sense of pride and self-worth. Teachers received copies of a teacher development manual entitled "What Shall I Tell My Children Who Are Black? Selected Material on Negro History and Culture for Head Start Teachers." The book included poems by Margaret Burroughs and Langston Hughes and a list of black Americans who fought in every war involving the United States.[98] Undoubtedly, this curriculum was new to some of the teachers, who had never before learned about black achievements. Tom Levin also requested that Johnson Publishing Company send issues of the monthly magazine *Ebony* to all center directors for use in their centers.[99] Perhaps he did this because he knew that the magazine projected an image of black material success that was otherwise beyond the imaginations of most Mississippians.[100]

A true understanding of African history and culture also evaded many in the CDGM community. CDGM Central Staff found that most local people thought of Africa as a primitive and shameful place. The radical Head Start program's curriculum included lessons on African dress and music as a way of connecting CDGM teachers and students to their ancestral past and correcting misconceptions about the continent. Preschoolers learned about the colorful, free-flowing attire that women wore in West Africa. To drive the lesson home, northern staff taught the children how to tie-dye clothing in order to create distinctive African patterns. The children complemented

In CDGM's program, learning was hands-on and creative. Whether making masks, acting out skits, or tie-dyeing cloth, CDGM youngsters tapped into their imaginations and had new experiences. Many of these lessons promoted African culture and racial pride. (Maria Varela, photographer/Doris Derby Collection, Manuscripts, Archives, and Rare Book Library, Emory University)

their attire with replicas of African beaded necklaces that were made of dyed macaroni. The simple, age-appropriate introductions to African culture helped to dispel notions of African savagery and foster racial pride.[101]

Moreover, to make sure that the concept of black self-worth was consistently applied, resource teachers worked with CDGM women in creating discipline techniques that corrected student behavior without using the then-common expressions that originated in slavery, such as "I'll tan your hide" or "I'll whip you til you can't sit down."[102] Teachers aimed to help students learn to respond to adults out of respect instead of fear. The use of fear to control behavior was a lesson that had to be unlearned, for the threat of violence had governed black life for so long.

The goals of CDGM's early childhood education program resembled those of the earlier freedom movement in that both tried to change the way people thought about themselves and their potential. The systematic denial of quality education had taken its toll on black expectations. Polly Greenberg found indifference when she approached one family in Clarke County about enrolling their children in a CDGM center. After Greenberg explained the benefits of early childhood education, the grandmother informed her that she dreamed for her grandchildren to have electricity, so that when they took in washing and ironing for a living, as she did, they did not have to walk half a mile to fetch wood for the fire.[103] CDGM worked to incubate more expansive dreams for both the grandchildren and the grandmother.

As a community action program, CDGM gave black parents the opportunity to participate in institutional change on a local level. They might not have had any say in the operation of the public school system, but their voices mattered in Head Start. Their opinions carried weight, just as those of experts did. Many educational specialists believed that children should have been the only focus of Head Start. For these professionals, shapes, colors, and the alphabet were the cornerstone of any preschool program, and trained teachers could better teach those lessons than undereducated parents. CDGM maintained that the best way to help children was to help their parents through job development and training. The battle between prioritizing community action or early childhood education, an appropriate debate, would cause CDGM to face opposition from expected allies in the program's later years.

CDGM also addressed black children's physical needs, in addition to focusing on their intellectual potential and giving their parents a say in their education. In Kemper County, a survey of sixty-three CDGM families showed that 75 percent of them did not have a sufficient amount or variety of foods in their households. The overwhelming majority attributed this problem to lack of money. Fifty-three percent of those surveyed received their only food from the state's commodity program—the same program that state officials had started phasing out prior to CDGM's inception.[104] The diets of CDGM families lacked sufficient protein and consisted mainly of starches available from the federal food commodities program. Like all Head Start children nationwide, CDGM students received a hot lunch daily that included foods such as fried steak, salmon croquettes, buttered cabbage, creamed potatoes, lima beans, carrot sticks, apple pie, rolls, and milk.

The Head Start lunch program often made the difference between survival and starvation in Mississippi. At the Tougaloo center, teachers found it necessary to cook breakfast in addition to lunch because the children normally arrived listless and weak.[105] Grace Simmons attended a Holmes County center and she recalled relishing mealtime. "I remember waiting for those string beans and pear halves," she wrote much later in an article for the

CDGM students preparing for mealtime. Nutritious meals were an integral part of Head Start's program because hunger negatively affects health and academic performance. (Presbyterian Historical Society, Presbyterian Church [U.S.A.])

Jackson *Clarion-Ledger*. Before Head Start, Simmons had never tasted a variety of foods and had only eaten once per day.[106] A teacher in Wayne County remarked that several of her students "had never had a balanced meal, never drunk milk, nor eaten an orange" before CDGM.[107]

The availability of hot and nutritious meals was simply one part of CDGM's comprehensive health program. A significant proportion of black Mississippians—adults and children—had never seen a doctor. Many felt suspicious of white physicians, who were often members of the local Citizens' Council. Additionally, the state had only fifteen to twenty practicing black physicians in Mississippi. Their short supply, coupled with the limited financial means of black residents, meant that it was more common than not that black Mississippians never received professional medical care. Moreover, after Congress passed Medicaid in 1965, Mississippi refused to sign on until 1971, so black Mississippians truly had little or no access to healthcare. CDGM changed this. Following national Head Start directives,

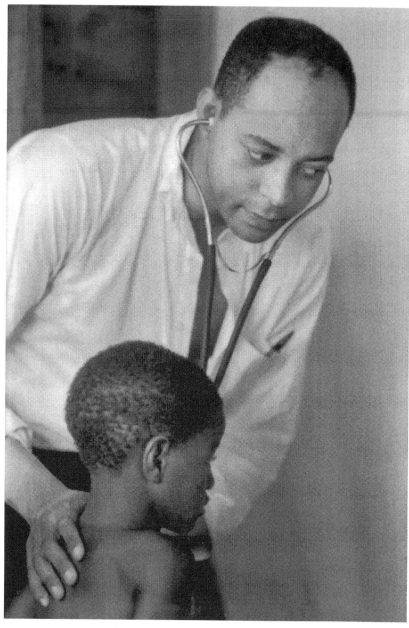

Head Start required its students to have physical and dental examinations, tuberculin screenings, and vision, hearing, speech, and blood tests. The overwhelming majority of CDGM students had never visited a doctor or a dentist. (Matt Heron/Take Stock/ The Image Works)

students had dental, vision, hearing, speech, tuberculosis, and psychological screenings. Children also received immunizations and had urine tests.[108]

Doctor Robert Smith, an African American physician and Mississippi native educated at Tougaloo and Howard University and a cofounder of the Medical Committee for Human Rights with Tom Levin, provided much of the medical care for CDGM.[109] Smith recalled that almost all white physicians opposed CDGM from the beginning and many black physicians shied away from it because it "didn't come down through the traditional channels." Smith became the nemesis of Doctor Archie Gray, Mississippi's chief health officer, for his work with Head Start. Gray argued that CDGM's health component was unnecessary because black children rarely had health problems, and if they did, they had access to healthcare through local health departments. In reality, most health departments in counties where CDGM operated refused to treat black patients or forced them to sit in segregated sitting areas and endure humiliating treatment. CDGM confronted hostility from health departments by securing sympathetic healthcare providers. Smith identified physicians to work with the program, securing the support of black doctors such as Aaron Shirley, James Anderson, and Gilbert Mason who saw students in their offices and in Head Start centers. These physicians, like Smith, had participated in earlier civil rights initiatives. For example, Mason led a 1959 "wade-in" against segregated beaches on Mississippi's gulf coast.[110]

CDGM doctors treated a host of ailments and diseases prevalent in impoverished communities, including high rates of anemia, intestinal parasites, and malnutrition. In the Philadelphia center, teachers noticed that six-year-old Janice Peeden often fell into a deep sleep. A CDGM doctor diagnosed her with having low blood pressure and poor nutrition. A young boy who teachers believed had learning difficulties simply had visual impairment that an eye specialist treated.[111]

Sometimes, even materials purchased for playtime were co-opted for medical purposes. CDGM purchased plastic wading pools for the Head Start center in Liberty. Rather than use them as pools, the teachers turned them into bathtubs, since many of the children lived in homes without tubs or running water and had impetigo. Teachers washed the children in the pool with medicated soap prescribed by a CDGM doctor to alleviate the skin rashes and sores.[112] At the Harmony center, Winson Hudson claimed that the medical examinations children received saved two or three lives. Employees at the Glen Allan center reported the enrollment of sixty new preschoolers after the community saw that CDGM children received eyeglasses at Head Start's expense.[113] Mississippi had the nation's highest infant mortality rate and the lowest median death age, making the Head Start's medical program all the more important.[114]

Healthcare had long been an issue in the Mississippi freedom struggle. Liberty, where the teachers used the wading pools to bathe students, was the county seat of Amite, known by movement workers as the "ninth circle of hell." Here, in 1961, a white state legislator murdered a black man with impunity. Amite County had not, by 1965, witnessed one civil rights sit-in or march and still only had one registered black voter. Yet the county was 55 percent black, suggesting the level of violence and fear that governed black life.[115] Teachers in Liberty perhaps viewed it as too dangerous to march through downtown, but they resisted the hold of Jim Crow on their children's minds with something as mundane as a bath.

Healthcare, like education, was inextricably linked to political power. The Liberty children's skin rashes did not result from lack of interest in cleanliness or from improper housekeeping, but from racist negligence that kept municipal water lines from the black residential areas. Additionally, African Americans' lack of hospital access or inferior hospital facilities also contributed to poor health. In 1946, Congress passed the Hill-Burton Act, which provided federal funds for hospital construction and expansion. Federal tax dollars built several of Mississippi's hospitals, yet many refused to accept black patients; those that did provided inferior accommodations. In Madison County, where black people made up 70 percent of the population, the largest local hospital, built with Hill-Burton money, reserved only twenty-two of the sixty beds for black patients. The hospital not only required an admission fee of fifty dollars, an amount few black people had, but denied them air conditioning.[116] CDGM's medical program sought to promote conversations between activists and non-activists. The program used activist physicians, so that when kids received health screenings, their parents would be informed of the links between racial discrimination and poor health. The causes of the most common and preventable illnesses plaguing the Head Start youngsters had their roots in racial oppression, and CDGM helped to expose those social determinants.

Health Services Director Helen Bass Williams, one of the few black middle-class staff members, knew the program's large, working-class black workforce would be watching her actions and behavior when she interacted with white staff. She carried herself in a way that proved instructive for the students and staff, giving them a model of leadership and affirming their dignity and self-worth. It was common knowledge that at the few health clinics in Mississippi that served black Head Start preschoolers "the child might leave with an inoculation, but also with the impression that his mother, who has been called by her first name throughout the transaction and made to enter through a side door, is a useless blob in a mass of shiftless people who make up the masses of blacks." Williams worked to change such treatment by challenging clinic personnel who called her by her first name, and she sometimes retaliated by calling the attending health care providers "Sally Lou."[117]

Williams's example proved instructive. Following her lead, the women at the Sunny Mount center in Holmes County stood up to racist health department officials who did not want black children visiting the clinic for urinalysis testing. The women vehemently refused to collect the urine at the center and bring it in as requested. Instead, they insisted that black children had a right to go into public health departments.[118]

Transforming the community was as integral a part of preparing black children for school as teaching them their colors. CDGM sought to help black parents recognize the links between their second-class livelihoods and their lack of political power. Something as simple as seeing Helen Bass Williams challenge white disrespect went a long way toward changing the mindsets of those who had not been reached by earlier movement activity. In an effort to promote change, CDGM centers had monthly or sometimes bimonthly community meetings where Central Staff met with parents and other community residents to discuss a host of issues, including the Head Start program, welfare rights, and racial discrimination. It was not unusual for more than half of the parents at a CDGM center to attend the evening community meetings. They "showed great happiness in being able to come together for the first time to talk about their children." Several meeting observers were pleasantly surprised at how talkative the parents were, "because at public school PTA meetings, these same parents set back and said nothing."[119] The parents' outspokenness in a CDGM setting shows that in the Head Start program, Mississippi society's underpaid, underemployed, and ignored citizens moved to the center. Poor black parents' ideas, input, and voices were welcome additions in this untraditional educational setting, and it was safe to speak up.

These Head Start center meetings disseminated information about such issues as "freedom of choice" school integration plans, welfare recipients' rights, and the proper way to cast a vote on a ballot. A significant percentage of teachers and other center staff knew the information presented, but most parents did not. Parents attended a seemingly harmless meeting about their children's education when they otherwise feared attending a political meeting.[120] Education became the conduit to discuss other forms of activism and empowerment.

CDGM meetings thus provided places to discuss black subordination and the need for independence. This lesson was readily apparent in the all black unincorporated community of Tougaloo near the college. One week after the Tougaloo CDGM center opened, the entire neighborhood was without water. The Tougaloo community drew water from a well owned by a white woman in Jackson who charged a monthly fee to tap into her line. After a Head Start center opened at Tougaloo, the well owner cut off the black residents' access to the water line. Tougaloo residents learned in CDGM community meetings how to form a water association and apply for a loan to dig their own well. They also learned how to incorporate their community to secure water and sewage. The owner of the well, once aware of these discussions, made her well available again, thwarting CDGM efforts at creating an incorporated all-black town.[121] The speed with which local people gave up on the idea of an independent water source demonstrated that CDGM's social services program was not always successful in helping black Mississippians to imagine and achieve outcomes where they were not merely the recipients of services.

At center community meetings, staff also implored parents to become involved in their local Agricultural Stabilization and Conservation Service (ASCS) elections, even going so far as to offer to drive parents to the meetings. ASCS committees decided the average crop each farmer planted and appointed the surveyors who measured each farmer's land. Mississippi ASCS committees excluded black farmers, who always received significantly smaller allotments. The situation in Amite County demonstrated the problem. That county had 3,400 black farmers and 2,600 white farmers in 1965, yet no black individuals sat on the ASCS committee. In 1964, COFO ran black candidates in the ASCS elections in heavily black counties, and CDGM continued that campaign. The ASCS elections did not require registration, literacy tests, or poll taxes. Black farmers in fourteen counties ran in ASCS elections in 1964, and that number increased to twenty-three counties by the end of 1965. These farmers attended ASCS meetings in impressive numbers, upsetting their white counterparts. When former Mississippi governor Ross Barnett appeared at polling places to "watch," and the wives of white farmers who had never attended meetings began to attend and vote, the United States Department of Agriculture changed the election process. Elections in the future occurred through the mail.[122]

No other Head Start program in Mississippi politicized parents or challenged existing social and political systems. The other Head Start programs skirted the issue of integration by occasionally using a white volunteer in an all-black center or by employing a black custodian in an all-white center. The focus of these programs was solely school readiness. In blending community action and early childhood education seamlessly, CDGM staff carried out OEO's national Head Start directives. CDGM's opponents would later point to its community action component to argue that its educational program was of poor quality.

CDGM also differed from other programs in terms of size, personnel, and classroom climate. CDGM did not turn down any communities that wanted to be a part of its initiative, making it a statewide program. Most other programs were confined to one school district or were countywide. Additionally, other programs neglected teacher and community development by using credentialed educators and favored preparing children to be obedient first-graders rather than inquisitive children. When Polly Greenberg visited a Mississippi Head Start center run by a public school system, she found children sitting at desks with their hands folded. Brand new Little Golden Books were placed on a high shelf so that the children could not "mess up the books." CDGM, by contrast, operated its centers in a way that encouraged students and staff to unleash their creativity and realize their potential.[123]

The untraditional Head Start program, by its structure and mission, built upon and extended earlier civil rights work in Mississippi. Just as SNCC cultivated indigenous leadership in black communities, CDGM nurtured the development of ordinary people through its center committees, teaching opportunities, and community organizing. For the first time, working-class black Mississippians had significant resources at their disposal and they used those resources to challenge white supremacy in new ways. The education of black children had always been political in the state, and Head Start made it possible for veteran activists to continue their work through a preschool program. Not since Reconstruction had African Americans played such a major role in their own education.

CHAPTER THREE

I'd Do It for Nothing the Way I Feel

I prefer CDGM to any other organization because it sees a person not as what he is, but what he can be. It takes the person with a minimum amount of education and gives him a chance to elevate himself.
—Mrs. Esther M. Holmes, St. John CDGM center employee

Out of the Headstart and the War on Poverty will come a generation of self-supporting, self-confident people.
—Mrs. N. A. Theodore, Gulfport, Mississippi

Alice Giles worked at a CDGM center that served Sunflower County children. The center, however, was physically located in Washington County's Leland township, because no black church or community center in Sunflower would open its doors to the Head Start program. One day, a young student hit his head while playing on the swings and needed medical attention. CDGM policy required that Giles take him to an integrated medical facility. She worried over how to follow policy and still get help for the child. Giles decided to take him to the nearest doctor and sit in the whites-only waiting area. She recalled that the medical workers were "scared to death. They hurried up and waited on me and got me out of there."[1] Giles's actions did not make the front-page news, but they embodied the mission of the grassroots Head Start program.

CDGM's program did not merely teach shapes, colors, and numbers but sought also to build children's self-confidence. The young child in Giles' care on that hot summer day learned that there was nothing inherently different about him that required him to sit in an all-black area. He also learned, by seeking medical care in a white waiting room, that he had a right and an obligation to assert his equality. Teachers offered black preschoolers an education intended to prepare them to stand up to white racism.[2] Freedom fighters understood that in addition to marching, boycotting, and registering to vote, they had to raise another generation to carry out their mission and test their successes. CDGM set out to create that generation.

Alice Giles, born in 1920 on a plantation outside of Drew in Sunflower County, attended a black Baptist private grade school. She went to school longer than most of her counterparts, although she recalled picking cotton while watching white kids ride by in school buses. She later took courses at Mary Holmes Junior College in pursuit of a high school diploma, but did not finish because her mother fell ill.[3]

The public school system would not have considered Giles, who lacked a high school diploma, for a position in the classroom. Yet, she was an ideal candidate for CDGM's program: her history of resistance was the credential that garnered her CDGM employment. In 1946, Alice and her husband, Oscar, opened a grocery store in Indianola, providing sandwiches to children whose segregated schools did not have cafeterias. The Gileses belonged to the NAACP and regularly attended meetings about voting and other civil rights issues. Oscar Giles later served as a Mississippi Freedom Democratic Party alternate delegate to the 1964 Democratic National Convention. White supremacists firebombed the couple's store and adjoining home on Alice Giles's birthday in 1965. "They threw two Molotov cocktails through the windows," she recalled, "because of our organizing."[4] Alice Giles did not stop agitating after the bombing. She and her husband rebuilt their store. She accepted a CDGM job soon afterward and positioned herself to teach preschoolers how to agitate themselves.

CDGM opened up an avenue for black women to lead—particularly when their advocacy was directly related to helping children—and gave them opportunities that were not typical in major civil rights organizations with the exception of SNCC. Both the NAACP and the SCLC, at the national and local levels, treated women as subordinates and favored male leadership. For example, Septima Clark recalled SCLC treasurer Ralph David Abernathy questioning her membership on the organization's executive board. Abernathy failed to recognize the integral roles that women played in terms of increasing membership, organizing campaigns, and providing behind-the-scenes leadership. Similar problems were present in the NAACP. In Clarksdale, Mississippi, Vera Pigee did the heavy organizational lifting, yet state NAACP leader Aaron Henry is the name mentioned in most records and reports.[5]

CDGM was the only institution of sizable scope and budget that had significant numbers of diverse black women at every level of administration. Marian Wright (now Edelman), the first black woman admitted to the Mississippi Bar and one of the few attorneys handling civil rights cases in the state; Victoria Gray, the Hattiesburg activist who ran against the segregationist U.S. senator John C. Stennis (D-Miss.) in the 1964 senatorial campaign; and Arenia Mallory, founder of Saints Industrial School, a private secondary school in Holmes County, all sat on the CDGM Board of Directors. Despite these women's presence, men outnumbered women eight to three on the board, replicating the black church's gendered pattern of predominately women audiences being shepherded by men leaders. Black women served on the CDGM Central Staff as the health coordinator, the professional staff coordinator, the roving staff person, and as one of the reading coordinators, but their contributions were most readily seen in the eighty-four centers that dotted the state. Black women made up the vast majority of the teaching and support staff in these centers. These women were also fifty-three of the eighty-four chairpersons of the community governing committees that oversaw hiring, firing, and center administration.[6] CDGM provided black women—regardless of their personal backgrounds—with occasions to lead the struggle for education and freedom.

The women's work connected them to a much longer tradition of black women's activism that began with the black clubwomen's movement of the late nineteenth century and spanned several generations to include NAACP youth councils and Citizenship Schools. No matter the time period and despite differences of class, black women found creative ways to dismantle racial subordination and advance the race. Just as women had earlier organized around issues of housing, health, employment, and welfare, CDGM women mobilized antipoverty resources to resist the region's one-party political system, the tradition of cheap labor, and the stunting of black children's opportunities for development.[7]

Minnie Ripley, a community chairwoman of the Mayersville CDGM center located in Issaquena County, illustrates how CDGM provided opportunities for black women to wield grassroots leadership. Ripley, born in Vicksburg at the turn of the century and raised by grandparents who were former slaves, did not complete school because of financial constraints. She cooked and cleaned for white families to support her family. Her grandmother had also worked as a domestic, so young Minnie's first encounters with whites came from following her grandmother to work. "I could play with the children's things, their little play things," she recollected. "I ate meals over there; naturally I didn't eat at the table with them."[8] Ripley shared an occupation with the woman who raised her, but she made sure her own daughter completed school. Ripley, through hard living and saving, sent her daughter to trade school where she studied stenography, quite an accomplishment in the 1940s for a black woman from the Delta.

CDGM women had long histories of working for quality education in Mississippi. Minnie Lewis (*far left*), who faced white retaliation after enrolling her six-year-old daughter in a previously all-white school, speaks with activists Dovie Hudson, Winson Hudson, and Marian Wright in 1966. All four women worked in CDGM's program. (Johnson Publishing Company, LLC)

Ripley's neighbors held her in high esteem, not only because her daughter had completed school, but also because in 1964 she had been one of the first African Americans in Issaquena County to attempt to register to vote. Early the next year, she passed the registration test. Ripley became involved with Head Start because "a young lady asked me would I help them to get it started. And we didn't have no place but the church house at that time." Ripley attended a meeting at her church to decide whether the building could be used as a Head Start meeting place. Many members grumbled, saying "the church isn't a schoolhouse no more."[9] Sixty-five-year-old Minnie Ripley stood up and made her case for why the church must open its doors to an educational program. She convinced the parishioners in attendance to allow their place of worship to double as a Head Start center. Ripley, who had never finished school, understood the importance of collective support for CDGM's long-term success. Her own days as a young mother determined to provide her daughter with the best education possible led her to back the early childhood education initiative.

Ripley's neighbors rewarded her commitment and tenacity by electing her chairperson of the Mayersville CDGM center, where she oversaw hiring and day-to-day operations. She encountered obstacles, such as when she tried to buy food for Head Start meals. "One firm didn't let us have milk for the children cause he thought it was a civil rights program. So we just got it from another firm."[10] The influx of federal Head Start dollars meant that Ripley did not have to beg, hat in hand, for the opportunity to purchase goods from a recalcitrant merchant. CDGM gave her the resources and the confidence to become a skilled broker, ceasing to do business with racist vendors as she ordered supplies and negotiated contracts.

In 1965, black women comprised at least 90 percent of CDGM's 1,100 employees and their numbers grew in later years. Their employment gave most a new sense of importance.[11] Women like Ripley, who had previously worked as domestics in white homes or chopped cotton in the fields, now suddenly found themselves overseeing preschool centers, planning menus, and teaching youngsters how to count. CDGM employment also provided these women with new status as teachers, a revered occupation in black communities. Thus, CDGM employees stood out in a region where the majority of adults—black or white—worked in agriculture. For most women, running classrooms represented an important departure from tradition, but they did much more than teach. Black women at the Shaw center, for example, worked until two in the morning tearing out old sheet rock because

Many CDGM centers were housed in black churches, since public school buildings were off limits. A CDGM teacher at the Pilgrim Rest center leads her students back inside their sanctuary-classroom. (Matt Herron/Take Stock/The Image Works)

their Head Start facility "was an old dance hall in awful shape."[12] In Holmes County, Cora Lee Roby recalled that "it was tough starting out. Me and Virgie had a time. We had to wash and scrub and paint. A lady gave us an old wood-cooking stove. We would decide what we were gonna carry the next day. If I was gonna carry milk, meal, eggs and butter, maybe she was gonna carry some flour, sugar."[13] They gave freely of their time, talent, and treasure, because CDGM was their institution, benefiting their children and their community.

Black women oftentimes received help from black men when performing manual labor in the centers. These men made significant contributions to the program, especially in bus transportation and in carpentry work. CDGM fathers made badly needed physical repairs to Head Start centers and constructed playground equipment including swings, seesaws, and climbing bars. The men turned vacant fields into colorful playgrounds complete with sandboxes made out of tractor tires and wooden platforms for children to play house on. They also constructed life-size dollhouses and building blocks. These hands-on tasks provided a way for everyone to be involved in the educational process. Most importantly, it allowed young children to see that their fathers were so concerned with their education that they freely gave of their time and talent to improve the educational facilities and provide toys. There was also a practical reason for drawing on the physical labor of men in the community. In order for CDGM to use the bulk of its grant money for new careers for the poor, the program had to be creative and resourceful in repairing buildings and acquiring equipment. Every dollar not spent on the latest recreational toys for children was a dollar that helped those children's parents to put food on their tables.[14]

Despite the vital contributions of men to CDGM's construction projects, black women dominated the program. The most obvious reason for their overwhelming participation lies in the reality that women were the primary caregivers for children. Many CDGM teachers had prior experience working with children as mothers and grandmothers, or as nannies to white children. Annie Mae King, who worked alongside Alice Giles in the Sunflower County center, explained her employment in these terms: "I myself raised up fifteen children of my own—healthy fine children of my own." She later added, "everybody knows how to raise their children—they done raised up all the white children."[15] In other words, King asserted that no one could better run Head Start centers than mothers who had ample experience working with children.

While women played significant roles in CDGM operation, the program took great pains to also involve men. One way of fostering male interest was through carpentry work. Black men constructed playground equipment and made the necessary repairs to CDGM buildings. In doing so, the men demonstrated their concern for and interest in their children's education. (Matt Herron/Take Stock/The Image Works)

King, born in Sunflower County in 1904, had only an elementary education and worked as a cook in the public school system until she attempted to register to vote in 1964. She failed the registration test and still lost her job. That reprisal made her more determined than ever to become involved in the movement. King opened her home to white movement workers. In 1964, Klansmen threw a teargas bomb in King's house because of her decision to house civil rights workers. The unrepentant freedom fighter asserted, "I fed the civil rights boys when they came in; I slept them; gave them a place to stay. I was paying my own taxes and I thought I had a right to have my own decisions about who came in my house."[16] In Head Start, King recalled, "we were working for principle. We were working for freedom and to be able to govern our own affairs and our own businesses and to teach our own children."[17] King's life and work embodied community action among women.

The War on Poverty and Head Start in particular mobilized poor mothers in impressive numbers. CDGM women exhibited "activist mothering" by organizing to provide early childhood education, hot meals, and medical screenings to black children. Their Head Start work derived from a concern for community children's welfare. At the center of "activist mothering" is a commitment to fighting oppression in all forms. When Alice Giles took her injured pupil to the waiting area for whites, she attended both to the child's physical needs and internal sense of self by refusing to sit in a segregated and dirty area that reinforced African Americans' supposed inferiority. She used the normative woman's role as a caretaker and nurturer to promote her politicized community work of challenging racial discrimination wherever she found it. CDGM's activist mothers devised innumerable ways to address the needs of black children through Head Start.[18]

For certain, motherhood and political activism on the part of women did not always constitute "activist mothering." A black woman who supported school desegregation in the 1960s was not necessarily an activist mother. She exemplified "activist mothering" when she championed school desegregation out of concern for a biological child or fictive kin's well-being and future success, taking up the mantle of motherhood as a source of empowerment and activism. Mary Frances Jordan was an activist mother whose daughter attended the Durant CDGM center. She worked as a nanny to a local white family until her employers fired her after learning that she had enrolled her daughter in CDGM's program. Rather than quietly accept her termination, Jordan fought back. She told her former employers that "everyone's interested in better things. The most important thing is better education for the children. I want them to have better than I did."[19] Jordan used her role as a mother to advocate for quality educational opportunities for black children at the expense of her livelihood. She did not have formal leadership credentials or celebrity status but she had firsthand knowledge of the importance of education, so she took rights for herself and her child, as activist Fannie Lou Hamer had earlier encouraged black Mississippians to do.

Moreover, one did not need to be a biological mother to engage in "activist mothering." Not all CDGM women had biological children enrolled in the program, but most assumed a mother-like role on behalf of their students. Taking on what sociologist Patricia Hill Collins has called the "othermother" role, CDGM women assisted biological mothers in ensuring that their children received nutritious meals and quality education.[20] For example, twelve black women resolved to keep the CDGM center at the Mount Carmel Baptist Church in Vicksburg open after the 1965 summer grant from OEO expired, even though only five of those women had children of their own. When asked why they freely gave of their time to run a preschool program for other people's children, they explained that they were "interested in the welfare of all children, especially in our home town."[21] Essentially, CDGM othermothers understood that black children's prospects for advancing the race lay in part with adults' ability to secure educational opportunity for them.

Activist mothers ran Head Start centers during a time of heightened scrutiny of working-class black mothering. Daniel Patrick Moynihan, the assistant secretary for Policy Planning and Research in the Department of Labor, published his study "The Negro Family: A Case for National Action" four months before CDGM centers opened. The report, which focused on urban areas, linked black poverty to the relative absence of nuclear black families. Moynihan's report suggested that black "matriarchy" harmed black communities just as CDGM women exerted their leadership and influence over one of the largest Head Start programs in the country.[22] Their presence as teachers, center directors, program administrators and board members served as an indictment of the chauvinistic ideology that labeled black women's leadership and independence as pathological. The women's work in an antipoverty program that was closely affiliated with civil rights rightfully placed the blame of poverty on racism and discrimination rather than on black women's alleged deficiencies.

In addition to their experience as caretakers of children, black women also dominated CDGM employment because they saw the program as a continuation of their prior movement activities geared toward black self-determination. Several of these women had participated in SNCC's earliest Mississippi initiatives or had served as teachers in the Citizenship Education Program that Septima Clark had developed in the 1950s to link practical literacy with community empowerment. CDGM board member Victoria Gray recalled that Citizen Education Program alumni brought "citizenship education to Head Start, issues and all."[23] Preschool education became the next step in their organizing campaigns. By the time Unita Blackwell heard about CDGM, she had already served as a Mississippi Freedom Democratic Party delegate to the Democratic National Convention in 1964 and had sued her local school board for not allowing her son to wear a SNCC lapel pin. She later explained that she sought Head Start employment because she saw it as a way to continue her community work for a better life.[24]

Pinkie Pilcher and Mary Lane, two movement stalwarts, helped to organize Leflore County's four CDGM centers in 1965. The women revealed how Head Start employees ran the gamut in age: Pilcher was born in 1899, Lane in 1940. Neither woman was a stranger to organizing. In 1938, Pilcher wrote to President Franklin Roosevelt to voice her concern about the Works Progress Administration's lack of hiring black women to visit the sick in Greenwood. "Let the colored people look after the colored people old sick and the white look after white. If we can't have colored home visitors, we don't want any." Before Head Start, Pilcher attended SCLC Citizenship School training in Dorchester, Georgia, then returned to her hometown to help prepare black citizens to pass literacy tests for voting. Soon, Pilcher served as the area supervisor for the Citizenship Education Program. She also ran for Greenwood commissioner of sanitation in 1965. Pilcher, elderly at the time of CDGM's inception, joined forces with other Greenwood activists to provide much needed services for children.[25] For Pilcher and women like her, Head Start involvement represented a natural next step in their activism.

Pinkie Pilcher worked under the direction of Mary Lane, a twenty-four-year-old SNCC staffer who became involved in the Greenwood movement in 1962 at the insistence of Bob Moses. In this capacity, Lane informed black people of their right to vote and took them to the courthouse to register. In time, she became the director of SNCC's Greenwood operation. After attending the 1964 Democratic National Convention as a delegate with Unita Blackwell, Lane spent much of the fall trying to persuade discouraged Greenwood residents to stay active in the struggle.[26] For her part, she saw Head Start as a way to continue her movement activities. "CDGM was really another SNCC thing," she noted. "The local people were beginning to control it." She sprang into action to bring the program to Leflore County, recalling "it was hard, but we set it up."[27]

Lee Bankhead, a Mississippi Freedom Democratic Party chair and SNCC organizer, oversaw CDGM centers in Bolivar County. Born in 1936 in Critten County, Arkansas, Bankhead fled to Mississippi with her parents to escape white terrorists. Her father was a member of the Southern Tenant Farmers' Union, an integrated union of sharecroppers and other agricultural laborers. Once Bankhead came of age, she crafted her own civil rights agenda around voter registration in Cleveland, Mississippi. By 1965, Bankhead had become a SNCC project leader in her county, where she organized many voter registration drives and sharecropper strikes. Police arrested her in Jackson two weeks before CDGM centers opened, for demonstrating against the undemocratic election of Mississippi's congressional delegation. Head Start provided a way for Bankhead to continue her organizing; she now had material benefits to offer hesitant potential voter registrants. As a center chairwoman, she offered jobs to impoverished parents and ensured that their children received medical care and food.[28]

Finally, CDGM employed more black women than men because women had fewer alternative employment opportunities. Agriculture continued as the predominant occupation of both groups, while its mechanization and low wages caused many black men to seek employment in cotton gins, lumber mills, and factories. These labor-intensive jobs were dangerous and dirty, but they provided some income not readily available to black women. For example, in 1953, Greenville Mill, a carpet factory owned by New York industrialists, opened in the Delta. Three years later, black men comprised 10 percent of its work force and by 1963 they were 24 percent. Yet, the factory had a policy of not employing black women, insisting that the employment of white women increased the need for black domestics in white households. Black women, with the assistance of Delta Ministry officials, reported the factory's employment discrimination to federal authorities. Greenville Mill then added six black women to its 1,100-person labor force in 1965.[29] The discriminatory employment practices and the mechanization of agriculture left domestic work as the only employment option available to black women. Aside from the low wages, such work made black women vulnerable to sexual harassment. Winson Hudson's father chose to lose 105 acres of valuable family land in 1924 rather than allow his daughters to work off debts as domestics in a white man's home because the threat of rape was so real. He was the product of sexual violence. His father, a white slaveowner, raped his enslaved mother.[30] CDGM was an employment option that kept black women out of white households where sexual assault was a possibility.

Lillie Ayers, of Glen Allan, found CDGM to be her most viable employment option. She became her family's main breadwinner after her husband Jake's activism cost him his Greenville Mill job. She made more than fifty dollars per week as a Head Start teacher and she encouraged her pupils' parents to go to the courthouse and vote. CDGM "changed us economically," she recalled. "It changed our mind about how we'd been treated as black people. It started us to thinking that black people are people. Because our skin is not white does not mean we should be treated any differently."[31]

While many black women viewed CDGM as an extension of their civil rights work, some women worked for the program because they failed to see its civil rights connections. As one anonymous woman explained to Polly Greenberg, "I'm the cautious type. I never got involved in civil rights activities. But CDGM's different. It's not civil rights, its education. So I got involved."[32] Black education in Mississippi had always been political, whether the cautious employee realized it or not. White planters collaborated with public school officials to sustain the region's agricultural reign and deny black Mississippians quality education well into the twentieth century. CDGM women ensured that black children were mentally, physically, and academically prepared to do well in school. In so doing, they offered a powerful rebuke to the southern way of life that had denied so many of them education. The Head Start program's curriculum and community outreach measures illuminated the connection between education and civil rights.

Those who had shunned civil rights did not easily join the CDGM sisterhood. Prior civil rights activity had helped some to secure CDGM employment, and the absence of it prevented others from obtaining it. Nareatha Naylor inquired of Congressman William Colmer (D-Miss.) if the federal preschool funds had "specifically been designated to be used as rewards for local Negro residents that work with the civil rights movement."[33] Naylor reported that CDGM denied her and five of her colleagues summer employment because they had not participated in movement activities in Forrest County.[34] The thirty-seven year old Naylor was a graduate of the historically black Lincoln University of Missouri and a fourth-grade school teacher in the Hattiesburg public school system. She was also the daughter of the Reverend Ralph Woullard, who had prevented an NAACP chapter from starting in his church and who had assisted the State Sovereignty

CDGM's educational program drew upon the wisdom and talents of working-class women. Here three teachers engage students in a classroom exercise about body parts. (Matt Heron/Take Stock/The Image Works)

Commission in trying to dissuade Clyde Kennard from desegregating what is now the University of Southern Mississippi.[35] CDGM officials maintained that Naylor was not hired because her application did not come through the proper channels, but it is plausible that the absence of movement work and her father's stance on civil rights hindered her chances for employment.[36]

CDGM's application did, in fact, ask applicants to list their civil rights activities. Of the eight CDGM centers in Hattiesburg, seven had women chairpersons, and most of these women had formidable civil rights backgrounds. For example, Erlene Beard, chairman of the Kelly center, was the sister of Vernon Dahmer, one of the leaders of the local NAACP. The Dahmer and Beard families housed SNCC workers and funded local organizing activities. Beginning in the 1950s, Erlene Beard took local youth, including Dorie and Joyce Ladner, to state NAACP meetings. Vernon Dahmer, Beard's brother, and the Reverend Woullard had been at odds since the late 1950s over the organization of the NAACP in Hattiesburg.[37] Some CDGM community chairpersons probably refused to hire individuals who had not been willing to risk their livelihood earlier for the freedom struggle—not least because they had earned less trust.

CDGM's pattern of giving movement veterans hiring priority was a double-edged sword. The jobs ensured that many of those who had risked everything during the movement's earliest days now had the opportunity to enjoy the fruits of their labor. On the other hand, prioritizing movement veterans for Head Start jobs led to self-serving behavior and meant that many of the poorest citizens who needed jobs were shut out. During the 1950s and early 1960s, local people who participated in movement activities did so mainly for personal satisfaction and a sense of efficacy. Tangible rewards were few and white reprisals were guaranteed. The Head Start program's well-paying jobs not only attracted individuals with selfish motives but also caused some of the earliest activists to expect monetary reward for their sacrifices. For example, many people in Bolivar County alleged that long-time activist Amzie Moore profited nicely from Head Start, since his rental property served as a Head Start center and federal money paid for property renovations.[38] Whether or not there was any truth in the allegations that the local leader received more than his fair share, the fact remained that Head Start offered the possibility of profit that had not previously existed.

Black women participants in CDGM all credited the Head Start program with improving their lives financially, giving them the opportunity to further their education, and providing new avenues to continue prior movement work. Eva Tisdale, born in 1942, worked for CDGM in Neshoba County, an area infamous because of the 1964 murders of the three civil rights workers. Tisdale credited CDGM for allowing her and many other black people to make more money than they had ever made. She recalled that many of her Head Start coworkers previously worked as maids in white homes and did not register to vote out of fear of upsetting their white bosses. Once securing CDGM employment, the women quickly made their way to the courthouse.[39] The job produced the financial freedom to register, but equally important was the sense of confidence that came from having the status of an educator and government employee. Essie Chaney, Lillie Ayers's sister and fellow teacher at the Glen Allan center, exuded that confidence in a conversation with Polly Greenberg. Thirty-year-old Chaney remarked that "we have BS degree teachers who think we are not qualified, but we have the answers to the questions and they don't."[40]

Black women who, for years, had heard that they had nothing substantial to offer now ran early childhood education centers. Hattie Belle Saffold, born in 1927, used to work in the fields before she became a Head Start teacher. When SNCC came into Holmes County, Saffold and her husband got involved in local organizing activities and became active Mississippi Freedom Democratic Party members. Saffold attended the CDGM planning meetings at Mount Beulah and secured employment as a Head Start teacher at the Second Pilgrim's Rest CDGM center. The Klan responded by shooting into her house several times, but she was undeterred, because the Head Start program had exposed her potential and given her an opportunity to contribute to black children's educations. She explained that CDGM taught "many things that we as parents can make at home to help our children—toys, games, and books—that do not cost a lot of money. This is something I have not known about before, never heard about them. My family are proud of me since I been working." Saffold went on to explain that in addition to CDGM giving her an arena of educational leadership, her employment also provided a much more practical benefit: running water. "We had been hauling water for about twenty years. One of the workers for CDGM came to my home and talked with us about a water loan [to install indoor plumbing]. We just couldn't understand at first, but he kept on talking to us. I cannot thank him enough for the water."[41] The overwhelming majority of black housing in the Delta was substandard. CDGM's social services program educated staff and parents about the ways to secure indoor plumbing and electricity.

In 1965, Hattie Saffold's Holmes County operated eleven different CDGM centers that varied in quality and size. The Mileston center was unique in that it grew out of a private kindergarten that local people and northern volunteers had opened a year earlier. The Holmes County Community Center in Mileston, built in October 1964 with northern white donations, housed the kindergarten and served as a meeting place for local black residents. After six months of operating the kindergarten with inconsistent donations, Mileston citizens secured CDGM funds, and their volunteer teachers finally received a salary. White volunteer Sue Lorenzi Sojourner relocated to Mileston from Berkeley in 1964 along with her husband to work in the county's freedom movement. She recalled that "the gigantic funding boost from CDGM provided training resources and greater advancement for staff, children, parents and the community." Celia Bell "Sweets" Turnbow became a cook. She had opened her home to SNCC workers during Freedom Summer, and her husband Hartman, an independent farmer, had been one of the first to attempt to register to vote in Holmes County.[42] Her Head Start employment strengthened the family's economic independence, so that they could continue their political work in the face of pervasive racism.

Virgie Saffold, another CDGM woman in Holmes County, was no stranger to community organizing. Virgie, who was distantly related to Hattie Saffold by marriage, had been a Citizenship School teacher and had also housed Freedom Summer volunteers. She was one of the teachers at the Old Pilgrim's Rest center in Durant that was located in a former Rosenwald school building. Of her CDGM work Virgie Saffold recalled, "I felt real well about working for the government because it was really the first job I had that paid. The only way to raise money here was chopping cotton. And chopping cotton all day long you receive two dollars. And once I started with Head Start, it was a great big change for me. They started off paying me like sixty dollars a week. That was more money than I ever made."[43] Safford's employment allowed her to pay off a loan her husband had taken to buy cows—no small feat in a state where white planters had historically used debt to constrict blacks' physical and social mobility. "It was the only job in this area and it was the only source of income that we had," she explained. "Once we started receiving that income, we could get some of the things that we really needed."[44]

Mamie McClendon Chinn, born in Canton in 1939, also recalled how CDGM employment improved her life. Chinn, unlike most of her contemporaries, did not farm as a child. Her father worked as a carpenter and her mother as a cook. Despite her relatively well-to-do upbringing, economic necessity forced her to quit school before graduating. She married into the prominent Chinn family that owned over one hundred acres in Madison County. Her father-in-law, C. O. Chinn, was a well-respected and courageous man feared by whites because of his "unwillingness to bend to white power."[45] Chinn rented one of his numerous buildings to CORE, which used it as a meeting place to plan voter registration drives. The patriarch paid dearly for his outspokenness and movement activity, losing almost all his property and serving on a chain gang. Mamie Chinn worked at a CDGM center in Canton, and her employment acted as a buffer against further white retaliation against the Chinn family. Though her husband was the family's main breadwinner, her CDGM job allowed the family to buy a new home. "I would save a part of my check and we finally saved enough money to pay down our home, which we're still in. That was Head Start money. The house was upscale, and it was central heat and air."[46]

CDGM benefits went beyond the material. Chinn recalled that her Head Start employment gave her a sense of importance that she had never experienced. "We had staff cars and the tag was U.S. Government. Black people had never had a car with U.S. Government. That was a sight to see."[47] More importantly, black people used those vehicles for organizing activity. CDGM employees sometimes drove the cars to the courthouse to register voters or to evening community meetings. Sidney Alexander, a CDGM community organizer, admitted that on one occasion while driving the car to Rolling Fork on official business, he gave a ride to five people who wanted to register to vote. Another employee used her program vehicle to transport Mississippi Freedom Democratic Party speakers to various engagements across the state.[48] A year earlier, Lyndon Johnson's Democratic Party had overlooked voter discrimination in the state, but now, using money from one of Johnson's domestic programs, CDGM found a new way to resist the white power structure.

In addition to appropriating program vehicles for their extralegal uses, CDGM women's militancy is revealed in their statements about their Head Start work. Gaynette Flowers, a supervisor of teachers along the Gulf Coast, stated that if CDGM ended, she would never go back to being a maid. "I would probably try to set up a garment and sewing shop. I wouldn't be satisfied with anything less than that."[49] Born in 1916 in Grove Hill, Alabama, Flowers had an eleventh-grade education when she learned of CDGM. Lack of money for tuition forced her to drop out of school; she found work in a garment shop and later as a domestic for a white family in North Gulfport. Like most women, Flowers came to CDGM with movement credentials. She was the longtime Gulfport NAACP secretary and she had housed many white Freedom Summer volunteers in 1964. Head Start employment helped Flowers, a single mother of four, to send her children to college. Flowers knew that it was "education and money, not aptitude" that stood between her and her goals.[50] The Head Start opportunity had made this clear. CDGM had created a revolution in expectations and self-esteem.

New attitudes and new ideas about black potential soon spread across the state. Holmes County teacher Hattie Saffold remarked of her CDGM employment, "I've experienced too much now. I'd rather pack up my little bag and leave the state than go back to what I used to do." Saffold, no longer afraid of white opposition or hindered by the oversight of local white employers, enrolled her daughter in the previously all-white public school in the fall of 1965. White people who opposed integrated schools put up fliers on telephone poles in Durant branding her as an "integrationist," yet she remained steadfast.[51] In Glen Allan, the Ayers family also used the financial protection of CDGM to assert their son's state constitutional right to a quality education. They enrolled their son Vernon in the second grade of the previously all-white elementary school. White residents retaliated by burning a six-foot-high cross in the Ayerses' yard. Young Vernon remained in the school despite the terror. In Panola County, Mona Miles, wife of a CDGM chairman, also resolved not to be intimidated after she enrolled her sons in the local white school. She recalled, "A Klansman called me and said an accident had been planned for my husband and nigger children. Some calls have told us that we have only about twenty-four hours to get out of town. As of today we are still around." Mona Miles could not be moved.[52]

Lavaree Jones of Hollandale also translated her CDGM employment into an opportunity to continue her earlier activism and improve her children's educational opportunities. In the fall of 1965, Jones sent her six-year-old daughter Katherine to the previously all-white elementary school in Hollandale. White men retaliated by burning crosses in her yard and attempting to run her off the road on several occasions. She also experienced backlash much closer to home. Her daughter's father, a prominent carpenter in the area, lost several of his white contracts because of Jones' decision to desegregate the local school. Jones ignored his pleas to remove their child from the white school, because she wanted her daughter to receive the best education possible. Local whites decided otherwise. A group bought the previously all-white elementary school from the Hollandale School Board at the end of the 1965–66 academic year and tore it down, preventing other black children from attending the white school.[53]

CDGM also awakened something in those parents who lacked previous civil rights experience. One parent who worked as a teacher's aide summarized her CDGM experience like this:

When they [whites] gave us the Headstart program they thought it would be a real quiet-like thing. But we have some real good people teaching our children, and they give us food for them, and a woman like me, they've given me a job, not sweeping after Mrs. Charley for five dollars per week and maybe a donut I'd get to share with the dog and the coffee that otherwise would be spilled out, but a real job and one that pays me good to do what's important for me and my family. I never believed that there were jobs like that, where you could get paid a good salary, to spend your time helping your own children and your people's children instead of the white man's kids. They call me an aide and pay me, but I'll tell you I'd do it for nothing the way I feel.[54]

THE FOLLOWING ARE NAMES OF PARENTS AND/OR GUARDIANS OF CHILDREN INTER-GRATING THE DURANT PUBLIC SCHOOL:

Barbara Carroll	Odelle Durham
Lillie Mae Cox	Eula McGee
Henry D. Hill	Albert Patterson
Amanda Ellis	Meetis Powell
Ruth Sara Hill	Mildred Coffey
Mary Louise Ellis	Ellowise Power
Laura Cox	Annie Mae Robinson
Rubertha Glover	Hattie B. Saffold
Lillie Mae Cox	Connie Bell Wright
Annie Lee Green	Jimmie Higgins
Katie Mae Griggs	Bessie Mae Huntley
Martha Hightower	Nathaniel Bailey
Annie Dora Eskridge	Elnora Lewis
Zebedee Larry	Curtis Lee Carter
Andrew Durham	Pearlie C. Carter
Sarah Artin	John Allen Wright

White supremacists often used economic intimidation to prevent African Americans from registering to vote or enrolling their children in a previously all-white school. Hattie Saffold's name, along with that of others, was placed on fliers displayed throughout town in hopes that creditors or prospective employers might pressure her and other parents not to go forward with the desegregation effort. (James W. Loewen)

For once, this woman had a say in her children's education. Cleaning up after whites and being expected to make do with their leftovers took a toll on the spirit. CDGM offered a way out of the degradation and elevated the woman's status to someone whose experience and talents were needed, valued, and recognized. Tom Levin had envisioned just this: preschool centers staffed with working-class black parents fostered the self-esteem, confidence, and drive needed to challenge the status quo and improve their communities.

Women who did not teach at CDGM centers still found opportunities that provided dignified employment, financial freedom, and the chance to shape the educational destinies of black youth. Flossier Miller, born in 1928, worked as a cook in a Bolivar County center where she planned and prepared nutritious meals. She had previously worked in a café nine hours per day, six days per week for fifteen dollars per week. She quit after "he [the boss] promised me a raise and never gave it to me." For her, Head Start was "was just like Christmas and Santa Claus."[55] CDGM employment allowed Miller to buy a house and send her children to college. It also gave her the chance to shape the educational trajectories of black youth. "Let me tell you, I loved the children so, and they loved us. . . . When they'd get to school, some of them would be smelling like peepee, and we would carry them in the room and heat some water and give them a bath and grease them down, put them on clean clothes. Most times, the next day we had to do the same thing."[56] Miller, like other activist mothers within CDGM, understood that she was raising up a generation to protect the civil rights gains already won and to continue to tear down racist barriers. She washed, clothed, and fed CDGM pupils to instill pride, letting them know that they were important and had potential. There are countless stories like Miller's where CDGM staff took personal interest in their young pupils, addressing both their academic development and their basic needs.

CDGM met the needs of many black women whose civil rights movement involvement left them unemployed. Roxie Meredith lost her job after her son, James Meredith, desegregated the University of Mississippi in 1962. Though her son was twenty-nine years old when he entered the state's flagship institution and had not lived at home in years, white supremacists punished her as a way of condemning her son's actions. She reentered the workforce as a CDGM employee. Meredith saw her job at the Kosciusko center as "my chance to get sort of a Head Start too, and it really have helped me."[57] Meredith, born in 1903 in Attala County, Mississippi, had a fourth-grade education when she secured a CDGM job as a cook.[58] Roxie Meredith's story was not an anomaly. Susie Morgan of Greenwood lost her job working in a white family's kitchen after her daughters talked back to a police officer at a 1962 demonstration. She later secured work in CDGM. Some women, like those in Mamie Chinn's Madison County, formed a sewing cooperative with the Poor People's Corporation to earn a living after they lost their jobs for attempting to register to vote or for attending evening civil rights meetings. CDGM communities supported their efforts by contracting with the cooperative to supply 6,000 children's smocks and other clothing for the Head Start centers.[59]

In addition to providing jobs for those who had suffered retaliation for their proximity to the movement, CDGM ensured that local people gained practical and professional skills that were transferable to future jobs. Velma Bartley, who worked at a Cleveland center, understood that her CDGM job was based on potential, rather than experience. Bartley, born in 1922, grew up in Bolivar County, where her parents rented farmland from white landowners. Economic necessity forced her to quit school after the seventh grade. She made money in the early 1960s selling cosmetics door to door until she became a CDGM community organizer. Bartley visited homes in the area to ensure families were aware of the opportunities available to their children and themselves. "That's something else this movement [CDGM] did was broke that down, that job qualification, you know, where you had to have certain qualifications for the work in certain jobs," she explained. "That helped a lot. And we went to school. We learned more about how to deal with children."[60]

Black women in CDGM, through the leadership and confidence cultivated through their work as Head Start professionals, struck a mighty blow to the widely held Mississippi supposition that black women belonged in white men's fields or in their wives' kitchens. Their participation also continued the century-long tradition of black Mississippians mobilizing for educational advancement. Moreover, black women's presence in classrooms and cafeterias as active leaders rather than as passive observers allowed them to have a say in the education of their children and allowed those children to see them in roles of institutional authority.

CDGM, in offering positive examples of black leadership, served as a source of community pride previously unknown. Unita Blackwell recalled that "CDGM centers truly were about our black Mississippi Delta people for the first time being totally in charge of running and staffing an educational program that was not controlled by the white establishment." She spoke of individuals such as "Mr. Dukey White and his buddies," who "brought tires and a wagon wheel and created playground equipment."[61] By the time Annie Seaton Smith's center opened in Tougaloo, with the help of students from the local college, the community had painted the building, built tiny tables, and constructed a playground complete with a sandbox.[62] Black communities, from McComb to Winterville, banded together to teach preschoolers their ABCs and to ensure that children received two hot meals per day and medical attention. Erlene Beard, a Forrest County CDGM employee remarked, "Now with Head Start, we have a chance to develop the potential that lies within our immediate community of a few people."[63]

CDGM's untraditional teacher corps racked up numerous successes. Yolanda Ammons, a four-year-old enrolled at the Tougaloo center, was "virtually incomprehensible" to her teachers during the first few weeks of school due to speech impediments. Over time, however, she became "an inquisitive conversationalist," initiating conversation with her white neighbors and correcting her mother's grammar. Just north of Tougaloo lived Floyd Pierce, an eight-year-old who lived with his grandparents and who had never attended school. Pierce enrolled in a center in Madison County, but refused to talk to anyone once there. He normally sat quietly, intently watching his teachers and classmates. One day a teacher showed him how to use modeling clay by making a cow and placing little "tits" on its underside. The demonstration caused Floyd to laugh—the first sound teachers heard him make. A few weeks later, Floyd spoke his first words.[64] CDGM encouragement equipped children to break out of their shells.

Stories abound of CDGM interventions. Evan Gibbs was a troubled five-year-old girl who attended one of CDGM's Greenville centers. She often threw temper tantrums, fought with other children, swore, and wet her pants. One of the center's teachers visited Evan's mother to discuss her behavior. With parental permission, the teacher took Evan into her home for four days. She bought the child new clothes, gave her love and attention and took her on trips to local stores and institutions. Within weeks, Evan's temperament changed dramatically. On a later field trip to the police station, Evan—without prompting—serenaded the police caption with a song about traffic. Deborah Washington, another CDGM student at a different Greenville center, was often too tired to sit up and participate in classroom activities. She rubbed and held her stomach most days. Deborah's teacher realized that the child was hungry and took her into the kitchen to get food. From that day forward she gave Deborah two lunch servings, a temporary

Students and staff from the Richmond Grove CDGM center standing in front of the life-size dollhouse that community members built for the Head Start program. CDGM encouraged its supporters to construct as many of the program's toys as possible so that the bulk of grant funds could be used for salaries for the poor. (Presbyterian Historical Society [U.S.A.])

solution to a long-term problem. As the concerned teacher explained, "I hate to think what's going to happen to Deborah without Head Start. There are five other children at home, without a father, without enough food."[65]

CDGM children had different living situations and competency levels, but their need for the program was the one great equalizer. Head Start provided poor children with preschool education, healthcare, and nutritious meals, and children certainly needed all those things. Before CDGM, many youngsters had never left the plantations where they lived. A four-year-old at a Greenville center arrived at school for the first time undernourished and dirty and with a baby's bottle in his mouth. A seven-year-old boy and his eight-year-old sister appeared at another Head Start center eager to learn. They had never been to school before, because their parents were unable to buy clothing for them. CDGM teachers met their basic needs and worked to get them in school.[66]

Quality varied. At many of the centers, women learned on the job, leaving much to be desired in terms of accountability and efficiency. OEO officials in Washington, D.C., did provide CDGM with funds for consultants who offered administrative assistance and training, but trial and error ruled the day. Supplies and paychecks often did not arrive on time. Local people, unfamiliar with accounting procedures, lost receipts or forgot to get invoices for center purchases.[67] Some children stayed home as often as they came to the centers, missing out on hot, nutritious meals and enrichment activities. Other centers operated way above capacity. Batesville requested summer funding for sixty-five children, but 165 students enrolled. Many came from remote plantations. The Batesville chairperson, despite not having the money to adequately serve that many children, refused to turn away any child. He explained, "We have one child in our preschool that is eight years old that has never been to school before."[68]

The chairperson understood the great need to educate black children. Problems even existed when trying to send the kids home, for many did not know their last names or where they lived. Workers at the Hollandale center solved that problem by cocking their heads at unidentified children and saying "I think that there's a Bowdre or this here's a Carter."[69] Despite these shortcomings, former sharecroppers and domestics operated eighty-four Head Start centers and oversaw one of the largest federal preschool budgets for eight weeks during the 1965 summer, contesting the notion that black Mississippians were incapable of running programs.[70]

Forrest County boasted ten centers during the first summer. In 1964 this county had more freedom schools than any other locale and now had one of the largest CDGM operations. Central Staff identified Erlene Beard's Kelly Settlement center as the best in the district. The center met in an abandoned black school that the local community had renovated. The forty-eight enrolled children easily reached books arranged on low bookshelves or played "make-believe" in the child-size town constructed out of cardboard. The Kelly Settlement center, however, was the exception. The Walthall center in Hattiesburg had so many students that the community chairman decided to split the center to teach 140 children in two different locations, meaning one of the locations lacked regular leadership and resulting in duplicated equipment and operational expenses. The greatest liability in splitting the center was the lack of real supervision of teachers. Resource teachers began to routinely arrive later and their casual attitudes about when the workday started affected lesson planning and classroom management.[71]

Leflore County had both poor and exceptional CDGM centers. A 1965 Central Staff report noted that at one Greenwood center no eye contact existed between teachers and students, only an "emphasis on rote alphabet and rote number memorization," and that "the toys and materials are crammed in disorderly heaps on tables."[72] The center at Itta Bena was the complete opposite. Willie Ester McGee, its director, had worked with Stokely Carmichael as a SNCC staff member. Teachers at McGee's center engaged in impressive small group interaction with the enrolled sixty-eight preschoolers. The young pupils took field trips to the local fire and police stations and often utilized a nearby playground rather than the one at their center, which lacked any shade. Head Start guidelines specified both small group interaction and field trips in each program.[73]

The 1965 schedules of all CDGM centers were similar. Students arrived at 8 A.M. Some students walked in groups to nearby centers, but most came by car or bus, many traveling as much as forty miles round trip. The day officially began at 8:30 as teachers helped the youngsters settle in. Free play began at 8:40 and continued until 9:30 when breakfast was served. During free play, centers offered children a variety of activities that encouraged dramatic play and social interaction. Various stations allowed youngsters to flip through picture books, build blocks, or play house. Teachers went around the room and had one-on-one time with the children as they played. Standard activities included storytelling, reading-readiness games, music hour, and science exploration. During the arts and crafts period, teachers encouraged the children to use their imaginations to create new things. The CDGM teacher manual reminded employees that "the results are not important, but the work and eagerness he puts in the painting and the pride he has in it is what CDGM IS ALL ABOUT" (caps in original document).[74] Most centers served lunch at noon, and it was followed by naptime. Children slept on blankets under the trees outside the center or on pallets inside. At some centers, students rested their heads on tables as teachers waved paper fans in the hot room. Before the 1:30 P.M. dismissal, the children normally engaged in more free play or in a class discussion with teachers.[75] Students whose parents worked until five stayed at the centers after the official dismissal.

CDGM women succeeded throughout the eight-week summer program because they received hands-on training and assistance from northern resource teachers and other professionals brought in to provide support during the summer. Doris Derby, a young black SNCC veteran and the cofounder of the Southern Free Theater, lived with Hattie Saffold and mentored teachers in Marshall and Holmes Counties.[76] Derby had degrees in elementary school education and cultural anthropology, and she had previously worked in preschools and as a third-grade teacher, so she knew how to manage classrooms. In the Newell Chapel and Second Pilgrim's Rest CDGM centers, Derby helped local women develop innovative lesson plans that promoted reading and counting skills. Years later, when recalling her CDGM work, Derby spoke about the white resistance she encountered in Holmes County. One day, when passing the church that hosted one of the centers where she worked, she "saw something strange on the ground." Within seconds, Derby realized "there was a fire slowly moving up through the doorway of the church." After yelling for help, she and other employees of the Durant center stamped out the fire that local white people had set.[77]

White northerners formed the majority of resource teachers who assisted in CDGM centers. Local people had formed relationships with northern white students during the 1964 Freedom Summer, so working with them in CDGM was not unusual. For many CDGM children, however, the Head Start program provided them with their first daily contact with white people. Peter Titelman, a white student at Earlham College, was the resource teacher at the Rolling Fork center in Washington County where he oversaw the reading-readiness program. Like Derby, Titelman endured many local threats and other forms of white resistance. He spent most nights guarding the Head Start center with a shotgun, even though he had never held a gun before joining CDGM. Titelman came from a progressive family. His mother served as the principal of the Bank Street Teacher's College, where some CDGM women later attended classes. He first became involved in civil rights in 1963 when he participated in SNCC's Albany movement. After he had a seven-day jail stint, his parents requested that he return home to New York because of concerns for his safety.[78] Ironically, his safety was threatened in a Head Start program, rather than in an Albany SNCC office.

White supremacists routinely intimidated northern resource teachers. Bernard Dinkin, a Jewish student from Temple University, encountered segregationist hostility as soon as he arrived in Mississippi. He came to Jackson and waited for CDGM representatives to pick him up from the bus station. A white man stood on the opposite corner and yelled anti-Semitic slurs at him. This introduction foreshadowed other acts of intimidation. Dinkin, like Derby, had civil rights movement and educational credentials. He had been active in the northern SNCC movement and ran an all-black boys club at a Philadelphia housing project. He attended orientation at

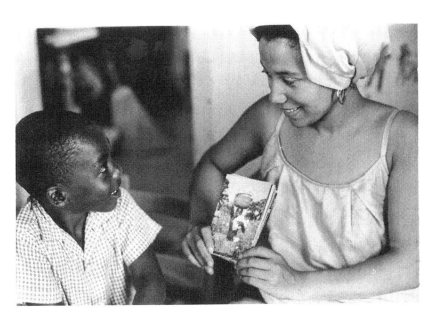

Resource teacher Doris Derby, a SNCC member and cofounder of the Free Southern Theater, educates a Head Start child about West African culture. (Maria Varela, photographer/Doris Derby Collection, Manuscripts, Archives, and Rare Book Library, Emory University)

Mount Beulah and then set out for McComb with other employees. On the way there, someone threw a large object through the windshield of the car he was traveling in, injuring him and the other passengers. The gravity of their injuries forced them to return to Mount Beulah.[79]

Once Dinkin finally made it to McComb, he established meaningful relationships with the local people. McComb had been the site of both SNCC's first voter registration project and several bombings. Yet, black people continued their organizing activities. Dinkin quickly became friends with several of the local activists. He and black SNCC worker Roy Lee once visited the Tylertown courthouse where they defied segregationists by desegregating the water fountains. Dinkin drank out of the fountain set aside for blacks and Lee out of the one for whites. These kinds of activities scared many CDGM supporters in McComb, but also showed them Dinkin's commitment to helping to dismantle white supremacy. Dinkin served as a resource for CDGM women in the classroom rather than as the individual in charge. "We didn't tell them what to do," recalled Dinkin. "If they had a problem, they came to us and we offered advice. They knew their children best."[80]

One teacher who had natural talent around impressionable youngsters was Marilyn Lowen, one of the many nonnative Mississippians brought on staff in 1965. Lowen came from a progressive Jewish family that had opposed segregation in housing, public accommodations, and education in Detroit in the 1950s. She enrolled in Bennington College in 1962, but left after a year to continue her political work as a tutorial organizer, tutor, and dance teacher in the Northern Student Movement's Harlem Education Project. She went south in 1965 to work in SNCC's Atlanta photography department. Lowen joined CDGM's Living Arts Project as director, traveling to different centers with a team of six who introduced CDGM teachers and students to theater, puppetry performances, and dance. She brought learning alive for the preschoolers and taught them how to express themselves through sound and creative movement. They acted out stories, moving uninhibitedly in front of others. They made puppets and performed with them. On one occasion, segregationists spotted the integrated Living Arts team traveling together in a car and proceeded to chase after them in two pick-up trucks. Lowen used quick thinking and a lead foot to protect her vehicle's occupants and end the terrifying encounter.[81]

Unlike many other teachers from the North, Lowen remained with CDGM after the first summer. From the fall of 1965 until 1968, she worked for CDGM's Department of Teacher Development and Program for Children. She conducted workshops throughout the state that provided CDGM teachers with extensive training and familiarity with folk music, fingerplay, language development songs, and dance. Lowen also spent three months on special assignment in Panola County. At the invitation of Robert and Mona Miles, she lived and worked with them to maintain Head Start's presence in that area. She also worked closely with Winson Hudson in Leake County for several years as a liaison from CDGM's Central Office. Lowen endeavored to bring the best of early childhood educational theory and practice to create an active and experiential learning environment in CDGM centers.[82]

Resource teachers played a big role in helping black women run CDGM classrooms, but no one was more central than Polly Greenberg in preparing local people to serve as Head Start teachers. Greenberg left OEO in June 1965 because she believed in Tom Levin's vision that ordinary black women had the ability to teach their own children. She wanted to play a part in such an empowering movement. Greenberg had specialized in early childhood education and had a master's degree in developmental reading and work experience in day care centers, elementary schools, and the United States Department of Education. Motherhood, however, was the credential that allowed her to form common ground with black women in Mississippi. Greenberg, when she relocated South, was the single parent of four little girls—aged four, six, eight, and nine. Other than Jeannine Herron, none of the other out-of-state staff brought children with them. CDGM mothers responded warmly to Greenberg and her children. Greenberg, in turn, established trust with and instilled confidence in black women by emphasizing the value of motherhood.

Greenberg recalled that CDGM women did not initially believe in their ability to impart knowledge and skills to the preschoolers. She encouraged them by suggesting that they teach their students songs. "I asked them if they knew songs. They said they didn't. I said, 'Didn't your mom sing to you at night? Don't you know church songs? Don't you know freedom songs?'"[83] Most did in fact know songs that their own mothers had passed on to them. One song passed down from generation to generation stemmed from the era of black codes. Oftentimes, those who violated the codes ended up on chain gangs supervised by former Confederate officers. CDGM women shared the songs with their young charges. The chain gang song introduced students to lyrics that contained the lines, "I don't want no white man's justice," and "a nappy-headed nigger ain't my name." In another song, four-year-olds who had not yet learned to tie their shoes cheerfully crooned and clapped:

Da-da-da-da-da
da-a-da-da-da-da,
oh well I read in the paper
just the other day
that the freedom fighters
were on their way.
And they came by bus
and a-airplane too.
They'll even walk if you ask them to.

The tune's refrain included a message to Mississippi Governor Paul Johnson. Children who had been placed in cotton fields as early as age three sang: "O Johnson, you know you can't jail us all. O Johnson, segregation is bound to fall."[84] Even music hour fostered resistance in the radical Head Start program. CDGM students also learned more traditional rhymes including "Little Sally Walker," "Miss Mary Mack," and "If You're Happy and You Know It," but the freedom songs showed that CDGM's Head Start program meant to change Mississippi.[85]

Greenberg understood that a strong teacher development program that included indigenous dancing, singing, and storytelling chipped away at the lack of agency that Mississippi's exploitative way of life induced in black adults. She visited centers all summer in 1965 to observe what worked and what did not. She created and distributed packets of information that contained suggestions for songs, arts and crafts, and children's games. For example, Greenberg invented the Sound Table to teach CDGM women how to prepare youngsters to read. She instructed women to decorate a table in the center where they gathered with their pupils to study a different starting sound each week. When they taught the letter "p" they taught the sound of the letter. Preschoolers learned that every time they saw a "p," it made a starting sound like "pig," "penny," or "pencil." They placed items that began with the "p" sound on the table. Greenberg understood that such an exercise trained children to listen to the beginning sound of a word and gave black women the chance to serve as role models to black children even if they had no formal training in reading readiness. Additionally, she introduced a monthly newsletter that allowed staff at the eighty-four centers to communicate with each other and share successful lesson plans. These efforts bore fruit, for, despite racial and class divides, CDGM women came to see Greenberg as a fellow mother and educator rather than a supervisor who wielded power over them.[86]

At the end of the 1965 summer, Greenberg worked to strengthen CDGM's educational component in anticipation of another OEO grant. OEO announced in August 1965 that Head Start would become a year-round program. Greenberg created the Area Teacher Guide system of "each one, teach one." Greenberg, in consultation with district coordinators, center chairpersons, and other community members, selected thirteen women who represented CDGM's regional diversity. These women received intense pedagogical training weekly and in turn shared what they learned with Head Start teachers and parents in their home communities. Mary Emmons, a twenty-one-year-old white graduate student from the University of Chicago, and Greenberg trained the guides, who included Hattie Saffold, Lillie Ayers, Erlene Beard, Gaynette Flowers, and Laveree Jones. Guides also learned from notable early childhood education consultants from around the country who agreed to visit the warehouse in Tougaloo that CDGM rented for training sessions.[87]

All guides had experience working with children, but not all had worked for CDGM during the 1965 summer. Polly Greenberg tapped Clarice Dillon Coney, a public school teacher by profession, to serve as the guide for Canton and the surrounding area if CDGM was refunded. Coney, born in 1926 in Bogue Chitto, an unincorporated area of Lincoln County, grew up in a relatively prosperous family. Her father worked for the Illinois Central Railroad and her mother was a homemaker. Black men who worked for the railroad formed a privileged group, because they had consistent employment free of local white control. Coney, after graduating from high school, studied education at Alcorn Agricultural and Mechanical College. She married Eddie Coney in 1947 and the couple became active in the 1950s in Madison County civil rights activities. They were members of CORE and the NAACP. A public school teacher, Coney was a CDGM anomaly, but her positive personality, history of engaging in what early childhood educators called "developmentally appropriate practice," and her prior movement work made her an ideal Area Teacher Guide.[88]

Each guide oversaw eight centers. They received rental cars or were reimbursed for fuel costs for driving to the weekly Wednesday meetings with Polly Greenberg. At the meetings, Greenberg and Emmons discussed early childhood education theories and classroom dynamics, including how to transition from one activity to another and how to improvise gap-filling activities when planned lessons ran shorter than expected. One highlight included the model classroom set up to demonstrate how to use everyday items to create interactive and welcoming centers. Visiting the Jackson library became another favorite guide activity, as the majority of the women had never been to a library. Hattie Saffold recalled being scared to enter until Greenberg told her that librarians, not Klansmen, ran the library. One successful visit to check out books led Saffold to visit the library regularly.[89]

After attending the Wednesday meetings, guides returned to their respective communities and shared what they had learned as teaching supervisors. They visited two centers every Monday, Tuesday, Thursday, and Friday to share the information Greenberg provided. Many of the women faced a dangerous three-to-four-hour drive each way along many dark back roads, yet they took the risk, because they wanted the best possible programs for their communities' children.[90]

Guides also traveled across the country to work with renowned child specialists in preparation for their new roles as teachers of other teachers. Head Start teachers all over the country attended training programs, but CDGM sent more of its staff than usual to these training sessions, because Polly Greenberg was close friends with Ed Kieloch, the OEO official who oversaw teacher training. CDGM women took classes at prestigious schools, including the Bank Street College of Education and the Peabody College for Teachers (now the Peabody School of Education at Vanderbilt University), for further instruction in early childhood education. One center's newsletter boasted that its guide, Lillie Ayers, had spent a week in Washington, D.C., "learning things that will be a help to the different centers."[91] For the women, the exposure gained from attending the national workshops was just as important as the material learned. Women who had never ventured far from home now traveled on airplanes and stayed in hotels.

In later years, many CDGM women returned to school and received GEDs, associate degrees, bachelor degrees, and even master's degrees. Velma Bartley, who took courses at Delta State University, Mississippi Valley State University, and Jackson State University, proudly stated that "these folks have had me up in more universities since I've been in Head Start."[92] Elizabeth Rankin, who taught at a CDGM center in Moss Point, spoke of a similar experience. Her Head Start employment afforded her the opportunity to travel to the University of Nebraska for early childhood education training. The training workshops inspired Rankin to complete the education she had begun at Alcorn before dropping out because her parents could not afford the tuition. A wife and the mother of seven children, she still enrolled in a local college, determined to earn her degree.[93]

CDGM women returned to school with financial assistance from the Head Start Training Course fund and from the Field Foundation. OEO spent more than $100,000 training seventy-one CDGM teachers at Tuskegee Institute, the University of Texas, and the University of Alabama.[94] Hattie Saffold of Durant, Mamie Chinn of Canton, Alice Giles of Indianola, and Lillie Ayers of Glen Allan all obtained their GEDs through their CDGM employment. Saffold and Chinn earned bachelor's degrees. In 1986, Saffold became a kindergarten teacher in a public school. Gaynette Flowers went back to school later and credited CDGM as the inspiration. She earned a bachelor's degree in early childhood education from the University of South Alabama after she retired from the classroom.[95]

Head Start led women throughout the country to return to school, but CDGM's program stood out, because no other state had so dramatically and successfully denied black people a quality education. Such deprivation ensured that they had only the most menial job opportunities. With farm mechanization nearly complete by 1965, the poorest black Mississippians who for so long made their living off the richest land now found themselves expendable. Head Start, as a community action program, addressed a root cause of poverty in Mississippi: the lack of opportunity to earn a decent living.

The autonomy and confidence CDGM fostered in black women, however, sometimes led to racial tensions with white staff members. While the guides had already established meaningful relationships with Greenberg, they were not familiar with other white instructors who came to assist them. Valentine Blue, a Jackson native, was the youngest guide on staff. Blue disliked the teacher-student relationship that she and her fellow guides had with some of the white visitors who came to offer guidance. She found them condescending and quick to belittle African Americans' suggestions. She maintained that every time she placed something in a certain spot in the demonstration classroom, one of the white resource people came behind her and moved the item to a different location. Blue did not believe that white people had the best ideas all the time. Her anger and suspicion were also fueled by the fact that the resource people were unfamiliar. Blue asserted, "We had never seen her before. She was new to us—we had just heard about her."[96] While CDGM women had developed a rapport with Greenberg, it was much harder to take instruction from those they did not know.

Valentine Blue's indignation was not uncommon. As she threw off the remaining psychological chains of white supremacy through CDGM, anger at a system that perpetually supposed that blacks had nothing to offer and everything to learn caused her to rebuff any white-initiated efforts, no matter how well intentioned or how liberal the individual. SNCC underwent a similar tumultuous period when some members questioned the utility of white participation in empowerment programs for blacks.[97] More and more black CDGM employees questioned the structure of CDGM and critically considered the implications of white leadership. CDGM's founders, the chairperson of the board, and the director of teacher development were all white individuals. Ironically, CDGM, an institution founded by white people, became the medium through which women such as Valentine Blue could express their frustration. On one hand, it meant that parents and staff alike were taking to heart the CDGM message to challenge, question, and confront. They knew that they had valid opinions. Moreover, moving forward depended upon more dialogue and less didactic speech, since increased decision making on the part of the previously marginalized was one of the program's primary goals.[98] On the other hand, black women's frustrations and the tense black-white interactions that resulted jeopardized key political and financial alliances that sustained CDGM.

CHAPTER FOUR

Senator Stennis Is Watching

Could it be that we are going half way around the world to fight communists and at the same time supplying money for the communists in this country to train our young people to be communists.

—C. Frazier Landrum, CDGM opponent

Agreeable to instructions from [Mississippi State Sovereignty Commission] Director Johnston to check on the Head Start programs under the direction of Mt. Beulah at Edwards, Mississippi, I journeyed to Shaw, Mississippi.

—Mississippi State Sovereignty Commission investigator

When OEO officials announced in August 1965 that Operation Head Start would operate year-round, CDGM activists believed they stood a strong chance of securing a year-round grant. The predominately black preschool program received praise from renowned child development experts. Famed Harvard child psychiatrist Robert Coles visited several CDGM centers and concluded that "the Head Start programs I saw throughout Mississippi achieved a truly extraordinary degree of success in reaching and significantly improving the physical and mental health as the well as the future educational competence of many children involved." Doctor Keith Osborne, director of the Merrill Palmer Institute and OEO's early childhood education consultant, remarked that even though CDGM "training was not as much as we would like, the quality of the program was good for the children. The parents were involved in a very creative fashion."[1] CDGM's chances looked promising, given the praise emanating from those who had no stake in its continuation.

Those directly involved in the Head Start program also added their commendations. A northern resource teacher summed up his summer experience by informing CDGM director Tom Levin that the children at his center did not learn to read and write in eight weeks, but he still saw the program as a success. "Some of our kids can't read a word. Some can't count to ten, but almost all have a measure of human dignity that they didn't have before."[2] Winson Hudson asserted that CDGM prepared Head Start graduates in the Harmony community for the first grade, correctly predicting that they would stand out in the classroom. Some public school teachers complained that when CDGM students entered the public school system, they were rebellious, inquisitive, and too independent.[3] This proved to CDGM teachers that their nurturing had produced confident students.

Creating self-assured black children was not what everyone had in mind, which caused CDGM's program to receive critical publicity. The *New York Times* ran an article featuring Ardella Jordan, a fifty-four-year-old black woman with an eighth-grade education, who quit her job as a maid to work as a CDGM teacher. Jordan created a classroom chart about hygiene, but misspelled the word "brush," omitting the letter "s."[4] Memphis's leading paper, the *Commercial Appeal*, pointed out the grammatical mistakes in the children's books that CDGM staff had created. The books included direct quotes from center students including sentences such as "he taste good," and "my dog named Chipper."[5] The article conceded that five-year-olds wrote the stories, but failed to realize that CDGM valued content over grammar. Program officials supposed that the best way to help children learn to enjoy reading and feel comfortable communicating verbally was to allow them to see their words in print without constant correction. The newspapers' attention on grammatical errors in CDGM materials sent the message that black working-class women did not have the competency to teach and privileged the idea that the best education was one provided by university-trained teachers.

While establishing strong grammar and spelling skills are important parts of school readiness and success, CDGM's goals were less academic in the traditional sense and prioritized personal development and empowerment. Perhaps the question should not have been whether grammatical errors and misspelled words signified poor-quality education, as the newspaper suggested. Rather, a more appropriate question given CDGM's goals would have been how does a poor black child think differently about himself or herself after seeing his or her thoughts, fears, and daily happenings in print. Another relevant question would have explored how the use of working-class black parents in CDGM classrooms influenced the educational achievement of their children. These questions were not ones that could easily be answered.

Certainly, there was legitimate criticism of CDGM, especially in terms of its approach to early childhood education. Was preschool education sacrificed in favor of social justice? Were undereducated women the best teachers to adequately prepare disadvantaged children for school? These types of questions were valid. Quality education requires more than caring individuals standing at the front of classrooms. All criticism directed at CDGM, however, did not stem from a genuine interest in black education.

Most white Mississippians opposed CDGM and the entire War on Poverty. Every member of Mississippi's congressional delegation had voted against the Economic Opportunity Act. These segregationists recognized that the antipoverty effort was an indirect way to bring desegregation to their communities. Thus, while state officials in Georgia and Alabama set up state agencies to coordinate antipoverty programs and funds in 1964, officials in Mississippi originally pledged to have nothing to do with them.[6] Not a single Job Corps camp or Volunteers in Service to America program existed in Mississippi. The only institution of higher education in the state that initially took advantage of the work-study program created by Title I of the Economic Opportunity Act was Tougaloo College. Despite public officials' antipathy toward the antipoverty program, Tom Levin went so far as to send personal invitations to Governor Paul Johnson and his state poverty coordinator to speak at CDGM's orientation. Neither individual participated nor responded in any way.[7]

Months after other governors set up state agencies to coordinate federal antipoverty funds, Mississippi governor Paul Johnson established the State Technical Assistance Agency to coordinate Mississippi's antipoverty efforts. Martin Fraley, a confidant of the governor and state director of the Pardon and Parole Board, oversaw the state office. CDGM had no dealings with the state OEO office since it was exempt from the governor's veto. Its officials mainly corresponded with OEO's southeast regional office in Atlanta and the national OEO office in Washington, D.C., which directly provided its funding. Delay by the state's political establishment opened the door for CDGM and three other private organizations to control the bulk of OEO money allocated to Mississippi through 1966. The other organizations were Mid-State Opportunities, a community action agency run by Rex McRaney, a former state legislator; STAR, a vocational training and employment program administered by the Catholic Diocese of Natchez-Jackson; and Coahoma County Opportunities, a biracial nonprofit community action group based in Aaron Henry's home county.[8]

CDGM received the most scrutiny and opposition from local and state officials. The attention from Mississippi's politicians, who had shown little interest in antipoverty programs or in black education, stemmed from CDGM's commitment to integration and its close association with civil rights veterans. Opponents feared the liberatory education that CDGM offered its students and the financial freedom it afforded its staff. Moreover, CDGM's foes disliked the program's disruption of the historical tradition of white southerners controlling federal largesse. CDGM officials had anticipated such opposition, insulating the program from gubernatorial control and retaining legal assistance prior to the first day of operation.

Those who opposed CDGM employed various methods. Blatantly racist language was no longer acceptable discourse in 1965, so the Mississippi State Sovereignty Commission used its extensive espionage powers to undermine CDGM.[9] The Sovereignty Commission infiltrated CDGM's Central Office with a paid informant posing as a secretary who furnished copies of all correspondence and memoranda to commission officials. The preschool spy also reported alleged civil rights activity conducted during business hours and recounted purported employee acts of drunkenness and immorality. Commission officials airmailed copies of every report to United States Senator John C. Stennis (D-Miss.) in order to "influence the cancellation of the 'Head Start' project as it is now organized."[10] Commission officials did not mention CDGM by name, but of the many Head Start programs operated in the state during the 1965 summer, they only investigated CDGM.

Most of the information uncovered by the commission simply proved that CDGM perfected the ideas of participatory democracy and community control. Poor people who could not vote for mayor, sit on a school board or a county crop-allotment committee, or even challenge their boss verbally sat on Head Start governing boards, ran classrooms, and allocated large sums of federal funds. Espionage agents noted that Head Start's payroll included Nola Mae Coleman. Coleman was the daughter of Andrew Hawkins, a forty-five-year-old former cotton chopper and Mississippi Freedom Democratic Party alternate delegate to the 1964 Democratic National Convention. He had testified before Congress that United States senator James Eastland used convict labor on his 5,400-acre plantation. Hawkins was also the leader of the Mississippi Freedom Labor Union, an organization that conducted sharecropper strikes in several Delta counties. Sharecroppers organized to contest the three dollar wages they received for a ten-hour day of chopping cotton.[11] During the spring of 1965, dozens of black families were kicked off plantations for demanding higher wages. The Head Start program and the jobs it provided not only created a safe space for poor people to speak out with less fear of white reprisals, but it also gave them the confidence and know-how to navigate various channels of power. Hawkins's daughter, Nola Mae Coleman, served as the CDGM committee chairperson for the Shaw center in Bolivar County and also worked as a full-time teacher there alongside her mother, Mary Lou Hawkins.[12] Coleman hired employees, entered into contracts for supplies, and had a say in the education of black children. Segregationists recognized the danger in an autonomous Head Start program that taught rank-and-file black Mississippians how to make their communities more responsive to their needs.

Private citizens and elected officials collaborated with the Sovereignty Commission in fighting CDGM. Klansman defaced the sign on the road leading to one CDGM center. C. Frazier Landrum, a medical doctor from Edwards, inquired of Senator Stennis why the country was fighting communists in Vietnam while simultaneously funding a Head Start program whose faculty "are former members of the communist sponsored Highlander Folk School."[13] Bryce Alexander, Indianola's police chief, sent Senator Stennis a copy of a check drawn on CDGM's account and made payable to Alice Giles. The police chief also added that it was his "personal knowledge that Alice Giles and her husband, Oscar Giles, are actively connected with the Civil Rights Movement here in Indianola."[14] Letters from the Magnolia State poured into Washington, D.C. Mississippi House of Representatives speaker Walter Sillers sent Stennis a list of people arrested for disturbing the peace in Rosedale, Mississippi, noting that five CDGM employees were among those arrested.[15] Congressman John Bell Williams (D-Miss.), whose district included Mount Beulah, requested from OEO a list of all CDGM employees receiving salaries greater than $5,000. Williams, who planned to show that Head Start money gave movement workers the financial freedom to continue organizing, shared the information with other members of the Mississippi congressional delegation and with the Sovereignty Commission.[16] The real problem was that CDGM gave meaning to nascent civil rights laws by opening up new channels for black participation in the governance of local communities and the distribution of federal funds. White supremacists used this movement affiliation to suggest that CDGM was not truly a program for preschoolers but instead a vehicle for revolution financed by the federal government.

Even Mississippi governor Paul B. Johnson, who had taken a more moderate approach on civil rights in 1964 in the wake of John F. Kennedy's assassination, criminalized CDGM. He provided Senator Stennis with a copy of a CDGM check drawn on the Freedom National Bank of New York. The governor reminded Stennis that integrationist Jackie Robinson was the

The Ku Klux Klan defaced a sign on the road to the Mount Pisgah CDGM center. Vandalism of CDGM centers was common throughout the program's three-year tenure. (Presbyterian Historical Society [U.S.A.])

president of that bank. Not only did the Head Start program have sizable financial resources independent of local white Mississippians, but the program deposited those funds in a black-controlled financial institution. In the letter to Stennis, Mississippi's chief executive also pledged to do his part in "nailing down these high-binders."[17] "Highbinder" was a term for a corrupt politician. Johnson had no proof that CDGM misused funds, but the accusation provided political cover to undermine a program that he disliked for other reasons. Governor Johnson's disdain for CDGM reflected his 1963 campaign persona; he boasted of blocking federal officials from escorting James Meredith into the Ole Miss Administration building. In a speech at the Neshoba County Fair, he referred to the NAACP as "niggers, alligators, apes, coons and possums." However, in a January 1964 inauguration address, for a more national audience, Johnson vowed that "hate or prejudice, or ignorance will not lead Mississippi while I sit in the Governor's chair."[18] The assassination of President Kennedy might have tempered Johnson, but it is more likely that he, along with Indianola sheriff Bryce Alexander and state house speaker Walter Sillers, understood that fanning the flames of racist hatred was no longer in vogue. Instead, Johnson and others set out to bring the radical Head Start program into disrepute by collecting potentially damaging information and forwarding it to Stennis.

Inquiries and letters of concern about the Head Start program from ordinary white citizens and politicians reveal that not only members of extremist groups such as the Ku Klux Klan were troubled by CDGM and its progressive mission. These opponents, acting in the name of local government and under the guise of fiscal responsibility and local control, had the same goals and concerns as racist demagogues. They understood that the antipoverty program created a shakeup in local power relations, as OEO bypassed the traditional leadership in Mississippi's towns and worked directly with poor black people. By displaying newfound interest in CDGM, white leaders in the state covertly protected their undemocratic leadership and inequitable distributions of power.

No one had a larger platform to oppose CDGM than United States Senator John Cornelius Stennis, a powerful player on Capitol Hill who leveled the most potent opposition to the Head Start program. In 1965 Stennis sat on both the Senate Armed Services and the Senate Appropriations Committees, assignments that gave him control over funding for the war in Vietnam and the War on Poverty. A son of the segregated South, in 1956 Stennis signed the Southern Manifesto, which decried the United States Supreme

John C. Stennis was a U.S. senator from Mississippi serving from 1947 until 1989. Stennis was one of CDGM's most vocal and powerful foes. (U.S. Senate Historical Office)

Court's *Brown* decision. He referred to Freedom Summer as a northern invasion and voted against the Civil Rights Act of 1964 and the Voting Rights Act of 1965. His antipathy to racial equality and black empowerment spilled over onto CDGM, but he chose tactics that appeared neutral on the matter of race.

Born in 1901 in Kemper County, Stennis came of age in De Kalb, the county seat of an area known for its red soil and tall piney woods. Unlike counties in the Delta, Kemper County had a white majority that generally made its living through subsistence farming. Stennis's father was a farmer and merchant who raised seven children in modest but comfortable circumstances. After graduating in 1919 from Kemper County Agricultural High School, John Stennis headed to Mississippi State University in Starkville. Stennis was "the intellectual who helped others with their homework." After graduation in 1923, he entered the University of Virginia Law School and earned a law degree in 1928. The following year, he married Coy Hines, a local home demonstration agent in De Kalb. They remained married for fifty-four years until her death in 1983. They had two children: a son, John Hampton, born in 1935, and a daughter, Margaret Jane, born in 1937.[19] Stennis's son recalled, "daddy taught us patriotic things and poetry. In teaching us the Pledge of Allegiance to the flag, he made sure that we understood the meaning." Stennis first won election to the United States Senate in 1947 to complete the term of Theodore Bilbo, who died in office.[20]

Often in the shadows of his senatorial colleague James O. Eastland (D-Miss.), Stennis wielded significant influence in the Senate. His reputation for sixteen-hour days on the Hill gained him admission into the Senate "club," an elite group of legislators who "exercised decisive influence over crucial institutional processes and decisions."[21] His colleagues knew him as the devout Presbyterian who led a Wednesday morning congressional prayer group and took attendance to keep a record of who missed the weekly gathering. Once, he took a group of his staffers to church with him and "was miffed when the collection plate passed down the row and the staffers didn't put anything in the plate." The following Sunday, he lined up the staffers like children and passed out dollar bills insisting that they put something in the church offering.[22] He was the first Democratic senator to publicly denounce Senator Joseph McCarthy (R-Wisc.); his peers rewarded this independent streak by choosing him to sit on the six-man panel that considered disciplinary action against the demagogic anticommunist.[23] His committee assignments gave him oversight of both domestic and foreign affairs.

Stennis saw the war in Vietnam—not the War on Poverty—as the most pressing issue in the country. He called for an all-out air attack to maintain the United States' military credibility and win the war. Total war was costly, but Stennis insisted that nothing was more valuable than the country's honor, which he perceived to be at stake. On the speech circuit in 1966, he maintained that Congress needed to increase war funding "at the expense of other less important matters, such as Great Society-type welfare programs."[24]

The junior senator was genuinely interested in winning the Vietnam War, but it was politically irresponsible for him to dismiss the utility of the anti-poverty effort. Poverty was so widespread in the state of Mississippi that the relief payment per person was minimal because of the large number of citizens requiring assistance. The state's average per-person payment from the Old Age Assistance Program was $35.20, while the national average was $76.92. Mississippi's average Aid to Families with Dependent Children payout was $8.91, while the national average was $30.95.[25] Mississippi also remained at the bottom in education. Over 67 percent of the state's draftees examined for military service in Vietnam were rejected in 1964 because they failed to pass the written and oral entrance exams.[26] Public education in the state was patently substandard.

Stennis's lack of concern about the widespread poverty and rudimentary educational opportunities in his state reflected his priorities. The man who represented the state without any public kindergartens opposed CDGM. Stennis insisted that the Head Start program wasted taxpayer dollars and usurped local white control. As he explained to one constituent, "It is shocking and almost unbelievable to know that almost $1.5 million is being spent by this group for completely illegal and unauthorized purposes. I want you to know that I am not going to drop this matter but fully intend to expose this program. I just hope that through this effort, we can make more people in the nation realize just how foolish many of these new federal programs are."[27]

Stennis saw as threatening OEO's empowerment of working-class black women to make decisions for themselves and become socially, financially, and politically independent of their white neighbors. He opposed a breakdown of Mississippi's established order of social relations that set white people in the dominant position, yet that is exactly what CDGM promoted with its integrated Central Staff and numerous white college students in Head Start centers. Stennis found further proof that his state's social mores were changing when he read a copy of one of Head Start's founding documents, the Cooke Committee Report. He underlined a section advising

Head Start programs to "introduce a variety of adult figures of different races . . . so that the children can learn to understand and appreciate the variety of roles in our society."[28] While the senator had not expressed interest in the dismal conditions of black public schools in Mississippi, he remained vigilant about defunding CDGM.

Senator Stennis began his pitched attack against CDGM in June 1965, before a single CDGM center had opened its doors. Having undoubtedly read about CDGM's large grant in the newspaper, he dispatched Paul J. Cotter, the Senate Appropriations Committee's chief investigator, to Mississippi to examine CDGM's financial records and interview its employees. Cotter's presence allowed Stennis to focus on financial figures rather than on race or CDGM's proximity to the movement.[29] By questioning the leadership, qualifications, and bookkeeping of CDGM teachers and administrators, Stennis, who had never before expressed interest in black education, raised what appeared to be valid criticisms. This method, while less dramatic than a southern filibuster on the Senate floor, was a means to the same end: the preservation of white supremacy.

Stennis understood that a Senate investigation proving corruption and waste within CDGM could undermine the program without appearing overtly racist. He also understood that his white constituents back home in Mississippi expected him to fight black advancement just as his predecessor, Theodore Bilbo (D-Miss.), had done. Bilbo had been the consummate white supremacist who believed the deportation of African Americans to Africa was the solution to race problems. Stennis, however, understood that racist grandstanding simply portrayed the South as backward. Because southerners were "fighting a losing battle in the forum of public opinion throughout the nation," he would "make no appeals based on prejudice or passion, even if the prejudice happens to be one I share from my natural experience of growing into maturity in the South."[30] Stennis shared Bilbo's views on white supremacy while he understood that the times required a new approach.

Stennis's political strategies infused his CDGM critique. Rather than directly castigate the program for fostering black financial independence and self-determination, the junior senator focused his attacks on administrative errors and irregularities, charging that CDGM "demonstrated a serious lack of fiscal responsibility in attending the administration of the whole project." He also lamented the lack of local participation in the Central Staff and questioned the role of civil rights in the program.[31] It was not unusual for a member of the Senate Appropriations Committee to be concerned with possible fiscal mismanagement. However, there were many different Head Start programs operating in Mississippi during the 1965 summer, and not one program had officially started when Stennis sent investigators to Mount Beulah.[32] Stennis's premature and sole investigation of CDGM appeared to be based on long-standing hostility to any and all programs with movement ties.

Stennis charged that CDGM funds subsidized civil rights work, citing a $30,710 payment to the Delta Ministry for orientation expenses.[33] CDGM had an agreement with the Delta Ministry to rent a building on the Mount Beulah campus for Central Staff members to work and live. Each Central Staff employee paid the Delta Ministry sixty dollars per month or two dollars per day for room and board. Tom Levin agreed to pay the Delta Ministry eight dollars per day for room and board for each orientation attendee, a fee that was exactly half of what OEO had budgeted for orientation costs per teacher nationwide. The senator wanted to know why the Delta Ministry charged orientation participants eight dollars per day to use the same facilities that Central Staff employees paid two dollars per day to use. Moreover, the timing of the payment disturbed him. On 17 June, Levin gave the Delta Ministry a check for over $30,000 as an advance payment on orientation conference costs to be incurred in July. The Mississippi Freedom Democratic Party held demonstrations at the Mississippi Capitol in Jackson on 14–19 June to protest the special session of the legislature that Governor Johnson called to revise Mississippi's voting laws because of the impending federal voting rights legislation. The grassroots political party's leaders correctly assumed that Governor Johnson wanted to change the state's laws to be in a better position to challenge the new federal voting rights law. The voting rights demonstrators stayed at Mount Beulah during the days of their capitol protests. Stennis alleged that CDGM paid orientation fees early to offset the costs of Mississippi Freedom Democratic Party demonstrators who resided at Mount Beulah.[34]

In addition to questions about lodging costs at Mount Beulah, Stennis's investigator uncovered other troubling aspects in the program's administration of federal funds. Program checks only required one signature—that of Director Tom Levin or Board Chairman Adam Beittel—and a twenty-one-year-old, Lenore G. Monsonis, had the only keys to the automated check-signing machine.[35] The investigator argued that there was no system in place to prevent Levin, Beittel, or Monsonis from stealing money. He also questioned the frequent salary advances given to CDGM employees to cover bail and fines. Five Central Staff members and several teachers were arrested during the Jackson demonstrations in June 1965.[36] Program books showed that many were given salary advances as bail money, although there was no written procedure for how those funds were to be paid back. Another problem uncovered in the committee's investigation was the purchase of over 3,000 preschool chairs at a cost of $6,000, even though the grant's conditions explicitly prohibited the purchase of furniture. Actually, Jule Sugarman had given Tom Levin verbal permission to buy the chairs so that children did not sit on the floor in some centers.[37]

Stennis's antagonism toward CDGM grew out of his disapproval of a program that usurped white Mississippians' control over black people rather than out of abhorrence for government spending or administrative errors. He remained conspicuously silent as his senatorial colleague James Eastland annually collected very generous farm subsidies ($170,000 in one year) for reducing his cotton production.[38] Moreover, Stennis remained silent about other Head Start programs in Mississippi that had sloppy bookkeeping. OEO audited the Head Start program run by the Biloxi Municipal Separate School District, whose superintendent was a Stennis ally. Auditors found that the ledger did not balance, staff attendance records did not support salary payments, and staff who did not travel received a flat monthly travel allowance. OEO investigators also found that the daughter of the president of the Biloxi school district's board of trustees received a Head Start job solely on the recommendation of the superintendent, and that the superintendent's daughter also secured employment and received the same salary as preschool teachers who held degrees, although she did not have one. Not only did Stennis not condemn the Biloxi administrative irregularities, he vigorously lobbied OEO to give the program additional funds.[39] Thus, his attack on CDGM displayed a clear agenda.

Shriver, after learning that Senator Stennis had sent investigators to Mississippi, dispatched former Louisiana congressman and assistant OEO director for congressional relations Gillis W. Long to observe CDGM operations. Long visited Mount Beulah on July 5 and 6, and reported back to Shriver that "Levin and his group are trying hard and within the objectives of the program, but they could have serious administrative/management problems."[40] The next day, senior OEO officials began scrambling. Theodore Berry, OEO director of community action programs, sent a memo to Project Head Start Deputy Director Jule Sugarman suggesting that the director of audits make a field check in Mississippi and determine what kind of help CDGM needed. Most telling about Berry's concern was the last sentence of the memo: "Senator Stennis is watching!"[41]

In response to Berry's request, an audit team from the OEO Office of Management traveled to Mississippi and audited CDGM's management and financial aspects. William Kelly, the assistant director of management, recalled putting "auditors into the field to determine whether or not there was an accounting system extant." It was common for Office of Management officials to visit programs that the national office suspected of having administrative problems. Management officials reported that there was some "fiscal amateurism," in CDGM but no willful misuse of funds. During that same time, Julius Richmond, Head Start's national director, visited fourteen centers to evaluate the quality and content of CDGM's program.[42]

By sending an audit team to Mississippi, Shriver appeared responsive to the senator's concerns, although some officials in the Washington, D.C., office privately insisted that CDGM's only fault was employment of known activists. Jule Sugarman later explained, "I think it [Stennis's investigation] had its origins in the fact that many of the people who were involved in the program had been members of the Freedom Democratic Party." According to Sugarman, Senator Stennis, "did not feel that [employment of movement veterans] was appropriate."[43]

OEO did not share Stennis's views, but the agency did find administrative problems within CDGM. Sugarman outlined CDGM's weaknesses in a letter to Dawson Horn, president of CDGM's sponsor, Mary Holmes Junior College. OEO requested that CDGM discontinue the use of their New York public accounting firm in favor of a local firm that could provide cheaper and prompter service. Additionally, OEO advised the program to reduce its printing office, which had unnecessary expenditures, to stop using grant money for legal fees, to stop conducting business through cash advances, and to maintain a travel log for CDGM's fleet of automobiles, showing the time, destination, and use of the vehicles.[44] Before the letter listing the stipulations arrived in Mississippi, OEO sent its assistant general counsel, Jim Heller, to meet with CDGM's board; at the meeting the most controversial demand was shared in person.[45]

On 1 August, at a Mount Beulah meeting attended by CDGM board members and several Central Staff members, OEO insisted that the program move its headquarters to Mary Holmes Junior College. Heller informed those assembled that Mount Beulah "had received too much unfavorable publicity and had acquired a bad reputation."[46] The request for relocation suggested that OEO had limits to its willingness to help bring about full freedom. Since CDGM's headquarters troubled Mississippi's congressional delegation, OEO attempted to exert control by separating CDGM from a place perceived to be a hotbed of activism. The relocation call, nothing more than an attempt to put out political fires, demonstrated that those holding the purse strings influenced the agenda and climate of the organization. SNCC staff had anticipated such control.

Years later, Jule Sugarman confirmed that the OEO request for CDGM relocation was political. "We had enough problems from the reports that we felt some change in the operation was necessitated." The "accusation was made," Sugarman continued, "that we were in fact subsidizing Mount Beulah."[47] OEO officials hoped that by moving CDGM's base of operation they could placate Mississippi's political elite. It was true that civil rights activity emanated from Mount Beulah. However, it was also true that Mount Beulah was closer to CDGM centers than Mary Holmes Junior College.[48]

OEO at all levels made some effort to conciliate southern officials who opposed the radical possibilities of the antipoverty effort. The southeast regional office, for example, allowed Alabama to maintain a segregated state economic opportunity office for years after the Civil Rights Act passed.[49] The realities of politics forced OEO to accommodate CDGM opponents and other segregationists. For one thing, the agency faced annual budget reauthorization hearings until 1967, when it received its first two-year authorization. If it did not placate southern congressmen, then these lawmakers might have joined forces with Republicans and placed OEO programs in established federal departments. To head off such an unholy alliance, OEO sacrificed some of CDGM's autonomy. Jule Sugarman had stated as much in his letter to Dawson Horn when he maintained that both CDGM and the national Head Start program stood to lose if CDGM did not implement OEO's recommendations. Frank Mankiewicz, director of the Peace Corps in Peru and one of Shriver's confidants, recalled years later that Shriver's backing down to Stennis on CDGM was "a tactical matter. It may have saved the program by not making explicit what was implicit."[50] Headquartering a movement-affiliated Head Start program at Mount Beulah was explicit political agitation that put Shriver in the crosshairs of one of the most powerful men in the United State Senate, John C. Stennis.

The OEO director had made such hard choices before. In August 1964, it appeared that the Economic Opportunity Act would not pass in the House of Representatives, because a majority of southern Democrats joined

Republicans in opposing it. North Carolina congressmen wanted assurance that Adam Yarmolinsky, Shriver's right-hand man in developing the War on Poverty, would have no job in the actual implementation of the program in exchange for their votes. Yarmolinsky's greatest crime was his progressive politics. While working at the Defense Department, he "was instrumental in declaring segregated facilities off-limits to military personnel in the South, which meant that bars, restaurants, and taverns near military bases had to be integrated or else military personnel were not allowed to patronize them." This did not sit well with southern congressmen. Additionally, Yarmolinsky was a "red diaper baby"; his mother had been a member of the Communist Party.[51] After meeting in the office of House Speaker John McCormack (D-Mass.) with chairman of the North Carolina delegation Harold Cooley (D-N.C.), Democratic House Whip Hale Boggs (D-La.), and with President Johnson on the phone, Shriver told Yarmolinsky, "we've just thrown you to the wolves."[52] The Economic Opportunity Act passed the House, but the price was high. Sargent Shriver could not employ Adam Yarmolinsky at OEO. A year later, as Shriver called for CDGM relocation to Mary Holmes Junior College, he once again found himself appeasing southern congressmen.

OEO's call for relocation brought CDGM's internal differences to the surface. The Central Staff, largely composed of well-educated, middle-class whites, opposed the compromise and urged resistance to OEO. However, Central Staff employees also had jobs and homes in other places that they could return to if CDGM ended. CDGM board member Jake Ayers, a local black Mississippian and Lillie Ayers's husband, was hesitant to challenge OEO on the call for relocation. He knew that thousands of black children had their first taste of decent education through CDGM and that through Head Start employment his family members and friends were making more money than they had ever made before. They had no other alternatives if OEO discontinued CDGM. Moreover, Ayers was looking toward the future. If OEO wanted CDGM to relocate, then Ayers was willing to acquiesce, if that meant that the program might secure a year-round grant. Joining Ayers in support for a move to Mary Holmes was board member and attorney Marian Wright, who also did not want to endanger future funding. Tom Levin, on the contrary, adamantly opposed the move and even threatened to resign in protest. After six hours of tense debate that ended at 3:00 A.M. on 2 August, the board voted for the move and adjourned the meeting.[53]

Both OEO officials and Central Staff members believed that the success or failure of the War on Poverty pivoted on CDGM's actions. No other program did a better job of adhering to "maximum feasible participation" of the poor, so if Stennis found flaws, then all programs had them. In a letter to Mary Holmes Junior College president Dawson Horn, Jule Sugarman warned that negative reports about CDGM could have implications for Project Head Start as a whole.[54] OEO officials demanded CDGM's relocation from the politically charged Mount Beulah to a more neutral site to keep the grassroots program's opponents at bay and inoculate the antipoverty agency against charges of subsidizing civil rights. Central Staff members believed, however, that a forced move belied the autonomous spirit of the Community Action Program. Furthermore, many staff members felt that OEO had singled out CDGM for unparalleled control. Although CDGM had several infractions, elsewhere such charges did not warrant a move. A Head Start program in Salt Lake City, Utah, for example, commingled its funding with that of the local public school district, preventing an audit from being conducted, yet neither OEO officials nor Senator Stennis called for major changes or the termination of that program.[55] OEO exacted uneven discipline because what happened in Mississippi had national consequences.

Neither Stennis nor OEO considered the possibility of public fallout from a forced relocation. However, Central Staff members did, and used it to their advantage. Days after CDGM's board agreed to move, Tom Levin called OEO's Washington, D.C., office and informed them that twenty-five Central Staff members planned to resign in protest of agency demands and would work in the program for the final three weeks without pay. The importance of the Head Start program to black communities necessitated that they complete the summer, but OEO's demands meant that they no longer wanted to associate with the agency.[56] Levin knew that neither the White House nor OEO wanted to be accused of bullying the poor. The employees who threatened to resign included college students and educators from the North who would surely tell the press about their ordeal: a federal agency committed to community action and local autonomy in theory demanded the complete opposite in practice. Levin had seen this public relations tactic work during Freedom Summer, as national media outlets finally covered black persecution in Mississippi because of the influx of northern, white student volunteers. To avoid questions about its dedication to bottom-up

community action, the federal agency reversed its call for CDGM's relocation. The program remained at Mount Beulah.[57]

Victory came at a cost. CDGM's board of directors set program policy,
and all Central Staff members served at the board's pleasure. Thus, the
board could terminate staff members if they overstepped bounds or jeopardized the program in some way. Four staff members, including Tom Levin,
attended the board meeting where OEO representative Jim Heller initially
demanded that CDGM relocate. Board members were not pleased with
Levin's ardent opposition to relocation; to them, his actions demonstrated
that "there were not proper relationships between the Board and staff."[58]
Marian Wright later recalled that she was appalled by Levin's behavior. "You
just don't threaten the government. I wanted the same thing he did, but he
antagonized everyone by fighting with OEO openly." Levin had attempted
to defy racist southern politicians, an extremely cautious OEO, and CDGM's
pragmatic board of directors in resisting relocation. His actions led board
members to plan his termination.[59]

The board voted to concentrate power and decision-making authority in
the hands of those most politically experienced to ensure that CDGM did
not fall out of favor with OEO. Thus, board members Marian Wright, Art
Thomas, and James McRee formed an Executive Committee that acted in
place of the full board when emergencies arose. The committee also oversaw all Central Staff hiring. Additionally, this select group handled all communication with OEO in Washington and passed down new agreements
and policies to staff in the Central Office and in the field. These changes
dramatically curtailed the full participation of local communities and served
as an indirect censure of Tom Levin for his antagonistic behavior toward
OEO.[60]

Many on CDGM's board considered Tom Levin a liability to the program's continuation, but Senator Stennis was the real threat. Board members had initially shared Levin's desire for a Head Start program that allowed
poor, rural black Mississippians to run their own affairs for the first time in
their lives. That shared goal was shaken to its core because a powerful segregationist disapproved of the program. As Stennis asked questions and
ordered investigations, CDGM supporters went scrambling. Thus, five
months after OEO sought out Levin as a progressive force to run the kind of
operation that they wanted, they recommended that he be fired. After several conversations with antipoverty officials in Washington, D.C., CDGM's
board relieved Levin of his director's duties and "promoted" him to a proposal

writer.[61] A board committed to grassroots leadership fired Levin and hoarded power among themselves in an attempt to curry favor with those who allocated grant funds for the poor.

Disputes between OEO senior officials, CDGM board members, and Central Staff did not go unnoticed by CDGM field staff and parents. The questions about Levin's leadership and the role of civil rights activity in the organization made many teachers and parents fear for the program's future. No grassroots participants wanted to jeopardize the availability of school preparation and nutritious meals for black children and high-paying jobs for their parents. Hollis Watkins, a SNCC organizer throughout the state, remembered that a lot of black Mississippians became afraid to attend mass meetings and other movement gatherings, even though they were held after hours. In his opinion, Stennis's inquiries were successful in re-awakening the fear that Watkins and other SNCC staffers had spent years trying to eradicate.[62] Winson Hudson, who taught at a center in Harmony, recalled an accident she had years later while driving a Head Start car on official business. Although she was badly injured and needed medical attention, she refused treatment until she had discreetly given the voter registration materials that were in her car to family members.[63] Hudson understood that if discovered the voting materials could be used against the program. Many CDGM supporters walked such a fine line, understanding that they had to be strategic about their efforts to bring services and political change to their communities. Others, as Watkins asserted, simply withdrew from movement activity because they did not want to lose access to education, healthcare, and improved living conditions.[64]

John Mudd, a twenty-six-year-old Harvard doctoral student in political economy and government, became Levin's replacement. While he did not have the former director's extensive civil rights background, he hailed from a prominent Philadelphia family that had championed many progressive causes. Mudd's parents had financially supported an initiative to improve housing options for Philadelphia's black residents in the fifties.[65] He himself first came to Mississippi in the fall of 1963 after meeting Bob Moses through his Harvard roommate. In the Magnolia State, Mudd met and traveled with Moses and Marian Wright to Greenwood and Liberty. The poverty and racism he saw caused him to return the following summer with a group of Harvard students and faculty in tow. He organized a summer project at Tougaloo where he used academic instruction to foster social action. Mudd remained in Mississippi after the 1964 summer and partnered with black farmers in

John Mudd (*far right*) confers with (*left to right*) CDGM's deputy director Martin Cohn and CDGM board members Rev. James McRee, Marian Wright, and Adam Dan Beittel. (Johnson Publishing Company, LLC)

Batesville to operate a vegetable cooperative. Thus, Mudd had some traction in the state when Marian Wright approached him about working with CDGM.[66]

As CDGM's acting director, Mudd tackled administrative issues. He recalled that initially Central Staff wanted nothing to do with him. "People were really angry. That's why instead of getting into any big policy stuff, I said that one of the things I could do is get payroll out, so I phoned around to see who had indeed been working."[67] By September, however, Mudd's attention turned to more pressing matters. CDGM's first grant had run out, so there was no more money. Except for Polly Greenberg, out-of-state resource teachers and Central Staff members had left Mississippi. Mudd began the arduous task of overseeing CDGM's application for a year-round Head Start grant.

OEO policies, however, had changed. Now, Head Start applications submitted through community action agencies received priority over statewide nonprofit groups such as CDGM.[68] Community action agencies ensured that mayors and other members of local political establishments, who had complained to OEO officials that community action usurped their power, had a say in what was going on in their communities. War on Poverty archi-tects had intended for community action programs to originate in local communities through agencies. However, by 1965, few communities had community action agencies or had applied for grants, so OEO developed "national-emphasis" programs such as Head Start and Legal Services to show Congress that antipoverty funds were being used. After the programs were created, logic held that local people sitting on community action agency boards would sustain their tenure, hence the OEO decision to fund Head Start programs through agencies after the 1965 summer. OEO did not initially have precise requirements about racial and economic representa-tion on local agencies, and some cities, towns, and counties formed agen-cies that did not include poor people or minorities and still received funding priority from OEO.[69]

In Mississippi, this policy meant that those opposed to CDGM could form a community action agency and control whether or not CDGM oper-ated in their community. This fact was not lost on segregationists. CDGM supporters in Amite County tried unsuccessfully to participate in that coun-ty's newly formed community action agency. Only after they complained to OEO officials were they allowed to work in the agency-run Head Start pro-gram, but most were relegated to cooking in the kitchen.[70] Mississippi State Sovereignty Commission director Erle Johnston would later explain to Stennis, "there definitely has been a change of attitude toward Head Start because local people now realize if they don't do the job themselves, some-one else will do it for them."[71] Community action agencies became a way for the white ruling class to strategically maintain the status quo.

John Mudd had little time to build relationships with local white citizens who sat on community action agency boards throughout Mississippi, because Stennis's continued inquiries into CDGM's program occupied his time. The senator publicly announced his plan to question OEO officials about CDGM in October 1965 when they appeared before the Senate Appropria-tions Committee in support of a supplemental appropriations request.[72] If Shriver, with Mudd's help and documentation, did not resolve CDGM's bookkeeping blunders and prove that the program had put systems in place to prevent future administrative errors, then CDGM would not have to worry about securing delegate agency status from local community ac-tion agencies because it would be ineligible for future grants.

On 14 October 1965 Stennis assumed a prosecutorial role and ques-tioned Sargent Shriver before the Senate Appropriations Subcommittee on Deficiencies and Supplementals. Buoyed by Stennis's passion, committee members spent three hours debating CDGM's $1.4 million grant from the 1965 summer and only one hour on the other antipoverty programs included in the $1.5 billion antipoverty appropriation.[73] The long and tense hearing began with Stennis explaining to committee members why CDGM troubled him. He mentioned the "racial zealots" that operated out of Mount Beulah and the outsider status of Tom Levin—even entering his curriculum vitae, which contained detailed civil rights activity, into the *Congressional Record*. The junior senator also lamented the way in which CDGM circumvented the authority of the governor's office.[74] Stennis then provided the committee with an overview of the results of the Appropriations Committee's investigation and OEO's audit. As evidence of subsidized civil rights activity, he entered into the record a CDGM document explaining under what conditions an employee's fine or bail would be paid by CDGM. He focused on a clause that read: "I (blank) agree that the personnel committee of CDGM shall decide whether the bail bond or fine in question is a result of my own action outside of my responsibilities to CDGM or is a result of harassments in the course of my normal work for CDGM. In the event the personnel committee decides that said fine or bail represents harassment, it will be provided by CDGM."[75] One of Stennis's many allegations was that CDGM used federal government money to pay fines and bail for protest activity.[76] Indeed, CDGM did pay the legal fees of employees in certain circumstances, but it did so with OEO's permission. Throughout the 1965 summer, local policemen and highway patrolmen arrested CDGM staff while they conducted official program business. Because of the frequency of these unlawful stops, Tom Levin requested and received from Jule Sugarman approval to reallocate $2,000 of the 1965 grant for legal fees.[77]

OEO officials showed a renewed commitment to CDGM during the committee hearing. Sargent Shriver, while acknowledging administrative mistakes, maintained his confidence in the program and asserted that Central Staff members had corrected accounting errors. He addressed many allegations, including the one widely circulated in newspapers across the state that CDGM rented a toilet for one hundred dollars. He explained that St. Peter's Church in Pascagoula, where the toilet was installed, was made available to CDGM free of charge as a center location, but the building had no indoor bathroom. To meet OEO requirements for Head Start center locations, the church purchased and installed two toilets, two sinks, and a urinal; the one-hundred-dollar CDGM payment was a fair portion of the church's expense. Shriver also corrected the rumor that outsiders ran CDGM. He showed that out of the 3,000 individuals on staff as volunteers, teachers, aides, and cooks during the 1965 summer, 2,850 of them were native Mississippians. He addressed the orientation costs at Mount Beulah by stating that he expected his programs to get the cheapest rate possible at all times, while also being mindful of the fact that organizations with rental facilities, including the Delta Ministry, had a right to charge different groups different amounts. As to the timing of the payment, the Delta Ministry's facilities manager asserted that the advance payment allowed him to purchase necessary supplies and make repairs before orientation began.[78] Finally, the OEO director reminded senators that "of the many charges leveled at this program, none has been aimed at the quality of the program, its content, its results, or its meaning to the parents and children who participated."[79] OEO stood by one of its model community action programs.

Stennis rebutted Shriver's findings, and his Senate colleagues assisted him. The senator reminded Shriver of a private conversation they shared in the vestibule of the Senate dining room regarding CDGM's headquarters. Stennis alleged that Shriver told him in good faith at that time that the program would relocate from Mount Beulah, but CDGM staff "rebelled and wouldn't leave."[80] Stennis insinuated that OEO officials had no control over CDGM, and so federal money would continue to be spent improperly. John Pastore (D-R.I.), subcommittee chairman and the senior senator from Rhode Island, joined Stennis in portraying CDGM as a defiant program. Pastore referenced recent newspaper articles about the arrest of two CDGM employees who demonstrated at the United States Capitol against American involvement in Vietnam. Jeannine Herron, a Central Staff employee, and Richard Dodge, a CDGM transportation worker, were among 1,000 marchers arrested 9 August.[81] Pastore asked Shriver if he employed "people like that in the poverty program." When Shriver answered that he employed "people who can exercise their rights as citizens on their own time," Pastore countered by saying, "but these are the people employed to help our young people get the proper perspective to be good citizens. I would have been very happy today if you had said, 'after we found this out, we fired them.' "[82] Shriver, defending CDGM, reminded Pastore that "university professors, paid by public money, [also] participate in these demonstrations, don't get fired and they teach your children."[83] For the time being, OEO's top official planned to carry the water for the embattled preschool program.

OEO director Sargent Shriver at a 30 June 1965 White House function celebrating the launch of Project Head Start. Pictured from left to right are Timothy Shriver, Robert Shriver, Danny Kaye, "Lady Bird" Johnson, Mrs. Lou Maginn (director of a Head Start project in East Fairfield, Vermont), and Shriver. (LBJ Presidential Library)

Debate over CDGM made for strange bedfellows. Stennis and Pastore were in the same political party, but they rarely held the same positions. Pastore, the first Italian American to sit in the United States Senate, was a liberal stalwart who played an integral role in the passage of the 1964 Civil Rights Act.[84] While championing Title VI on the Senate floor, Pastore engaged in heated debate with Stennis over whether racially discriminatory programs in any state had ever received federal funds.[85] One year later, in joining forces with the southern conservative to critique CDGM, Pastore complicated the argument that opposition to CDGM was covert preservation of segregation.

The *Jackson Daily News*, one of the leading newspapers in the state, joined forces with Stennis in castigating CDGM. One day after the Senate appropriations hearing, the paper ran a political cartoon that suggested a scandal brewed at Mount Beulah. The illustration carried the headline "phew" and served to cast a shadow over CDGM's operation despite Shriver's testimony to the contrary.[86]

CDGM still had not received a year-round Head Start grant three months after the Senate appropriations hearing. CDGM's board of directors had requested six million dollars for a nine-month preschool program, but had heard only that money was on the way. The new grant application included old and new communities that had requested Head Start programs. More than fifty communities operated centers on a volunteer basis while awaiting a new grant. Undoubtedly, the delay in Washington was largely due to Senator Stennis's lengthy investigations of the program. If Shriver refunded CDGM without making sure that safeguards were in place to prevent further errors, he would appear to be irresponsibly allocating federal money and would have a difficult time funding other antipoverty programs. The delay in refunding weakened the trust and partnership that his office had developed with CDGM supporters, who urgently needed the educational opportunity, food, and income that Head Start provided.

Desperation showed its face in Greenville, Mississippi, on 31 January, 1966, as forty black sharecroppers who had been evicted from local plantations broke into the empty Air Force base seeking shelter. The base contained 300 buildings that had not been used since 1960. The dispossessed sharecroppers unloaded blankets and boxes of food in the barracks, preparing to settle in for an extended stay. The break-in had been planned the day before at a Delta Ministry meeting held at Mount Beulah after a distress telegram to President Johnson went unanswered and two elderly black Mississippians froze to death in a Delta plantation shack. Several individuals with CDGM ties assisted the squatters, including board member Art Thomas and district organizers Thelma Barnes and Unita Blackwell.[87] When approached by the base commander about the unlawful entrance, the group spokesman presented him with a statement that read: "We are here because we are hungry and cold and we have no jobs or land. We don't want charity. We are willing to work for ourselves if given a chance." The prepared statement also called for CDGM's refunding.[88]

Troops flown in from as far away as Denver forcibly removed the occupants the morning after the base occupation, citing a rationale that was as cruel as it was ironic. The commander in charge maintained that the federal government was removing the sharecroppers because the building in which they had taken up residence did not have water or proper sanitation. Understanding the irony of the situation, one strike leader retorted, "all over Mississippi, homes don't have water or fire protection." Indeed, in the Delta, 90 percent of the homes occupied by black sharecroppers lacked indoor toilets or bathing facilities.[89] The government's newfound concern for decent living conditions rang hollow.

The decision to take over federal property on one of the coldest days in Mississippi history demonstrated just how determined the former agricultural workers were to bring attention to their plight. The state employment commission had earlier released the news that 6,500 tractor drivers living with their families on plantations would be jobless and homeless by spring because of automation.[90] The trespassing group hoped that the military barracks would be converted into housing for displaced tenants of some of the richest farmland in the world. The episode demonstrated CDGM's importance to impoverished black communities. While the Head Start program could not wipe out unemployment, it did provide a significant number of rural black residents with the livelihood to survive and become active participants in democracy.

The Air Force base takeover was unwelcome news for CDGM, which did not plan the event. All three broadcasting networks (ABC, CBS, and NBC) covered the incident.[91] CDGM could not afford to be associated with civil disobedience as it awaited refunding. The Head Start officials would have much rather preferred that media outlets report on the more than fifty centers that remained open on a voluntary basis.[92]

By the time of the January military base takeover, black women from the poorest sections of the state had run CDGM centers without any financial assistance from OEO since September. They provided 3,300 children with education and food. They also donated over $190,000 worth of free labor.[93] Supporters asked families who could spare the money to pay twenty-five cents per week. A center in Greenwood reported an average daily enrollment of ninety-three children during the unfunded period. Community chairman Ethel Brady wrote, "We have learned that money is not the only aspect. We are developing a more greater nation to come." Indianola teachers reported that while they had no building to hold the 300 children enrolled in their program, "we do have people that are donating rooms in their private homes for us to get started." At the Shaw center, community members donated heaters for the Head Start program to keep preschoolers warm.[94] In Cleveland, Velma Bartley talked black residents into letting her grow greens and corn on their property. She used the food grown to feed preschoolers.[95] Other women also improvised to meet nutritional needs. Area teacher guide Lavaree Jones recalled one teacher who "canvassed door-to-door and got a tomato from one person, a potato from another, and some spaghetti from someone else. She came back to the center and said 'I believe I am gonna make it' and at eleven o'clock as usual, she called all the children and said 'come, the food is ready.' "[96] The women in Minnie Ripley's Mayersville community "all had deep freezers" and brought food out of those freezers to feed preschoolers until federal money arrived.[97] They did this without the promise of a grant or reimbursement. These CDGM women were willing to stretch their households' budgets beyond imagination to keep community children fed, safe, and happy.

In addition to keeping the centers open, CDGM women embarked on a letter-writing campaign. In letters to President Lyndon Johnson, Sargent Shriver, and CDGM officials, the women extolled CDGM's numerous benefits and urged its refunding. Roberta Lewis, a woman from Durant, told the president that "Mr. Stennis does not represent us. He knows we never had the opportunity to live in decent homes or educate our children." Lewis asserted that CDGM "is the best and only program that has ever been in Mississippi to educate Negro children and train the adults." Shirley Williams, who worked in the Laurel center, wrote, "I don't know whether the things Stennis said about Head Start is true but I know he don't want to see our children progress."[98]

Educational progress was a common refrain among CDGM mothers. In Madison County, a woman told Polly Greenberg, "the best thing about CDGM was the children got something new each day: a song, a kind of art, a walk, a talk, something new to eat. I've never seen a time in Mississippi when poverty children of our race were daily offered something new to develop his mind."[99] The Head Start program was the kind of academic opportunity that black parents had mobilized and organized for since Reconstruction.

Black women's words demonstrated that CDGM was about more than a paycheck or an educational title. The program provided them with self-determination and their children with the educational opportunities they had sought for years. These women understood that their opportunity to have a say in black children's education and in their community's governance were hard-fought gains they could not relinquish without a fight. While they might not have been in an OEO board room negotiating with antipoverty officials, their resolve to keep centers open and to lobby public officials was resounding evidence of their desire to see CDGM refunded.

Women in other parts of the state who wanted the same opportunities for their children that CDGM women had secured began to open Head Start centers during the unfunded period and claim CDGM affiliation. Rankin County was not a part of CDGM's first grant, but by September

1965, a sizeable majority of its black residents in the unincorporated community of Fannin wanted preschool programs for their children. Alean Adams, the wife of the local NAACP president and mother of five children, desired something better for her family. Having heard of CDGM accomplishments in other parts of the state, Adams set about bringing the program to her community. Like other CDGM women, Adams came from humble beginnings and was active in the movement prior to Head Start's inception. She was born in 1935 in the Three Prong Road area of the Fannin community in Rankin County. Her family sharecropped on whites' land. As was the case for most black people in the Deep South, and specifically for most CDGM women, Adams's education was informal. She stopped attending school in the tenth grade. "I always had a burning desire to go to school, but there were few schools around here for blacks at that time. After a while school just kind of ran out."[100] School ran out for Adams because no other grades were offered in her community after the tenth grade.

During her short educational tenure, Adams met her husband, John, whom she married in 1953, and together they challenged unfair practices and laws in their county beginning in the early 1960s. John served as Rankin County NAACP president and he was often gone at night to civil rights meetings held in various churches in Florence, Pisgah, and Pelahatchie. Eventually, Adams decided that she should be at those meetings too. As she explained:

> Every time they would go, someone would get arrested. Either your headlight was out or you had a tag that wasn't right. They were really harassing us. Finally, I just said it is too nerve-racking to sit home and wait and see who was going to get a ticket or get arrested, so I said we're going too. I loaded the kids in the car, got their homework, and sometimes they wouldn't have had time to even eat very much. I would have them at the back of the church doing homework and I would be at the front and help talk about stuff up there.[101]

The same spirit that drew Adams from her home while her husband attended civil rights meetings galvanized her to bring Head Start to her community. She wanted the neighborhood children to have early childhood education, so she partnered with other women to run a center. "It was a coming together to make things happen. Whether you had any money or any food, we took whatever we had and we just shared that." Adams recalled that women came from various community churches and used whatever skills they had to get the program running. "There was always someone who knew how to sew and someone who knew how to cook. If you could cook, you'd end up in the kitchen, and if you could read a little bit, you ended teaching the class. As they figured out who knew what, you got some formal training."[102]

Black women mobilizing for the education of their children was not a story that the press cared to pick up. In addition to the unflattering news stories that did run, CDGM had to contend with an even more cautious OEO after the Air Force base takeover. Senator Stennis called for the eviction of the base squatters and told President Johnson that if they were not removed quickly, his only "recourse will be through the HEW [Housing, Education, and Welfare] appropriations bill."[103] Officials in the upper echelons of OEO understood that if Stennis could withhold HEW funding because of Greenville demonstrators, he could also hold up antipoverty program funds because of CDGM. They would have to tread carefully.

As January gave way to February with no word from OEO about CDGM's refunding, CDGM upped the stakes. They solicited support from the Citizens Crusade Against Poverty (CCAP), a coalition of organizations and individuals committed to ensuring that the War on Poverty lived up to its mission. Dick Boone, a former member of both President Kennedy's Committee on Juvenile Delinquency and President Johnson's Task Force in the War Against Poverty, created the CCAP in October 1964 to keep OEO accountable to its early goals. Boone had also been the government employee who inserted the phrase "maximum feasible participation" into the Economic Opportunity Act. CCAP functioned as a watchdog agency to make certain that OEO kept its promises to the country's poor. At Boone's urging, labor leader Walter Reuther, civil rights leaders Dr. Martin Luther King Jr. and A. Philip Randolph, and Rabbi Richard G. Hirsch, founder of the Religious Action Center of Reform Judaism, sent telegrams to Sargent Shriver urging him to refund CDGM.[104]

CDGM supporters also brought pressure to bear on Congress by traveling to Capitol Hill. On 11 February 1966, forty-eight preschool children, twenty-five Head Start teachers and parents, and two nurses arrived at the Rayburn House Office Building in Washington, D.C., on charter buses from Mississippi. Polly Greenberg's aunt paid for the two buses; relatives of Greenberg and John Mudd lived in the nation's capital and secured housing for the group among their social networks.[105] The preschool lobbying effort was not initially conceived as a political move. Raylawni Branch, a Hattiesburg native and mother of three, including one CDGM student, was in need of a babysitter in early 1966, but could not afford to hire one. She offhandedly remarked to Bob Beech, head of the Delta Ministry's Hattiesburg office, that she wished she could send her kids to "Lady Bird" Johnson for the day, because she was sure Johnson had people in the White House who could watch them. Beech liked the idea of CDGM going to Washington and shared it at a strategy meeting about the program's refunding.[106] Once in Washington, CDGM students and staff created a makeshift Head Start classroom in the House Education and Labor Committee hearing room. Spreading out crayons, scissors, construction paper, and even a wooden Donald Duck toy in the ornate halls of Congress, CDGM preschoolers refuted the allegations that their program was merely a front for civil rights. Mississippi's congressional delegation refused to meet with the group, but several other congressmen did, including Representative Joseph Resnick (D-N.Y.), who castigated his Mississippi colleagues and promised the group that there would be "good news in a few weeks."[107]

The Washington trip underscored the value of "street theater." Senator Stennis, after all, had access to national news outlets that he frequently used to condemn CDGM. In going to the nation's capitol, CDGM students and supporters gave their cause personal and persuasive imagery, similar to the way the televised scenes of water hoses being turned on young black children in Birmingham, Alabama, galvanized white Americans to support civil rights. Both the *New York Times* and the *Washington Post* prominently covered the preschool visit to Capitol Hill, because CDGM employees had sent press releases prior to leaving for Washington.[108] The latter outlet published a photograph of the romper lobby on the front page of the paper. Northern media attention to the CDGM situation suggested that if four-year-old black children could not get access to orange juice and story time in Mississippi, then something was wrong with the nation.

National news outlets highlighted the tranquility and innocence of preschoolers playing on Capitol Hill, but the real show happened behind the scenes. Led by CDGM board member Jake Ayers, members and teachers visited OEO's headquarters to inquire about their proposal for a second Head Start grant. Years later, Ayers recalled steering his group into an elevator and up to the eighth-floor executive offices where an aide told them that Sargent Shriver was gone for the day. Just as it seemed that they would leave empty handed, a door opened and Shriver appeared unintentionally. Ayers, seizing his chance to get answers, demanded a reception with the OEO director, who was also a member of the most powerful political family in the nation.[109]

The David-and-Goliath showdown on Capitol Hill forced Sargent Shriver to reflect on OEO's purpose and commitments. Shriver, although accustomed to negotiating on behalf of the poor, had little experience in negotiating *with* them. The OEO director began the accidental meeting by explaining that his office could not act faster on CDGM's application because of the many problems the program had and the trouble it caused with certain members of Congress (namely John C. Stennis). Shriver's words moved few in the crowd. Ayers, demanding answers rather than excuses, reminded Shriver that his top priority should be the children of Mississippi who benefited from hot meals and early childhood education. Lavaree Jones, a CDGM teacher, made an even more dramatic plea for a new Head Start grant. In frustration she exclaimed, "Sergeant Shriver, you don't care about killing and starving people in Mississippi."[110] Jones had no idea that Sargent Shriver was not in the military. She had just called him by his first name and accused him of being indifferent to those he was supposed to serve. The black Mississippians' appeals put Shriver in a tough spot. He could honor the letter and spirit of the Economic Opportunity Act and re-fund CDGM or curtail a radical Head Start program to avoid congressional attack on the entire antipoverty program.

The tense meeting demonstrated how CDGM had influenced poor black Mississippians. Ayers, who had not felt comfortable standing up to OEO officials in August of 1965, now went toe-to-toe with Shriver himself in February of 1966. The Head Start program had done more than offer black children early childhood education and drop manna on Mississippi. It had given the marginalized a taste of power that they were not going to easily abdicate.

Shriver was in a bind. The Head Start program made the perfect sacrificial offering to ensure southern congressional support for the War on Poverty's continuation. The lack of a two-party system in the region, coupled with widespread black disfranchisement, meant that southern congressmen wielded disproportionate power because of the seniority system. Shriver understood that taking a tough stance with CDGM would be looked upon favorably by the southern delegation and could be politically beneficial during the next appropriations hearings. Black Mississippians who made the trip to Washington and those who stayed behind, however, used every tool in their arsenal to convince the OEO director that refunding CDGM was the right move.

Black women back in Mississippi continued to write letters to the OEO director. They discussed student progress and pointed out black Mississippians' long history of exclusion. Mary Luckett, a CDGM mother from Cary, told Shriver that her daughter did not talk to anyone or play with other children until she attended a CDGM center. Alice Backwell, an employee at the Greenwood Center, wrote that Stennis did not "like for poor people to run anything that will improve their community and their children's education." She pointed out that black Mississippians "had been denied good schools, voter registration, good homes, proper food, clothing, etc."[111] Even though they did not sit at the negotiation table in the nation's capitol, these women found a way to express their support for a program that had changed educational and professional trajectories for the poorest of the poor.

Black Mississippians' sophisticated use of interest-group politics forced OEO to act on the long delayed refunding request. On 22 February 1966, ten days after preschoolers lobbied Congress and six months after CDGM's initial request, OEO approved a $5.6 million grant for Head Start programs in twenty-eight counties. The funds included areas that had not been a part of the first grant, including Alean Adams's Rankin County. The grant came with stipulations that CDGM relocate its headquarters to Jackson, hire a Jackson accounting firm that could provide day-to-day counseling, employ new senior staff officials with administrative experience, and diversify its board of directors.[112] The latter request addressed Stennis's complaints that CDGM promoted black separatism and suggested that OEO officials believed a larger white presence on the board would allow for more board oversight.

As expected, Mississippi's congressional delegation vehemently protested CDGM's $5.6 million grant, a sum equivalent to $41.2 million in 2014.[113] Federal payouts to the Mississippi Delta were common, but a grant of that size to black southerners was unheard of. Speaking on the floor of the Senate, James Eastland (D-Miss.) argued that CDGM was "a device to funnel funds into the extremist leftist civil rights and beatnik groups in our state." The senior senator from the Magnolia State believed that "education is the furthest thing from their minds."[114] In the House, dissent was led by John Bell Williams (D-Miss.), who called the new grant "inconceivable," and alleged that OEO refunded CDGM because of pressure from "preschool lobbyists." He suggested that his colleagues should look into the "mysterious source" that financed the trip.[115] Mississippi Governor Paul Johnson joined Eastland and Williams in denouncing CDGM. In a telegram to President Johnson, the governor called CDGM's refunding an affront to his state and incorrectly asserted that CDGM officials had opposed American policy in Vietnam.[116] These elected officials attempted to link CDGM to communism as a last-ditch effort to gain northern support. Accusations of black separatism and militancy would not win many hearts in Congress, because its members had grown tired of the tall tales coming out of the South. However, with American troops dying in Vietnam, the Magnolia State men looked to leverage anticommunism against Head Start.

Unlike his colleagues, Senator Stennis chose to continue employing the trope of incapable black leadership in his opposition to CDGM. He did so because questioning the administration of the program, rather than the program itself, allowed him to appear supportive of antipoverty initiatives even as he worked to weaken them. In remarks before the Senate, Stennis maintained that OEO refunded "an organization that is financially irresponsible and whose leaders are generally regarded at best of being incapable to conduct a school for children." He went on to warn, "if the poverty program fails in Mississippi, it will be because responsible, honest, and capable local leadership has been bypassed and rejected by the national and regional leaders of the program."[117] For Stennis, "capable local leadership" meant black public school teachers subject to the oversight and control of white school boards. It did not include the hundreds of working-class black women who ran CDGM centers and discussed everything from black history to voting. When CDGM's second grant was announced, Stennis publicly questioned OEO about why other Head Start applications from Mississippi still had not been processed. Within a week of Stennis's meeting with Sargent Shriver, the Mid-Delta Educational Association, a competing Head Start program operating in Washington County alongside CDGM and supported by Greenville's white mayor, received $441,000 from OEO. Even as Shriver defied Stennis in funding CDGM, he made concessions to him by approving smaller grants to Stennis-backed groups that rivaled it.[118]

The junior senator had perfected the art of "practical segregation."[119] He found a way to appear receptive to antipoverty programs and simultaneously keep power in the hands of the white ruling class. Stennis's calls for "capable local leadership" were coded language for white segregationists' control of antipoverty funds. Pleas for local leadership and the dismissal of "outside agitators" had been a white supremacist rallying cry every time

African Americans mobilized since emancipation.[120] CDGM's staff, of which over 90 percent were native Mississippians, might have appeared "foreign" to the senator, since black Mississippians had never before had the opportunity to run government programs.

Tellingly, the senator's concern for responsible leadership and school quality did not extend to public black education. In 1964, the black high school library in Fannie Lou Hamer's Ruleville only contained six incomplete sets of encyclopedias and a dictionary. Black parents who tried to enroll their children in better schools faced reprisals. For example, during the 1965–66 academic year, ten black families totaling seventy people experienced eviction from plantations in Issaquena and Sharkey counties because they dared to desegregate local public schools.[121] Stennis did not take to the floor of the Senate to publicize their plight or lament the insufficient outfitting of black schools.

Practical segregationists answered John Stennis's call for "local leadership." Prominent white residents in Bolivar County, including the vice president of Delta Pine and Land Company, created the Bolivar County Community Action Agency in June 1965 and moved to take over county Head Start operations that fall. For good measure, there were several middle-class African Americans on the agency's board. CDGM could not operate in counties with a community action agency unless the agency's governing board gave them the power to do so or CDGM supporters could prove that the community action agency had unfairly excluded them from participating. Over CDGM protests that the Bolivar agency did not represent the poor, OEO officials in Washington, D.C., excluded Bolivar County from CDGM's second grant and gave Head Start administration to the local group. They did so because Community Action Programs, of which Head Start was one, were supposed to originate in local communities and be tailored to a locale's particular needs. The Bolivar County Community Action Agency allowed OEO to maintain that local communities in the Delta had mobilized their own resources to fight poverty. Moreover, the biracial Bolivar County agency demonstrated that the War on Poverty penetrated "the most southern place on Earth." National antipoverty officials maintained that the Bolivar agency was "the greatest stride in the history of the county in race relations" and "would be a catalyst in moving the entire community toward the removal of present patterns."[122]

There were problems with OEO's Bolivar County Community Action Agency success story. It violated the spirit of "maximum feasible participation" of the poor. Working-class citizens, the very individuals who should have been at the center of antipoverty initiatives, were not represented. Standing up to local leaders and antipoverty officials in Washington, D.C., black women such as Lee Bankhead, Velma Bartley, and Flossie Miller attended local agency meetings and publicly challenged their exclusion. Sarah Williams, Mary Wince, and others wrote letters to Shriver in which they argued that if OEO funded the local agency instead of CDGM, "we will have lost all hope in benefitting from these programs." They urged OEO officials to investigate the leaders of the Bolivar agency, individuals who "will see to it that the white power structure continues to prevent the Negro and poor whites from developing in a social and economic way."[123] The women's words and mobilization efforts demonstrate that they understood the danger and deception of practical segregation.

In neighboring Sunflower County, Senator Eastland reportedly vowed that CDGM would be refunded in his home county "only over his dead body."[124] Before anyone could call his bluff, whites in Sunflower County organized a community action agency, Sunflower County Progress Incorporated (SCI). As told to Senator Stennis by a Sunflower segregationist, SCI's formation "was a direct result of OEO's action in recruiting alternative Head Start agencies in Mississippi."[125] In other words, the local power structure created SCI to keep CDGM out of Sunflower County.

White Mississippians and OEO supported community action agencies for different reasons. Many local public officials became involved in antipoverty programs to stymie desegregation. Southwest Mississippi Opportunity was the Community Action Agency in Pike and Amite counties. In 1966, the agency decided to allow the McComb public school system to run the Head Start program rather than CDGM. This was the same school system that had refused federal funds rather than comply with school desegregation.[126] White citizens in Bolivar and Sunflower Counties developed interest in Head Start to gain resources for themselves and curtail the economic power and financial freedom that CDGM provided African Americans. The radical Head Start program had invigorated Mississippi businesses, as preschool centers spent thousands on food and supplies, and local banks enlarged their deposits with the paychecks of CDGM employees.[127] Practical segregationists understood community action agencies to be a way to prevent African Americans from working outside of the traditional governing channels while ensuring that Head Start money continued to foster economic development. OEO championed the agencies for a different reason. Since community action programs such as Head Start were supposed to originate in local communities and give local people the chance to solve their own problems, countywide programs more closely adhered to the mission than statewide ones.[128]

In both Bolivar and Sunflower counties, the emergence of community action agencies allowed practical segregationists to make a mockery of "maximum feasible participation" and gain control over Head Start. By the time of CDGM's second grant, white leaders in Sunflower County had created SCI, and Indianola's police chief, Bryce Alexander, served as its first director.[129] Placing Alexander at the helm of a program for the poor was nothing short of intimidation. On Alexander's watch, law enforcement officials had used extralegal violence to restrict civil rights activity in the Delta town. Even after President Johnson signed the Civil Rights Act of 1964, Police Chief Alexander publicly vowed to enforce local segregation laws.[130] Alexander had also written to Senator Stennis complaining about CDGM; now he was expected to run the local antipoverty program and include CDGM supporters.[131] With Alexander in charge of Head Start, there would be no preschoolers desegregating waiting rooms in Sunflower County as there had been with Alice Giles in CDGM's program.

Segregationists in Sunflower County skillfully maintained the appearance of compliance with the Economic Opportunity Act's call for "maximum feasible participation." In their efforts, they inadvertently promoted integration as they handpicked black middle-class leaders to represent the poor. African Americans made up half of SCI's board of directors, although most of these members had financial ties with whites that prevented them from advocating for the type of program that CDGM sponsored. Five of the nine black board members worked as teachers or principals in local public schools where they reported to white school boards and superintendents.[132] Fannie Lou Hamer and several CDGM employees in Sunflower County charged that the board was not representative of the poor and asked for elections, but to no avail. Cora Fleming, CDGM's Area Teacher Guide for the county, asked SCI to join forces with CDGM, since the latter group was already operational and simply needed funding. SCI officials not only rejected Fleming's proposal in a public meeting but also allegedly used the word "nigger" several times in explaining why they would not work with CDGM.[133]

Black residents in Sunflower County who had long histories of mobilizing for full freedom did not simply abdicate Head Start to the ruling class. In protest of an organization whose board included white leaders "who got us into poverty in the first place," county residents including Fannie Lou Hamer and Alice Giles formed the Associated Communities of Sunflower County (ACSC) and continued to run their CDGM centers on a volunteer basis. They also protested their displacement to OEO officials in Washington, D.C., and demanded that SCI officials address them with courtesy titles.[134] This new nonprofit group was a testament to the leadership opportunities CDGM provided poor people to take control over their lives and create their own solutions to local problems.

Something similar happened in Bolivar County. Don Wiley, who was also director of the Chamber of Commerce in Cleveland, Mississippi, ran the Bolivar County Community Action Agency. Wiley admitted that he and other residents created the agency to "fight CDGM and keep it out of this county."[135] Just as in Sunflower County, the sixteen-member governing board of the Bolivar community action agency was equally made up of blacks and whites. None of the board's black middle-class members had previously engaged in civil rights activities, suggesting that the new group was a way to separate Head Start from the black freedom struggle.[136] In protest of an organization that did not include the poor, CDGM supporters formed the Association of Communities of Bolivar County (ACBC).[137]

ACBC supporters displayed a keen understanding of participatory democracy and proportional representation and protested the composition of the Bolivar County Community Action board. Led by Amzie Moore and Lee Bankhead, black residents objected to the undemocratic means for selecting board members. The all-white Bolivar County Board of Supervisors appointed the community action board members. Moreover, CDGM supporters argued that the board should reflect county demographics. Since African Americans comprised 68 percent of Bolivar County's population, ACBC supporters called for greater black representation on the Bolivar Community Action board. Over 1,700 black residents signed a petition supporting the reorganization of the board.[138] These emboldened black citizens also went head-to-head with white leaders in public meetings. When a white audience member remarked that "he did not appreciate outsiders coming in with a program" in reference to CDGM, black attendees led by Amzie Moore and Lee Bankhead stood and declared that they were long-time residents of the county. Black peopled touted their experience in CDGM's program when the superintendent of schools questioned the lack of credentialed employees to run Head Start centers in ACBC's program.[139]

On 3 March 1966, the ACBC submitted a Head Start proposal to the Bolivar County Community Action Agency board. The proposal named CDGM as the delegate agency, and, as expected, the Bolivar board rejected the ACBC application. CDGM supporters, as in Sunflower County, operated Head Start centers in Bolivar County on a voluntary basis and appealed to national OEO representatives for redress.[140]

Black Mississippians created parallel institutions to the ones run by the ruling class and thus called into question the poverty program's commitment to the meaningful inclusion of the poor. They forced OEO to consider whether or not it was willing to subsidize community action in a way that fostered significant local changes. White men such as Bryce Alexander and Don Wiley carried prestige in their own respective circles, but in no way did they represent the interests of the black poor in the Delta. Historically, these men's interests had been diametrically opposed to those of black Mississippians. In Washington, OEO officials realized that community action agencies in the Delta were unwilling to reorganize their boards so that they would be more representative. One agency employee concluded: "Although representing less than a third of the Negro population, [the CDGM group] is a potent and vocal force that must be recognized and included in any further OEO programs. Further postponement of funding will raise the level of emotional discontent of the Negro/poor from one of frustration, channeled into constructive efforts, to one of frustration resulting in overt demonstration. In other words, there had better be a Head Start and quick before the lid blows."[141]

Black women learned that participation in electoral politics was only one way to wield power. Through their work in the Head Start program, many realized that power was also found in their ability to say no. These women, by keeping preschool centers open on a voluntary basis and refusing to participate in new programs that did not comply with the spirit of "maximum feasible participation" of the poor, outsmarted Senator Stennis and other segregationists. In Sunflower County alone, eighty-two volunteers kept centers open. Parents provided jars of fruit or meat from their hogs. Their tenacity compelled OEO officials to act in their favor. In April 1966, the federal agency agreed to divide Head Start funds evenly between the Bolivar County Community Action Agency and the Association of Communities of Bolivar County. A little over a year later, OEO forced SCI to allow the ACSC to run Head Start centers for the county as a delegate agency.[142]

To Stennis's chagrin, activist-run Head Start centers continued to operate throughout the state. Segregationists, even when they used respectable means by Mississippi standards, found themselves unable to get rid of an early childhood education program that empowered black parents while simultaneously educating their children. They did learn, however, that the practice of auditing accounts and charging antipoverty groups with fraud could serve as a default strategy for the defunding, suspending, or weakening of organizations that challenged the racial, political, and economic status quo. In time CDGM's opponents realized that in order to control Head Start funds in Mississippi, their coalitions had to include not just handpicked middle-class blacks, but also moderate whites. The latter group provided a sense of "anti-discrimination legitimacy" that men such as Stennis and Alexander never achieved on their own.

CHAPTER FIVE

Say It Isn't So, Sarge

The people who come forward to help in the community action agencies are the same people who don't give Negroes good jobs.

—Mr. Joe Edmondson, CDGM board member

We're tired of being told what we can do and what we can't do. We decided we'd run this program on nothing before we'd let somebody else run it for us. We've been bought and sold too many times.

—Mrs. Matyln Loper, CDGM and FCM supporter

Winson Hudson, Lillie Ayers, and Lavaree Jones certainly had much to celebrate in 1966. The women's Herculean efforts to keep centers open on a voluntary basis had paid dividends. OEO refunded the embattled Head Start program in February after a five-month feud, and the Reverend James McRee, a local activist from Madison County, became board chairman. Yet, white supremacists continued to stymie change. In January 1966, Klansmen murdered Hattiesburg civil rights leader Vernon Dahmer by firebombing his home. Dahmer had urged black people to register and vote in the wake of the new voting law. His death signaled that white repression was longstanding and could not be eradicated with a new voting bill alone. Erlene Beard, Dahmer's sister, served as a CDGM Area Teacher Guide. She temporarily suspended her Head Start work to help care for her late brother's children.[1]

The Mississippi State Sovereignty Commission continued to provide its own brand of reprisals. In addition to surveillance, the Sovereignty Commission resorted to military draft selection to undermine CDGM. Throughout the 1960s, CDGM employee John Otis Sumrall led numerous demonstrations and voter registration drives in Quitman and Shubuta, small towns in Clarke County. Sumrall's mother, Jimana, served as chairperson of the local CDGM center.[2] Black residents in town formed the Shubuta Planning and Improvement Committee and presented a list of demands to the Shubuta mayor—the construction of sidewalks in black neighborhoods, the hiring of black employees in local businesses, and the free use of the abandoned high school building for a CDGM center. The demands were printed on a sheet whose letterhead read "Shubuta Head Start Committee."

In a report to Senator Stennis, Sovereignty Commission investigators noted that the newly organized Improvement Committee shared a physical address with a CDGM center, suggesting that CDGM and the Shubuta Planning and Improvement Committee were one and the same.[3]

Local white leadership, believing that John Otis Sumrall was behind the list of demands, mobilized resistance. Law enforcement had arrested Sumrall numerous times during civil rights demonstrations. These arrests and charges exempted him from military service. Quitman's mayor, however, wrote the local draft board and offered to drop all charges against Sumrall to make him eligible for induction into the service. Soon thereafter, Sumrall was drafted to fight in Vietnam, although he did not meet Army qualifications for induction. His draft number was called up to instill fear among black residents in the area, who learned that their involvement with CDGM and other freedom struggle activities could lead to the frontlines of another delta—the Mekong.[4]

The actions of a CDGM affiliate such as John Sumrall would have been enough to give Shriver a headache, but the OEO director had problems on all sides. Throughout 1965 OEO officials had battled with Syracuse, New York, Mayor William F. Walsh, because community organizer Saul Alinsky ran a community action agency in Syracuse that used federal funds to sponsor voter registration drives that dramatically increased the Democratic Party's voter rolls. Walsh, a Republican, who was up for reelection that year, did not waste any time in castigating community action programs. The mayor complained that "these people go into a housing project and talk about setting a democratic organization—small 'd'—but it sounds just the same as Democratic—big 'd.'" The Republican official went on to lament that "in a close election, it could be decisive."[5] Soon, other congressmen expressed doubts about OEO initiatives. In January 1966, Republican congressmen called for OEO programs to be placed in more established cabinet-level departments, such as the Department of Health, Education, and Welfare (HEW). Decentralization took the political teeth out of community action programs. William Phillips, OEO's assistant director for congressional relations, said as much. "If you spin off the programs into the old bureaucracy, the innovative quality will be lost. . . . The reason OEO could be effective was that it could be creative."[6] Proposals to do away with OEO were indirect censures of Shriver's leadership.

The attacks on OEO and its director kept coming. Activist and comedian Dick Gregory called the antipoverty chief the poor's "biggest enemy," suggesting that Shriver was not committed to their "maximum feasible participation." Months later, community action program workers from across the country, including Unita Blackwell, booed Shriver at an antipoverty luncheon and charged him with maintaining the political and economic status quo. By summer, congressmen on both sides of the aisle called the War on Poverty a "sham," guaranteeing a budget showdown on Capitol Hill.[7] Would CDGM once again be the focus during debate on the OEO appropriation?

The embattled Head Start program had made great strides since the 1965 summer. Polly Greenberg reported that during the second grant season she had seen improvement in nearly all CDGM centers. The five district coordinators were replaced with eight area offices to decentralize CDGM operations and foster increased local autonomy. John Mudd worked tirelessly to implement new bookkeeping systems to increase efficiency. He tried to bring new programs to CDGM, including a partnership with the Peace Corps. Sixty-two Peace Corps volunteers who were headed to India were supposed to spend a week in Mississippi studying CDGM families' health needs and strategizing about ways to improve the living conditions of the black poor. The experience would provide the volunteers an introduction to poverty before they began their stints abroad and it would temporarily diversify CDGM's ranks. As a year-round program, the Head Start program no longer had northern white college students on break to work. While a win-win situation for all groups involved, the initiative never materialized, because State Health Director Archie Gray refused to sign off on it. His recalcitrance underscored why it was necessary for antipoverty programs to sometimes bypass the local power structure.[8]

Senator Stennis, for his part, continued to protest CDGM, although he was no longer opposed to all "Great Society–type welfare programs."[9] Antipoverty programs had become a leading source of revenue in Mississippi. By 31 July 1966, the OEO had funneled over $23 million into the state, with another $25 million on the way. In comparison, the state's leading industry was construction, whose 1965 wages and salaries totaled $50 million. Wages and salaries from the timber and wood products industry totaled a little less than $39 million that year.[10] Thus, for Stennis, antipoverty programs were not all inherently bad. Only CDGM, which threatened old forms of white control, including his, was a problem.

Stennis saw nothing good in CDGM, despite meaningful improvements in program administration. In March 1966, he called for Senate investigators to routinely inspect the Head Start program's books.[11] By summer, the senator claimed to have plenty of evidence to back up his assertion that CDGM continued to mismanage federal funds. Investigators found that at the Richmond Grove CDGM center in Madison County, all twenty employees and the governing board were members of two interrelated families. OEO personnel policy for community action programs stated that "no person shall hold a job while he or his immediate family serves on a board or committee if that board or committee has authority to order personnel actions affecting his job."[12] OEO's policy was out of touch with the reality of rural people's lives. Richmond Grove was an isolated community that did not attract many visitors or new settlers. Its inhabitants were the descendants of people who had lived there since emancipation. Over time, Richmond Grove residents married each other, creating familial bonds. Thus, CDGM's board of directors, with OEO approval, amended the personnel policy to state that no more than one member of a household could be employed by the program.[13] It did not matter that OEO approved of CDGM's special hiring policies. The damage was done when Stennis hinted that something sinister was going on within the program's human resources.

The most damning accusation against CDGM in 1966 was the alleged connection between the Head Start program and the emerging Black Power movement. The *Clarion-Ledger* newspaper ran an article stating that CDGM's board had met with SNCC chairman Stokely Carmichael several times prior to the Meredith March Against Fear held to encourage African Americans to register to vote. The Meredith March began on 4 June 1966, when James Meredith, who had desegregated the University of Mississippi four years earlier, began a 220-mile walk from Memphis to Jackson. On day two of the trek, a white sniper shot him, prompting a coalition of civil rights organizations including SNCC, CORE, and the SCLC to continue the march in his place. Over 4,000 black people registered to vote, and over 10,000 local people marched in Mississippi over the course of the twenty-two-day journey. In Greenwood, local officials prohibited the marchers from setting up camping tents on the grounds of a black elementary school. Carmichael defied the order and was summarily arrested. When released from jail several hours later, Carmichael made his famous call for Black Power. He declared that he would not go to jail anymore and that African Americans had to control their own destiny. Carmichael's words resonated with a largely African American crowd frustrated by the slow pace of change and the lack of black control over black communities. The SNCC activist's speech brought completely different emotions in white communities.

White Americans across the nation feared the implications of Black Power, assuming that the phrase was veiled language for violence against white people.[14]

In that charged atmosphere, Senate investigators reported that some CDGM centers prominently displayed "Black Power" signs and that C. O. Chinn, who had a CDGM transportation contract, used Head Start buses to transport Meredith March participants. White hysteria escalated when Sovereignty Commission officials reported that over 500 participants in the Meredith March ate food purchased with CDGM funds and cooked at CDGM centers.[15] CDGM officials vehemently denied that the Head Start program had any link to Black Power. The program's board never met with Carmichael. Program officials also insisted that C. O. Chinn owned the buses and wagons that he used to transport CDGM children and that after he met his contractual obligations to CDGM, he was free to use the vehicles as he saw fit. Board members did concede that CDGM center cooking facilities were used to prepare food for Meredith March participants and that "Black Power" signs hung in some centers. However, CDGM operated in rented facilities and did not dictate to facility owners the displays on the walls and in the buildings. Board members maintained that Head Start operations were not disturbed by other non-CDGM events simultaneously occurring in CDGM centers.[16]

Segregationists had succeeded once again in casting a pall over CDGM and putting the program on the defensive. OEO southeast regional director Frank Sloan contacted Mary Holmes Junior College, CDGM's sponsoring agency, asking for documented evidence of the program's efforts to "recruit and employ white staff at the center level." Sloan also requested information on CDGM efforts to locate and enroll white children in the program.[17] The call for information implied that OEO officials saw white involvement as the best defense against Black Power charges. This rationale, however, was unfair for several reasons. First, Head Start centers in Milwaukee, Wisconsin, were "de facto segregated," but no one insinuated that Black Power was the source of the racial separation.[18] Second, white racism prevented staff integration in Mississippi. In Clarke County, a white woman approached about CDGM employment unabashedly stated that even though she needed a job, she would starve before working with African Americans.[19]

Moreover, the atmosphere of fear and tension that surrounded CDGM communities made it difficult for white people to be involved. At the Second Pilgrim's Rest CDGM center in Holmes County, a few local white people donated money, but none risked working in the center out of fear of being ostracized. Most of the twenty-eight CDGM counties funded during the second grant lacked local white participation.[20] Fear of bodily harm was also a real concern. In Winson Hudson's Leake County, for example, a twenty-two-year-old local white man agreed to work as a program recruiter. Two days after he started, a sniper shot at him several times. The employee quit a few weeks after the incident because of pressure from local whites. Kathy Price, a white native of Brandon, Mississippi, told Rankin County CDGM officials that "I have been thinking of filling out an application. I would like to help colored children, but I am just afraid of these other white folk."[21]

CDGM integrated its staff with white college students, an arrangement only possible during the summer. Paul Murray, a recent University of Detroit graduate, volunteered at a Madison County CDGM center during the 1966 summer. Murray had participated in several civil rights initiatives in the North and had regretted not volunteering in Mississippi during the 1964 Freedom Summer. After graduation, Murray went south to work in CDGM, after learning of the opportunity from an American Friends Service Committee flyer. Murray assisted eighteen-year-old CDGM teacher Emma Pearl Dinkins with her Head Start classroom. His presence and that of several other American Friends Service Committee work campers mitigated claims that CDGM lacked white staff participation at the center level.[22]

It was even harder to attract white preschool students. Many poor whites wanted their children to have the head start that the program offered but chose not to enroll them out of fear of being ostracized or physically harmed for aiding desegregation. They surely remembered what happened to Hazel Brannon Smith, the white newspaper editor in Holmes County whose editorials against racism prompted white Mississippians to boycott her paper and cost her husband his hospital administration job.[23] No white individual who was suspected of having civil rights sympathies was safe. In 1964, after Albert and Malva Heffner, the parents of the reigning Miss Mississippi, invited a Freedom Summer volunteer to dinner at their McComb home, the family began receiving harassing phone calls, their insurance business folded, and their dog died mysteriously, all of which prompted the family to leave the state.[24] White supremacy circumscribed the world of white as well as black Mississippians. The few white people who dared to challenge the order faced retaliation.

OEO's demand that CDGM increase its white involvement was just one sign among many that its partnership with the grassroots Head Start program was troubled. Six Howard University Law School students claimed that during the 1966 summer the national OEO office sent them to CDGM centers and instructed them to "act and dress like civil rights workers in order to infiltrate the project and check on whether funds were misused." OEO denied the allegations, but it is highly likely that the antipoverty agency had indeed attempted to engage in espionage. For one thing, OEO officials in Washington, D.C., wanted their own unfiltered reconnaissance of the Head Start program, to see if Stennis's claims had merit. Second, the allegations seem plausible, because of the person who brought them to light. Jean Cahn, an African American OEO employee and the wife of Sargent Shriver's 1964 executive assistant, made the law school students' claims public.[25] Cahn had no reason to discredit OEO.

The partnership between OEO and CDGM was indeed waning. The agency conducted its own review of program operations and found serious irregularities and conflicts of interest, including three cases where center directors held transportation contracts. Other conflicts of interest included one CDGM board member renting his church to CDGM while another board member's wife served as an Area Teacher Guide.[26] In 1965, OEO had awarded CDGM more money than the program requested. The agency had also shielded the organization from a gubernatorial veto and backpedaled on a demand to relocate. Continued problems and bad publicity, however, weakened the agency's commitment.

The chance of fraud was ever present. For certain, some saw the preschool program as a way to line their own pockets. Dishonest gain among employees was a reminder that the movement had changed since the earlier days when the main benefit to participation was self-satisfaction and personal empowerment. The antipoverty program essentially paid black Mississippians for doing the very organizing that they had once done for free. CDGM, unlike prior movement activities, increased the possibility of self-serving behavior. OEO officials discovered that thirty-three teachers received both CDGM salaries and OEO stipends for attending training courses. The teachers should not have been included on center payroll lists for days when they attended out-of-state training. Whether the payroll errors were malicious or novice mistakes was up for interpretation. It is highly probable that the error was an example of beginners' unfamiliarity with OEO rules, as columnist Carl Rowan surmised. "If Mary wanted off Tuesday, she got Cousin Sally to work. The time card showed Mary present, so Mary was paid. Then Mary paid Cousin Sally."[27]

Whatever the cause of the discrepancies, they played directly into the hands of CDGM opponents, who had argued for months that the preschool program misspent federal funds. The mismanagement also significantly reduced CDGM's chances of securing a third grant. It was one thing for Syracuse mayor William Walsh to complain, but it was real trouble when Senator Stennis had grievances; his congressional seniority gave him direct access to the White House and significant control over the federal budget. CDGM's current grant was set to expire on 31 August 1966, and OEO expected a proposal for a new grant by 1 July.

On 18 June, over 500 CDGM supporters assembled at the Masonic Temple in Jackson to discuss the program's next grant proposal. Fannie Lou Hamer sang freedom songs as representatives from fifty-four funded centers and forty-five unfunded centers began debate about CDGM's future. Based on discussions at that meeting, John Mudd submitted a Head Start proposal to OEO asking for $41 million to serve 30,000 children in forty-four counties. One week later, OEO officials rejected the proposal on the grounds that they would not fund CDGM for more children than the program had on the current grant. CDGM supporters, 2,000 of them, once again assembled at the Masonic Temple. The meeting was the largest gathering in the Masonic Temple since Medgar Evers's funeral and demonstrated local people's commitment to having a say in Head Start administration. From the second statewide meeting came CDGM's revised proposal calling for $20.3 million to serve 13,500 children.[28]

Unbeknownst to CDGM supporters, Sargent Shriver had made plans to replace CDGM with a less controversial multi-county Head Start program. The OEO director had lost confidence in CDGM and was steadily assembling its replacement in an attempt to woo congressmen before they voted on OEO's 1967 budget. In May 1966, Republicans had circulated one of the longest congressional minority reports in history, arguing that the antipoverty program was full of scandals, abuses, and mismanagement. The eight authors of the report saw the War on Poverty as a partisan effort that required a "complete new start" or else OEO "would stumble into another year of operations without the restraint of congressional directives."[29] Shriver once again found himself attempting to prevent an alliance between Republicans and southern Democrats. Congressman James Gardner (R-N.C.) had labeled the antipoverty effort as a "shield for the so called 'black power' struggle," an outlook he shared with Stennis.[30] To head off possible collaboration between Democrats and Republicans on Capitol Hill, Shriver took a hard line and decided not to refund CDGM. Years later, Shriver explained that he backed away from CDGM because if he refunded it, "the whole War on Poverty might have been stopped."[31] Thus, he moved to replace CDGM to save the rest of the antipoverty war.

In his attempt to save the War on Poverty and maintain early childhood education in Mississippi, Shriver summoned Aaron Henry, the president of the Mississippi NAACP, to Washington, D.C., to discuss setting up a new Head Start program.[32] Henry, born on a Clarksdale plantation in 1922, studied pharmacy at Xavier University in New Orleans with GI Bill tuition assistance. In 1950, he opened a drugstore in his hometown and within two years actively worked with national NAACP leaders on local issues such as white sexual violence against black women. After the 1954 *Brown* decision, Henry and over 400 other black people in Coahoma County presented a petition to the local school board demanding that it abide by the high court's decision. Their action incited swift retribution from whites. Henry recalled, "the newspapers carried our pictures and our names in the paper. Our names were put in obvious spots within banks and lending agencies and credit was a problem."[33] In 1962, Henry founded the Council of Federated Organizations, but later decided against collaborative civil rights work when SNCC began to overshadow the NAACP.[34]

At the meeting in Washington, D.C., Shriver told Henry that CDGM would not be refunded, but that OEO wanted to continue offering strong Head Start programs in the state. To this end, Shriver planned to form a new statewide nonprofit group to replace CDGM and he wanted Henry's support. Shriver acted strategically in contacting Henry, because the forty-four-year-old, middle-class, World War II veteran and civil rights activist provided OEO with civil rights movement legitimacy. If and when liberal news outlets and CDGM supporters accused OEO of turning their backs on the black poor, the agency could point to Henry and assert that segregationists had not won. Henry, however, had lost credibility among many poor black Mississippians. In contrast to Fannie Lou Hamer, he had favored accepting the two-delegate compromise offered to the Mississippi Freedom Democratic Party in 1964. At the national level, the NAACP leader still garnered high levels of respect from those who were sympathetic to the movement and unaware of internal tensions that surrounded him back home.[35]

The partnership Sargent Shriver formed with Aaron Henry brought several antipoverty program divisions to the surface. OEO employees Samuel Yette, special assistant for civil rights, and Hyman Bookbinder, assistant director, believed that the antipoverty agency had treated CDGM unfairly by discreetly creating a rival Head Start group. These employees circulated a petition in the Washington, D.C., office to save the program and upset Shriver by informing CDGM's board members of the furtive meeting with Aaron Henry.[36] The tensions within OEO demonstrated that some employees believed the agency had belied its mission by undercutting such a shining example of community action. Folks near and far from the nation's capital followed the situation. In Alabama, when the white power structure opposed the OEO-supported Southwest Alabama Farmers Cooperative, liberal groups warned OEO officials "not to make another CDGM" out of the cooperative grant.[37]

Tensions over Head Start in Mississippi came to a head in a meeting involving Marion Wright, the Reverend James McRee, and Aaron Henry. The NAACP leader maintained that his focus was ensuring that black children in Mississippi continued to receive nutritious meals, medical care, and preschool education.[38] During the private meeting, Henry also pointed out that NAACP leaders did not hold any of the top positions in CDGM. Competition among civil rights organization had been fierce ever since Freedom Summer and Henry did not think that the NAACP had received the recognition or respect that it deserved from CDGM. The activist-run Head Start program tended to employ working-class individuals who more readily identified with SNCC or the Mississippi Freedom Democratic Party rather than with the middle-class NAACP. While there were certainly exceptions such as Winson Hudson and Amzie Moore, the NAACP's membership in Mississippi largely consisted of teachers and other black professionals who had been hesitant to participate in CDGM during its earliest days.[39] Henry, who had run a much smaller Head Start operation in Coahoma County, now had the chance to run a large-scale preschool program with several job opportunities and to restore his organization's prominence as a state leader in the African American freedom struggle.

Publically, Aaron Henry stated that quality, rather than an organizational slight, was his main concern with the largest Head Start program in the state. He worried that CDGM's untraditional teachers could not give their students "the benefits of affluent society."[40] This was a legitimate criticism. Could parents who had educational deficits of their own give poor children the head start they needed to succeed in school? For those who privileged traditional book knowledge and correct grammar, the answer was no. For those who prioritized verbal communication, social development, and racial

pride—teaching children that they were important—the answer was a resounding yes: CDGM women had the mettle to teach. Aaron Henry, like
CDGM supporters, favored socially aware and intellectually curious black
children in Mississippi. He simply was not willing to achieve that by dismissing the importance of trained educators in Head Start operations.[41]

The clandestine effort to replace CDGM also involved Hodding Carter
III, whose father was a Pulitzer Prize–winning journalist and the founder of
the Greenville, Mississippi, *Delta Democrat Times* newspaper. Local white
people had boycotted the family newspaper for five years because the Carter patriarch spoke out against racial intolerance and the Citizens' Council.
Carter III graduated from Princeton University and served in the United
States Marine Corps, before returning to Greenville in 1959. Within three
years, he had taken the reins of his father's paper. His involvement with the
movement in Greenville came about unexpectedly. He recalled, "sixty-four
was for me personally a change." Before that, he had purposefully not gotten
involved in civil rights issues, because he knew the consequences; he had
witnessed his family struggle because of his father's editorials. "But sixty-
four did it. One too many killings and I knew too many of those folks so I
started getting involved one way or another."[42] Carter used the might of the
pen to speak to white Mississippians during the long and hot Freedom
Summer. When the three civil rights workers disappeared and many white
folks maintained that the young men "had been taught a lesson," Carter
fired back. "It may well be a lesson. It may be a lesson that there are people
living in this state who can see three men disappear without concern simply
because they felt the three men were unwelcome."[43] After FBI agents found
the men's bodies, Carter once again used his editorial column to prod the
consciences of white Mississippians. "Now that the three civil rights workers have been found, brutally murdered, many of us in Mississippi need to
take a long hard look at ourselves. The roll call of the dead is long. The list of
those convicted is still a blank page."[44]

This rare white courage attracted OEO's attention. In 1964, on leave from
working at the newspaper, Carter had been in Washington, D.C., working
on President Johnson's presidential campaign. In the nation's capital, he met
many Democratic Party officials with whom he stayed in contact after returning to Mississippi. According to Carter, one of the men he met during
the campaign called and told him that "Sargent Shriver is in trouble and he
needs an alternative [Head Start program in Mississippi]." Like Aaron
Henry, OEO officials told Carter they would not refund CDGM under any

circumstances and that a biracial group of established community leaders was the only way to keep a large-scale Head Start program in the state.[45]

Hodding Carter III had his own reasons for acquiescing to Shriver's request. In January 1965, Delta Ministry officials helped African Americans picket Greenville Mill in protest of the plant's refusal to hire black women and its restriction of black men to menial, low-paying jobs. When the Delta Ministry extended the picket to the mill manager's home, Carter spoke out, asserting that the group wanted "revolutionary change, of a kind which goes far beyond the question of an equal chance for all men."[46] As a business owner, Carter did not like the negative publicity that the Delta Ministry's activities brought to Greenville. In addition to the pickets, the Delta Ministry also played an influential role in the January 1966 Greenville Air Force base takeover that called for CDGM's refunding. The city's business leaders touted good race relations to attract more industry, and the ministry's activities hurt the image they tried to sell.[47]

Also, Carter understood that the new interracial Head Start program might function as a vehicle to further a biracial Democratic Party in Mississippi. A significant number of the state's conservative white Democrats felt betrayed by national Democratic Party leaders, who had offered the Mississippi Freedom Democratic Party two seats at the 1964 Democratic National Convention.[48] In spite of the dominance of the state Democratic Party, 87 percent of Mississippians voting in the 1964 presidential election cast their ballots for Republican candidate Barry Goldwater. Moreover, Prentiss Walker (R-Miss.), the lone Republican who ran for a congressional seat in Mississippi in 1964, knocked off an eleven-term Democrat.[49] The Democrats' New Deal coalition was in trouble, as white southerners began to look to the Republican Party to represent their interests. Democratic loyalists like Carter looked for ways to slow down, if not stop, white Mississippians' bolt to the Republican Party.[50]

Carter had first tried to save the Democratic Party in Mississippi in July 1965 when he partnered with Labor Council president Claude Ramsey and Aaron Henry to form the Mississippi Democratic Conference, an interracial organization committed to restoring the state's relationship with the national party. The National Democratic Party had pledged in 1964 not to seat any segregated delegations at future conventions. Despite this proviso, the regular Democratic Party in Mississippi continued to deny African Americans participation in party meetings. The Mississippi Democratic Conference functioned as an alternative to both the all-white regular state Democratic

Party and the Mississippi Freedom Democratic Party that alienated many white voters in the state. The Democratic Conference's architects, in order to build support among white loyalists, kept their distance from more radical civil rights organizations. In fact, no Mississippi Freedom Democratic Party or SNCC members were invited the Democratic Conference's founding meeting. The state Democratic Conference was integrated, but black membership was limited to middle-class black men such as Charles Young, an affluent businessman from Meridian, and Aaron Henry. Despite careful planning, the Mississippi Democratic Conference fell apart by early 1966 because of infighting, financial shortfalls, and lack of support from the White House and the National Democratic Committee. Support from the latter groups did not materialize, because national leaders did not want to upset United States senators James Eastland and John Stennis.[51]

Biracial Democratic politics in the Magnolia State was an uphill battle. Carter became active in the Mississippi Young Democrats after the Mississippi Democratic Conference's demise. The Young Democrats, while interracial, shunned more radical civil rights groups like the Mississippi Freedom Democratic Party in favor of the middle-class NAACP. Once again, national party leaders failed to support the Young Democrats out of deference to Mississippi's segregationist senators.[52]

Hodding Carter III saw a new, biracial, statewide Head Start program as laying the foundation for the integrated state Democratic Party that he envisioned. An apolitical Head Start program provided a way to build a coalition that included loyalist Democrats and middle-class and working-class blacks, while appeasing the state's senators who sought to replace CDGM. As historian John Dittmer poignantly acknowledged, Carter and Aaron Henry "must have been aware that control over millions of dollars of Head Start funds would give them political patronage and power, enhancing their position as a credible alternative to the Freedom Democratic Party." Carter himself admitted that one of the objectives of creating a new preschool program "was to destroy the [white supremacist] system that ran Mississippi."[53] The new Head Start program aided in that effort if it brought members of the white establishment to the table with the Mississippi Freedom Democratic Party rank and file and NAACP affiliates. Together, these groups could serve as a foundation for a new and integrated state Democratic Party.[54]

Aaron Henry and Hodding Carter III were not the only strategists who understood that the move to replace CDGM was about more than Head Start. Senior officials in the White House saw the embattled preschool program as a political impediment to Democratic victory. Harry McPherson, President Lyndon Johnson's speechwriter and special counsel, recalled that white moderates in Mississippi warned him "that CDGM's political activities would destroy any chance the national Democratic Party might have to carry the state in 1968." Acting on behalf of President Johnson, McPherson called for a replacement Head Start program.[55]

In September 1966, Mississippi governor Paul Johnson gave a state charter to a newly formed group called Mississippi Action for Progress (MAP), the product of Shriver's secret meetings to replace CDGM. In addition to Hodding Carter III, MAP's charter listed the white businessmen Owen Cooper and Leroy Percy as program incorporators.[56] The men served as founder/president and board chairman, respectively, of the Mississippi Chemical Company. Their membership on the board signaled that those who had the least in common with the poor would control the new antipoverty programs. Percy, a member of Mississippi's most prominent family, assuaged Delta planters' concerns about the program. Percy owned Trail Lake Plantation, a vast 3,000-acre farm in Washington County that had been in the Percy family since the antebellum period. At the plantation's postbellum height, almost 200 black families lived and worked as sharecroppers on the property. Cooper's appointment also troubled Mississippi's poorest black citizens because he had opposed the Delta Ministry, fought against a minimum wage in Mississippi, and refused to allow unions at the Mississippi Chemical Corporation.[57] Despite this history, Shriver approved of Percy and Cooper because they were native white Mississippians who had refrained from the vitriolic bigotry that characterized white resistance to black advancement in the state. In fact, Cooper broke ranks with state officials in 1962 when he signed his name to a petition urging the University of Mississippi's faculty and students to resume normal activity after James Meredith desegregated the campus.[58] These men's participation in the program allowed Shriver to maintain the existence of an interracial coalition concerned about early childhood education in Mississippi.

CDGM supporters, however, saw no common ground with MAP. The new organization's charter stipulated that the organization consult with the governor in all of its dealings and that only Carter, Cooper, and Percy could appoint members to the board of directors.[59] Governor Johnson had never shown concern for the interests of his black constituents, so his involvement suggested that MAP strayed away from the social justice initiatives at the center of CDGM's program. Black members on the MAP board consisted of people who cooperated with Mississippi's ruling class: the Reverend R. L. T. Smith, a Jackson supermarket owner and Methodist minister; Charles Young, a Meridian business owner; Merrill Lindsey, a West Point, Mississippi, minister who was Henry's brother-in-law; and James Gilliam, a Masonic leader from Clarksdale. All of these board members had histories of fighting racism in Mississippi, yet had also been whites' preferred contacts when dealing with black communities.[60] The board's white members included the Reverend William P. Davis, a Baptist minister who served as president of the Mississippi Baptist Seminary for Negroes and who led the effort to rebuild black churches burned during Freedom Summer; Jackson *State-Times* newspaper editor Oliver Emmerich, a moderate segregationist who once warned of "an easily manipulated bloc vote" if blacks were widely enfranchised; and Oscar Carr, a Clarksdale plantation owner.[61]

Neither working-class individuals nor women sat on MAP's board. This type of class and gender bias was nothing new. In 1964, Democratic Party officials rejected sharecropper Fannie Lou Hamer as one of the two at-large delegates for the Mississippi Freedom Democratic Party in favor of pharmacist Aaron Henry and minister Edwin King. Hamer, as the vice chair of the grassroots independent political party, was the ranking party official in Atlantic City and was the logical representative of the group. Hubert Humphrey allegedly stated, "The President will not allow that illiterate woman to speak from the floor of the convention."[62] Just as excluding Hamer from being a delegate demonstrated that the Democratic Party was not mindful of the political struggles of those at the bottom of society, the absence of those who knew firsthand about poverty and hunger on the new Head Start program's board insulted the spirit of "maximum feasible participation" of the poor.

Mississippi Action for Progress's lack of women was also in step with the NAACP's tendency to discount the role and work of women. When women did have official positions in the oldest civil rights organization in the country, they tended to serve as hospitality coordinators or secretaries.[63] Black women had wielded great organizing power in every civil rights battle in Mississippi during the 1960s. When the Freedom Riders came through Jackson, it was black women who provided them with toiletries, food, and housing. When SNCC field secretaries and northern volunteers fanned out across the state for voter registration, it was black women who supported their efforts in large numbers. Given their extensive social networks, history of activism, and the tendency to see education as women's work, black women's absence in the administration of the MAP program was alarming and suspicious. Their exclusion was an acknowledgement that MAP's program would not be connected with movement activity.

The composition of MAP's board was not the only sign that OEO had moved away from CDGM and toward a program more tolerable to the state's political establishment. Three days before the *Jackson Daily News* broke the story on MAP's charter, OEO denied CDGM's $20.3 million grant request, asserting that the "program in its present organizational form" could not lawfully be refunded, according to OEO guidelines.[64] The agency's phrasing suggested that with a few administrative changes, CDGM could receive a new grant. Yet Senator Stennis publicly boasted of CDGM's replacement before OEO had awarded MAP any funds. "I have been working toward turning this project [Head Start] over to local responsible people and I have been assured that a very significant announcement will be made very shortly. I fully expect the CDGM group to be replaced."[65] For a sitting member of Congress to speak about CDGM's replacement before MAP received OEO funds made clear that the antipoverty agency had already backed away from one of the most successful examples of community action in the country.

For certain, OEO was coy about CDGM's future. In mid-September, while the House of Representatives debated a War on Poverty appropriations bill, OEO led CDGM officials to think that a new grant was possible with changes to the program's "present organizational form." On 29 September, the House approved the bill. Four days after the affirmative House vote and before the Senate voted on the measure, representatives of the antipoverty agency mailed CDGM board members a report outlining its decision not to fund the program under any circumstances.[66] The timing of OEO's decision was critical.

Shriver dodged the wrath of CDGM supporters such as Adam Clayton Powell (D-N.Y.) by defunding CDGM after the House vote and maneuvered to avoid Stennis's by taking action before the Senate vote. On 11 October, the antipoverty agency announced a grant of $1.2 million to the historically black Rust College to administer a Head Start program for 600 children. Rust had not submitted an application, so the college's funding demonstrated how determined Shriver was to have Mississippi's Head Start allocation in new hands. As the *Washington Post* asserted, "manna from OEO" miraculously fell on groups in Mississippi that had not requested Head Start funds. One day after the Rust College announcement, OEO funded Southwest

Mississippi Opportunity with a $713,300 Head Start grant to serve 935 children. The antipoverty agency's press release for the Southwest Mississippi grant went so far as to say that the new program would "make use of many of the Head Start centers previously used by CDGM."[67] OEO did not intend to refund CDGM. A *Washington Post* reporter speculated that the federal agency was attempting "to give all its money away so that there will be none left to give" to CDGM.[68]

It appeared that CDGM's opponents had won the antipoverty battle in Mississippi. One day after Governor Paul Johnson approved MAP's charter, the organization hastily submitted a Head Start application to OEO, inadvertently including an unsigned copy of the charter. Despite this error, OEO funded the program, removing any doubt that MAP was indeed a replacement for CDGM.[69] OEO awarded MAP $3 million to serve 1,500 children. The agency placed an additional $7 million on reserve for future MAP centers. Shriver promised, when announcing MAP's grant, to add six representatives of the poor to the new organization's board of directors.[70] The NAACP national office lauded MAP in a telegram. Both Governor Paul Johnson and Senator John Stennis publicly gave MAP their blessing, and the Sovereignty Commission recruited "ordinary citizens" to send telegrams to Shriver expressing support for the new program.[71] MAP planned to operate in thirteen counties, including five former CDGM counties.[72]

Yet, the battle for Head Start in Mississippi was far from over. CDGM employees and parents had cut their political teeth while administering the first two preschool grants, so they quickly mobilized to contest the rival organization. Marion Wright and Rev. James McRee brought pressure to bear on NAACP leader Aaron Henry, causing him to do an about-face and urge OEO to refund CDGM, even though he had agreed to sit on MAP's board. Years later, Henry admitted that he supported CDGM's political component, but did not approve of its brazenness. "I don't give a damn about how many people he [John Mudd] ferried in and out of the Meredith March you see. But anytime a son-of-a-bitch write on a goddamn trip ticket, 'Meredith March!' he's a crazy son of bitch. He can't get by with that and the auditors were looking down his neck."[73] Most CDGM supporters, however, saw no problems with the program's close affiliation with the movement.

CDGM held a public meeting at the College Park Auditorium in Jackson after learning of MAP's incorporation. Over 3,500 black Mississippians attended and issued a vote of no confidence in the MAP board. Attendees also resolved to operate CDGM centers on a voluntary basis, to refuse employment or cooperation with MAP, and to send a petition to the national NAACP office requesting that all local NAACP chapters withdraw their support of MAP. The supporters issued a unanimous call for an Equal Employment Opportunity Commission investigation of the Mississippi Chemical Corporation's hiring practices, the company MAP board member Owen Cooper led.[74]

Attending press described the CDGM meeting in Jackson as a combined political rally and religious gathering. Marian Wright proclaimed, "if there isn't a political deal involved here, let them prove it. Shriver himself said this was the best program in the nation and what we are going to have to ask him is how that changed all of a sudden."[75] The gathering at the auditorium not only galvanized CDGM supporters but also gave voice to class conflict within black Mississippi.[76] Movement veteran Fannie Lou Hamer carried the day just as she had done while speaking at the 1964 Democratic National Convention. She implored those in attendance at the College Park Auditorium not to give up on CDGM: "we aren't ready to be sold out by a few middle-class bourgeoisie and some of the Uncle Toms who couldn't care less."[77] Mississippi Freedom Democratic Party chairman Lawrence Guyot, CDGM board members Reverend James McRee, and CDGM organizer Unita Blackwell also spoke.

Middle-class black involvement in MAP rubbed salt in a working-class wound that had festered since the COFO's collapse. In 1965, state NAACP leaders withdrew their organization and its middle-class constituency from the council, because they feared they had lost ground to SNCC and its offshoot, the Mississippi Freedom Democratic Party.[78] State NAACP leaders also found CDGM to be problematic because NAACP members had difficulty securing jobs in the program. Throughout October 1966, Charles Evers, Mississippi NAACP field secretary and the brother of slain NAACP leader Medgar Evers, sent letters to CDGM center directors encouraging them to participate in MAP's program. Evers identified himself in the letters as MAP's personnel consultant indicating that anyone seeking employment in the new program needed to go through him. Aaron Henry also signed the letters, although he later denied it. Nonetheless, it was clear that the NAACP was eager to reestablish itself as a major player in the state.[79]

Many CDGM supporters saw the letters as proof that some middle-class black Mississippians sacrificed self-determination for nominal power. Jimana Sumrall, whose family had been harassed by the Sovereignty Commission because of their CDGM connections, was one of hundreds who

CDGM supporters held a public meeting in Jackson on 8 October 1966 to renew their support for the embattled Head Start program. The gathering was one of the largest at the Masonic Temple since Medgar Evers's funeral. (National Archives, CSA [RG 381] series: Office of Economic Opportunity; Community Action Program Office; Records of the Director; Subject Files, 1965–1969)

believed MAP took away her freedom to further movement work through a Head Start program. She illustrated her commitment to the black-run program by asserting, "I'll go to jail before I give them [preschool children] to MAP."[80] Sumrall had developed her own political worldview that challenged the old-guard leadership. CDGM had exacerbated tensions and expanded horizons. Black people who in the past had put aside ideological differences now became enemies.

CDGM received support from friends near and far. Mississippi Freedom Democratic Party officials MacArthur Cotton, Jesse Harris, and Annie Devine set up an educational fund to support CDGM's boycott of MAP.[81] Kenneth Neigh, general secretary of the Presbyterian Church's Board of National Missions in New York, called the White House daily requesting to see President Johnson about CDGM's refunding. National representatives from progressive labor unions, faith organizations, and human rights groups rallied to CDGM's defense and lobbied OEO for a third grant. Both Senator

Jacob Javits (R-N.Y.) and Mamie Phipps Clark, a member of the national committee that founded Head Start, sent telegrams to OEO urging the agency to reconsider its decision to end support of CDGM.[82] Congressman Adam Clayton Powell and Ben Neufeld, executive secretary of the National Council on Agricultural Life and Labor, sent letters to Sargent Shriver expressing disappointment in the way OEO had handled Head Start.[83] Support for the beleaguered preschool program even came from within OEO. Hyman Bookbinder, OEO assistant director for private groups, publicly admitted that his office "was wrong to halt the CDGM program."[84] Bookbinder's admission, coupled with outcries from across the country, provided fuel for CDGM employees and parents to fight back.

The CCAP represented the biggest weapon that CDGM had in its refunding arsenal. The CCAP, Richard Boone's watchdog organization that had rallied to CDGM's defense during the first unfunded period, received most of its funding from Walter Reuther and the United Auto Workers and from the Field Foundation. The CCAP consisted of a coalition of over one hundred organizations and individuals, including the Brotherhood of Sleeping Car Porters, the Council of Jewish Federations and Welfare Funds, and the United Packinghouse, Food and Allied Workers. The organization also had the ear and the support of United States senator Robert Kennedy (D-N.Y.). The CCAP, with Kennedy's support, formed an independent Board of Inquiry to investigate OEO's charges and concluded that CDGM's program was "of the highest caliber and must be considered a striking success."[85] The CCAP sent a copy of their findings to OEO.

Nationwide support for the largest inaugural Head Start program in the country caused OEO officials in Washington, D.C., to prepare for public fallout. Herbert Kramer, OEO's public affairs director, sent a memorandum about CDGM to all OEO regional directors and public affairs officers. The memo outlined OEO's rationale for not refunding CDGM. The memo's very existence illustrated that antipoverty officials anticipated resistance and wanted to disseminate their own version of events.[86]

National OEO officials agreed to meet with CDGM's director and board members. A delegation led by Community Action Director Theodore Berry and Head Start Director Jule Sugarman met in Atlanta with CDGM representatives on 13 October 1966, led by board chairman Reverend McRee and CDGM director John Mudd. Sugarman explained to those assembled that OEO could not refund CDGM because the program's statewide board of directors had no control. Local centers operated autonomously, promoting disorganization and giving center directors the opportunity to prioritize civil rights work over early childhood education. Additionally, he asserted that the program lacked biracial participation and had not made a concerted effort to work with local community action agencies. These problems, according to Sugarman, necessitated that OEO approach other people about operating a statewide Head Start program in Mississippi.

John Mudd countered OEO's assessment by arguing that the agency's goals were unrealistic. Interracial collaboration with community action agencies was impossible, because there were two communities in Mississippi. Mudd explained: "Community means mutual cooperation of individuals who respect each other and have sufficient consensus to make cooperative endeavor possible. To gain this in a society where there have been such profound differences means you must work hard at developing the competence of those who have been deprived. A façade of biracialism in substance still preserves the dominant-subordinate relationship."[87] If working-class black Mississippians were to work effectively on community action agencies in the future, they needed time to overcome feelings of inadequacy and fear that had shaped their interactions with white residents. CDGM's autonomous and indigenous center governance provided that time and experience. Mudd's rebuttal was an indirect condemnation of MAP, its clandestine formation, and its biracial board, which was undemocratically selected and excluded working-class African Americans. While interracial, MAP still maintained existing power relations between the rich and poor, black and white.

Board chairman James McRee also took on OEO officials who called for greater coordination with local community action agencies. The Madison County minister asserted that OEO had not given CDGM credit for attempting to work with community action boards that were oftentimes created to replace CDGM. He reminded those assembled that two communities existed in Mississippi. Well-founded racism, fear, and mistrust prevented African Americans in many CDGM communities from participating in Head Start programs sponsored by community action agencies.[88]

Working-class black Mississippians also came to the program's defense during the meeting. Thelma Barnes, a community worker from Greenville and a CDGM board member, maintained that CDGM helped the most marginalized children and adults realize their potential. Barnes went to great lengths in 1965 to get black women in the Delta to apply for Head Start jobs. Most were hesitant to do so because they had low self-esteem. Perhaps she remembered the difficulty she faced in securing teachers as she responded to Sugarman's critique about lack of board control. "We were trying to help people grow by involving them in things they haven't been involved in before." While Barnes admitted "that there has been a slippage of control" in the board's oversight of program operations, she was quick to point out that CDGM was "the first nonpaternalistic relationship we have had with our government. Our people are feeling their self-worth."[89] CDGM provided poor African Americans with training, education, and supervisory experience. In doing so, the program modeled "maximum feasible participation" of the poor and gave black parents the skills and confidence needed to participate in existing institutions, such as public school systems.

The tense five-hour meeting between CDGM and OEO signaled that the leaders of the grassroots Head Start program had developed their political astuteness. African American board members had worried in 1965 about the consequences of standing up to the federal government, but in 1966, they demanded fair hearings and questioned OEO's commitment to ending poverty. Their refusal to take no for an answer made refunding a possibility. Before OEO officials adjourned the meeting, they held out the prospect of refunding CDGM, provided the organization improved its administration.[90]

Despite this change of events, or maybe because of it, CDGM and its supporters did not wait hat in hand for a new grant to appear. Clergy from mainline white churches that had come out publicly on the side of civil rights in the 1960s were some of the first to act. Days after the OEO-CDGM meeting in Atlanta, representatives of the Episcopal, United Presbyterian, and United Church of Christ denominations attending a routine meeting in Chicago received word from a National Council of Churches official that the Head Start program was in trouble. The ministers heard about CDGM's continuing funding battle and traveled from Chicago to Washington via a chartered plane on a day's notice. Seventy white clergy from the three major denominations picketed the OEO offices for three hours. In the nation's capital, the clergy threatened to withdraw their denominations' support of the War on Poverty if the agency continued to deny CDGM a new grant.[91]

The preachers' picket made front-page news in the *Washington Post*, but CDGM aroused the nation with a $10,000 advertisement that ran in the *New York Times*. The full-page ad supporting CDGM and denouncing OEO blared "Say it isn't so, Sargent Shriver," and contained the signatures of over 160 individuals who called themselves the National Citizens Committee for the Child Development Program in Mississippi. The advertisement was the brainchild of David Ramage, an executive officer of the Board of National Missions of Churches; Jon Regier, executive secretary of the National Council of Churches' Division of Home Ministries; and Kenneth Neigh. Richard Boone had asked the men to rally support for CDGM after learning about the program's funding status from John Mudd. Among the 160 signees were American Jewish Congress President Joachim Prinz; SCLC associate director Andrew Young; former CORE Director James Farmer; and United Auto Workers Union president Walter Reuther.[92] The advertisement wording was a play on the phrase "say it ain't so," which dated back to 1920, when baseball great "Shoeless" Joe Jackson admitted to participating in a conspiracy to fix the World Series. The newspaper ad suggested that Shriver engaged in his own political fixing because of "awesome political pressure."[93] CDGM, by placing the ad in one of the most influential newspapers in the country, hoped to force OEO's hand.

The attack on Shriver's commitment to the poor greatly upset him. Jule Sugarman recalled that he had "never really seen him as moved and as upset as he was" when the ad ran in the paper.[94] Angry, the antipoverty chief responded with a *New York Times* op-ed piece, defending OEO's decision to look for alternative programs in Mississippi. He argued that there was "no group of individuals which has sought and prayed for CDGM's success more than OEO." Moreover, he asserted that the decision to discontinue the movement-associated preschool program was "the unanimous recommendation of all the OEO officials involved—Community Action, Head Start, auditing, inspection, civil rights [and] legal."[95]

Adding insult to injury, two of Sargent Shriver's top civil rights aides resigned from the OEO in protest of the agency's stance on CDGM. Steven Lowenstein, deputy special assistant for civil rights at OEO, explained in November 1966 that "the War on Poverty has lost its initial thrust of helping the poor. One glaring example of this is CDGM. I had very strong feelings on the matter." Ruby Barrows, another employee in the civil rights division, resigned for similar reasons.[96] Samuel Yette, OEO's top civil rights aide, resigned three months later in protest of the OEO's lax compliance with civil rights.[97] Yette did not mention CDGM by name, but it is highly likely that he opposed OEO's stance on the program.

The newspaper advertisement and OEO personnel defections caused Sargent Shriver to have second thoughts about replacing CDGM. He decided to meet with John Mudd and CDGM's board in Atlanta. Others in attendance included Ralph Caprio of the CCAP; Joseph Rauh, CDGM

Advertisement that ran in the 19 October 1966 issue of the *New York Times* pressuring OEO director Sargent Shriver to refund CDGM. (Judith Schultheiss and *New York Times*) special counsel and a renowned labor and civil rights attorney; and Bob Patricelli, a representative from Senator Jacob Javits's (R-N.Y.) office. All three men participated at CDGM's request. Shriver and his lieutenants raised concerns throughout the meeting about CDGM's hiring practices, the lack of formal credentials for teachers, and its lack of white participation, but suggested that they might fund CDGM if the program made some changes.[98]

CDGM's representatives used every resource at their disposal to influence the refunding negotiations. In an eleventh-hour move, board members invited Dr. Martin Luther King Jr. to the Atlanta meeting without informing OEO. The civil rights leader arrived late, but once there he urged Shriver to refund CDGM, noting that the program accomplished the impossible in Mississippi. King admitted that "there may have been some mistakes here and there," but maintained that "the basic thrust of this program [CDGM] has been good. It has given new hope to the hopeless."[99] Shriver had not anticipated someone of King's stature at the meeting. Wherever King went, the media followed, and neither Shriver nor President Lyndon Johnson welcomed public criticism of the antipoverty program by the civil rights leader. Johnson, in 1964, had personally summoned King to the White House to sell him the War on Poverty, so the stakes were high.[100] The OEO director needed to create a solution that appealed to Congress, black and white Mississippians, northern white liberals, and the most famous black activist in the country.

Conspicuously absent from the negotiating table were working-class black women, who were the backbone of CDGM's program. As was often the case in public schools where black male administrators met with white leaders to negotiate funding and other issues, men on CDGM's board typically served as the organization's spokesmen. CDGM women, like black women public school teachers, rarely interacted with the power structure.[101] They mobilized and organized within the communities in which they lived. While nationally known figures in suits and ties chattered in offices in Washington and Atlanta, black women once again found themselves creatively pooling resources to keep centers open.

CDGM women operated sixty-seven centers on a voluntary basis during the unfunded period that began in August 1966. Teachers worked without pay, even though they often lacked other means of financial support. They got by with donations and loans from friends and family and with fundraisers.[102] In Neshoba County, CDGM supporters held a supper every Saturday night to raise money. Centers there opened five days per week on a voluntary basis. In Clarke County, Jimana Sumrall proudly watched residents in her community take up daily collections to buy food for the 167 children in her center. Some teachers sold barbeque plates.[103] Emis Mabry, who worked voluntarily at a CDGM center in Humphreys County, successfully appealed to the Field Foundation for financial assistance in early 1967, after months of carrying food from her house to feed Head Start children. The New York–based philanthropic organization had a history of supporting civil rights organizations in Mississippi, so her request was not unusual.[104] In Washington County, Lillie Ayers held cakewalks and canvassed door to door for donations. She used the $14.75 raised to purchase a turkey to provide a Thanksgiving meal for children at the Glen Allan center.[105]

CDGM women faced a tough battle to keep centers open. Flora Brooks, an Area Teacher Guide for Jones County, admitted that "all the centers need encouragement as they feel that this fight is more than we can stand."[106] Things appeared bleak, because after CDGM's second grant ended, OEO officials gathered all the toys, books, and other classroom items purchased with federal money and put them in a warehouse. By seizing CDGM inventory, the federal agency charged with stamping out poverty appeared to be closing the door on the possibility of a third grant. Brooks reported that in her county "even the crayons and paper had to be returned to OEO. The children miss these things very much. Yet there are toys that were made in the center. We have some pretty puzzles done by Miss Roberts. They are just plain cardboard boxes, painted and cut out."[107] Instruction at CDGM centers did not stop because of the absence of materials. Black women improvised with homemade hobbyhorses and musical instruments. They also focused classroom instruction on things that did not require teaching aids, such as fire drills and safety lessons.[108] CDGM parents, in sending their children to makeshift centers with rudimentary learning tools rather than to well-funded MAP-run preschools, resolved to maintain the program that they had built.

MAP's board members were surprised to receive a cold shoulder from so many working-class black Mississippians, because the new Head Start program's staff included several individuals with meaningful ties to black communities. Patricia Derian served as OEO's liaison to MAP. Derian, a white woman who relocated to Mississippi from Ohio in the fifties, had previously worked to desegregate schools in Jackson and improve rental housing conditions for the capital city's poor residents. She had also served as a Head Start program director.[109] MAP's board also hired Walter Smith, the husband of progressive newspaper editor Hazel Brannon Smith, as program director. The presence of southern white liberals, however, did not convince CDGM supporters to send their children to MAP. They recognized the fundamental differences between their program and its replacement. CDGM was an egalitarian project operating under the conviction that the best way to help black children was to fully incorporate their parents into the Mississippi mainstream through meaningful employment and leadership opportunities. MAP, in contrast, focused on preparing children academically for the first grade, with little emphasis on jobs for their parents or other forms of parental involvement. A MAP representative told black women in Clarke County that the purpose of his Head Start program was to get children "ready to attend school the next year." He made no reference to Shriver's own assertion that Head Start was a "child development program involving parents, volunteers, and families, not just pre-school training."[110]

MAP's deep pockets looked increasingly appealing as the struggle to feed children and to staff CDGM centers became more difficult. Black women in Clarke County reached out to the rival program when they were unable to operate because of insufficient funds. In conversations with MAP officials, the women learned that in the new program, black and white children learned in separate buildings. The arrangement was illegal and demonstrated that OEO was unable or unwilling to enforce desegregation in some locales.[111] Years later, Julius Richmond conceded that there had been isolated occurrences of racial segregation, but maintained that "communities kept learning that we were serious about this [racial integration]."[112]

Many working-class black Mississippians boycotted MAP not only because it practiced segregation and lacked the community action commitment, but also because it placed a premium on education and experience in its hiring in ways that excluded most CDGM workers. A newspaper advertisement for openings within the new Head Start program stipulated that the personnel manager needed a college degree plus previous experience in personnel. The requirements for the office manager included ten years experience in business or government. Administrative assistants needed five years of secretarial experience. White supremacy barred most blacks from obtaining professional employment even if they had the education, so the experience requirement shut out many. MAP also preferred trained teachers, which went against the basic premise of CDGM's educational program that through on-the-job training ordinary people could run an efficient pre-school program.[113]

The new Head Start program's personnel policies supposed that the program was for children and not for communities. MAP's leaders believed that poor children needed the intellectual stimulation that early childhood professionals provided, so they sought credentialed educators. Thus, language and emergent literacy skills, rather than job creation for the poor or political activism, was the primary focus of MAP's program. For certain, not all MAP supporters championed the program for the reasons that Senator Stennis did. Many believed that the best learning outcomes for children came from high-quality programs and that teacher training influenced classroom quality. Despite their noble intentions, however, MAP's commitment to trained professionals cut off one of working-class black women's few opportunities for professional employment and, in so doing, left them once again at the mercy of local white employers.

MAP's first centers opened on 22 November 1966, in Lauderdale County. MAP board member and cosmetic manufacturer Charles Young lived in the county and used his extensive contacts to get preschool centers up and running. Since MAP preferred teachers with formal credentials, CDGM educators received no preferential treatment in hiring, even though they had already run Head Start classrooms. To the chagrin of OEO officials, a committee comprised of middle-class black and white citizens decided MAP policy "with the intention of adding [poor] parents after the program begins." Antipoverty program employees in Washington knew that such an arrangement subverted "maximum feasible participation" of the poor and fueled CDGM supporters' distrust.[114]

As MAP went full speed ahead with its Head Start program, Sargent Shriver and other OEO officials remained in conversation with CDGM representatives. In early November, national Head Start director Jule Sugarman outlined OEO's preconditions for refunding CDGM. The stipulations included replacing John Mudd and James McRee, whom the agency believed symbolized lack of organizational control; increasing white participation at all levels; employing trained teachers in every center; and limiting community committees to the parents or guardians of enrolled or previously enrolled children. Officials designed the conditions to guarantee that CDGM was an interracial organization that had the managerial skills necessary to avoid previous mistakes. Additionally, the new conditions were supposed to strike a balance between community action and early childhood education.[115] Backroom negotiations continued when Vice President Hubert Humphrey spoke to the National Council of Churches in December 1966.

Clergy sympathetic to CDGM pulled Humphrey aside and made their case for the embattled Head Start program. The vice president left the meeting with tears in his eyes. Not long after these developments, Jule Sugarman recalled that someone in the White House encouraged OEO to award CDGM a new grant, and Humphrey offered to facilitate mediations.[116]

CDGM received a $5 million grant to serve 5,900 children in nineteen counties through June 1967. OEO also pledged a second grant of $3 million, subject to the availability of funds, for CDGM in the 1967–68 fiscal year. This third grant became possible because the Presbyterian Board of National Missions assumed full responsibility for any past, present, or future disallowances of program expenditures, weakening Senator Stennis's objections about money mismanagement. McRee and Mudd remained in their respective leadership positions, but CDGM officials agreed to increase the size of the board from seventeen to nineteen members, with six of those members being native white Mississippians. The program also agreed to hire Richard Davies, a Washington management consultant, who worked closely with Mudd and participated in management decisions.[117] The new grant included four counties not previously assigned to CDGM, including Senator Stennis's home turf of Kemper County. The senator made his displeasure known in a letter to President Johnson.[118]

CDGM had nine lives, to the disappointment of its opponents. Outraged that the radical Head Start program had received yet another grant, Federal District Court Judge Harold Cox refused to convene a grand jury to weigh evidence in the murder cases of Vernon Dahmer and the three civil rights workers. He said he would hold out until the federal government requested a grand jury investigation of CDGM. The judge, a Kennedy appointee and Senator James Eastland's college roommate, had no legal basis for his ultimatum. He simply attempted to cast a negative light on CDGM and delay Klansmen from standing trial.[119] Mississippi governor Paul Johnson joined the chorus of those who expressed anger about CDGM's third grant. His state had not desegregated its public schools, thus it stood to lose millions in federal aid, as the 1964 Civil Rights Act gave HEW the authority to cut off funding to discriminatory programs. Johnson said, "thirty-three of our school districts are threatened by the department of HEW with the loss of $45 million that would benefit both races and yet another agency has just handed on a platter a grant of $5 million to an agency that has proved to be irresponsibly managed."[120]

MAP officials were also unhappy with CDGM's refunding because they had not expected to compete for Head Start funds or children. Not only did CDGM survive, but it received five counties previously assigned to MAP. In a MAP executive committee meeting, Owen Cooper charged that OEO was in CDGM's camp and demanded that the agency honor its original county assignments and allow them to retain control over Head Start in Clarke, Humphreys, Leflore, Neshoba, and Wayne counties. Cooper threatened to take the dispute to the entire Mississippi congressional delegation if OEO amended the original agreement.[121] Shriver had endured enough criticism from United States senators Stennis and Eastland and Representative John Bell Williams (D-Miss.) to know that the wrath of the entire state delegation was a bullet he wanted to dodge. The OEO director thus awarded CDGM fourteen counties rather than the nineteen promised a month earlier when he finally signed the program's third grant. As was the case in other parts of the country, local politics influenced the antipoverty agency's commitment to the poor's empowerment.[122]

CDGM employees and parents in the five contested counties decided to operate voluntarily under the name Friends of the Children of Mississippi (FCM) rather than accept MAP's jurisdiction. The five disputed counties had been the sites of some of the earliest civil rights activities in the state, so it was no surprise that many black residents in those areas turned their backs on a Head Start program imposed on them.[123] Black people in Greene County, which had not previously been affiliated with CDGM, also took up the FCM name and ran Head Start centers. Fifteen hundred children and 400 employees operated under the FCM banner on an allocation of thirty cents per child from money raised among community members and from sympathetic organizations. MAP's better-funded centers in FCM counties only attracted 400 children. FCM supporters decided to either negotiate a contractual arrangement to operate Head Start centers on MAP's behalf or seek direct funding from OEO, since they had the majority of eligible preschoolers while MAP had the money.[124]

The widespread commitment to FCM demonstrated that the black poor wanted more than access to federal dollars and programs—they wanted to control the allocation of those resources. CDGM operated with poor people's input. Moreover, its curriculum eschewed whiteness as a standard and imbued black children with a sense of racial pride. MAP's program, in contrast, was top-down and focused on school readiness, without addressing black assertiveness. Many FCM volunteers had traveled two years earlier to Mount Beulah, where they learned that the community action program would include them in the planning and implementation of antipoverty programs. An FCM teacher from Greene County explained, "we're tired of being told what we can do and what we can't do. Poor people have been under other people's programs ever since they've been born. We decided we'd run this program on nothing before we'd let somebody else run it for us. We've been bought and sold too many times."[125] Working-class black parents resisted black and white middle-class leadership and challenged OEO to uphold its own policies by specifically supporting FCM. For over a year, the volunteer-run FCM offered to operate Head Start centers for MAP as a delegate agency. FCM, while rebuffed by MAP, received a Field Foundation grant of $425,000 to operate Head Start centers for fifteen months.[126]

The United States Senate Subcommittee on Manpower, Employment, and Poverty held hearings in ten states to assess antipoverty initiatives during the standoff between FCM and MAP. Senators Robert Kennedy (D-N.Y.), Jacob Javits (R-N.Y.), Joseph Clark (D-Pa.), and George Murphy (R-Calif.) traveled to Jackson for hearings in April 1967. There, Senator Stennis recommended that all antipoverty programs receiving federal funds be subject to a governor's veto. He also maintained that antipoverty programs with inaccurate accounting should not receive additional federal money.[127] Without ever naming CDGM, Senator Stennis sought to shut the program down. CDGM supporters, however, also attended the hearings and stressed the ways in which community action programs helped the poor.

Thelma Barnes, Marian Wright, and Unita Blackwell represented CDGM, along with FCM leader, the Reverend J. E. Killingsworth. Blackwell testified that Head Start was more than working-class black Mississippians' bread and butter—it was their entry into the political arena and a vehicle through which they could have a say in their children's education. "In 1965 there was talk about a Head Start program," Blackwell told the assembled group. "We worked to try to get the program started. That is the first time—that's the reason I suppose we love it so well, because it's the only program that ever reached down to where the poverty—, poverty—, poverty-stricken folks is." Blackwell continued, "mechanization [of cotton picking] took over and the people didn't have anything to do. Back in 1965 and 1966 people learned coming off of plantations that they could make some decisions," through antipoverty initiatives such as CDGM. "That brought dignity to the people, they also argued—like they do in Washington—on committees and these kinds of things. They learned they could make some decisions for themselves."[128]

Blackwell's testimony demonstrated that CDGM had achieved what Head Start's architects had hoped the preschool program would accomplish nationwide. CDGM engaged the poor in decision making regarding their children and their communities. Experts from on high did not tell black Mississippians how to improve their children's chances for long-term success. Rather, professionals worked with black parents to create an educational opportunity that met their needs. Designing curricula, sitting on Head Start center governing boards, and allocating large amounts of federal money provided marginalized citizens with the confidence to go after institutional change in other areas of their lives.

The Jackson hearings also shed light on CDGM's practical importance. Several speakers mentioned the widespread hunger throughout the state. Hundreds of black Mississippians in Leflore County, for example, had lost their jobs to mechanization in 1962 and were denied government surplus commodities because of their civil rights activity.[129] Despite documented cases of white reprisals, Mississippi governor Paul Johnson retorted, "nobody is starving in Mississippi. The nigra women I see are so fat they shine."[130] Such crass racial insensitivity drove home to visiting senators the importance of black citizens participating in community action programs to counter systemic racism. Senator Javits asked several of the working-class African Americans present which antipoverty program was most important to them. Fannie Lou Hamer answered unequivocally that the Head Start program was the most important, because "it give the children a head start but also give the adults a Head Start."[131]

CDGM supporters received another boost during the hearings when the Ernst and Ernst accounting firm released the findings of its latest audit of the program. Auditors told the senators that "the amount of disallowance, if any, will be relatively minor in amount." They found that CDGM officials misspent $14,000 out of the $1.5 million grant in 1965 and $653 out of the $5.6 million grant in 1966. Not only did the amounts negate the charges of widespread corruption that Stennis brought earlier in the day, but the steep drop in the second year suggested that staff had improved its practices.[132] The report vindicated the over 2,000 working-class black Mississippians who used federal money to offer education, food, and medical care to preschoolers. While the program did indeed have close connections with civil rights groups and movement activists, Head Start funds had not been seriously misspent.

Even after being cleared of allegations of fiscal mismanagement, CDGM faced many internal challenges. The refunding battles caused relationships among former allies to deteriorate as people became suspicious of colleagues' motives. Polly Greenberg had officially left the program in June 1966, although she worked behind the scenes for several more months. She recalled later that her departure did not bring any "parties, testimonials, demonstrations of gratitude or good-bye letters from the board."[133] The time was ripe for black leadership even, if CDGM's white staffers were not ready to leave. Pearl Montgomery Draine, a black public school teacher from Jackson, replaced Greenberg. Draine was born in 1926 in Lexington, Mississippi, to sharecroppers. She earned a bachelor's degree in education and social services from Jackson State University and master's degrees from Indiana University. The educator was no stranger to community organizing. She had taken bold public gestures for civil rights, including joining the NAACP against the wishes of her school superintendent, opening her home to Freedom Riders, and sending letters to state and national leaders demanding black voting rights. In 1965, she had risked her public school employment by writing an open letter to United States attorney general Nicholas Katzenbach and Governor Paul Johnson in which she offered to serve as a voter registrar to speed along implementation of the Voting Rights Act.[134] Draine's promotion to director of teacher development fulfilled Levin's vision of local people assuming leadership of a program created for their benefit.

John Mudd left the program fourteen months after Pearl Draine arrived. He stepped down, he later explained, because "it seemed time to make a transition to local black leadership."[135] Charles F. Thomas, a minister from the Gulf region, succeeded Mudd in September 1967, becoming CDGM's first black director. Thomas had spent ten years in the military and was the pastor of a rural Mississippi church that served as a CDGM center.[136]

The new director's first major task was to secure CDGM's refunding. The program's last grant had expired in June of 1967, and it had not received the additional $3 million that OEO had earlier promised. Thomas addressed perceived CDGM impropriety to speed up acquisition of funds from OEO. He first dealt with a scandal in the Reverend James McRee's Madison County. The Reverend McRee and his wife Christine had hosted freedom schools and conducted voter registration drives in 1964. They continued their movement work through CDGM. McRee served as chairman of the CDGM board, and his wife oversaw several centers in Canton. Many Canton Head Start employees alleged that they paid kickbacks to Christine McRee or to George Raymond, a veteran CORE organizer and Rev. McRee's close friend, to secure CDGM employment.[137] Thomas called for McRee's removal, and the minister soon left the program without admitting guilt. Whether or not the allegations were true, McRee's departure was evidence of the rifts among people who had labored together in the trenches for years.[138]

In October of 1967, CDGM received its last grant, as community action changed dramatically at the local level. OEO provided CDGM with the $3 million that it had promised earlier. That grant expired in January 1968 and proved to be the end of an era in many ways. During the long, hot summer of 1967, riots had erupted in eighteen cities, including Newark and Detroit. Several Republicans joined with southern Democrats, including Senator James Eastland of Mississippi, and alleged that community action program workers instigated the uprisings, in spite of a government-funded study that listed failed education, social services, and housing policies as the reasons for the violence. The riot allegations could not have come at a worse time for OEO, since its reauthorization hearings in Congress were scheduled for the fall.[139] As a defensive measure, top agency officials supported an amendment created by Edith Green (D-Ore.) that placed community action agencies under local governments' control. The Green Amendment specified that groups seeking community action funds had to either be affiliated with local or state government or be a private entity that local or state government selected to run community action programs.[140] "The amendment was a conscious effort on the part of this agency to satisfy some very negative attitudes, particularly among southern members of the House," OEO's deputy director, Bertrand Harding, recalled. "Unless some sort of compromise was put into the bill this agency would have come to a screeching halt."[141]

The political concession worked. By severely constricting the poor's ability to challenge local power structures through community action, OEO received congressional funding for two additional years. During the final debates on the Green Amendment, Senator Javits of New York, one of CDGM's most consistent supporters, lamented the agency's shift away from "maximum feasible participation" of the poor.[142] Javits correctly recognized that increasing the influence of local elected officials in community action agencies disrupted the grassroots spirit of programs such as CDGM.

The 1968 inauguration of a new governor in Mississippi compounded the Green Amendment's impact on CDGM. John Bell Williams, who had consistently opposed CDGM while a United States congressman, became Mississippi's governor just as CDGM's last grant from OEO expired. It was highly unlikely that state or county officials would contract with CDGM to operate Head Start on Williams's watch. Without the support of the white ruling class, CDGM was not eligible for OEO funds, according to the stipulations of the Green Amendment.

Moreover, to fund the war in Vietnam, the White House introduced deep cuts in the War on Poverty's 1968 fiscal year budget, including a $25 million reduction in Head Start funds. Mississippi saw its Head Start appropriation reduced by $8 million, a larger cut than any other state. OEO justified the drastic reduction by pointing out that Mississippi earlier had received a disproportionate amount of Head Start funds.[143]

CDGM sympathizers continued to wage their own freedom struggle even as the nation's attention drifted elsewhere. A delegation of CDGM youngsters traveled to Washington, D.C., in April of l968, just as they had done two years earlier. They found Capitol Hill a much different place. Sargent Shriver had stepped down as OEO director in March, and his successor, Bertrand Harding, did not have the same political know-how or commitment to struggling programs. When interviewed by reporters about CDGM's lobbying efforts, CDGM director of Teacher Development Pearl Draine explained, "all we are asking is $4 million when the riots cost $70 million." She went on to say, "if we must leave, we will be back. Mississippi has no public kindergartens so this is the children's only chance for better training. It is their only chance for two hot meals a day, too."[144] Draine had learned the political process and she was well prepared to make her case to anyone who listened, but her cause garnered few supporters after Dr. Martin Luther King Jr.'s assassination put the nation's attention on poverty and unrest in cities. Indeed, OEO never again funded preschool programs in Mississippi under the CDGM name.

CDGM, despite its brief tenure, had been tremendously successful in helping working-class black people take rights for themselves and challenge the social order that had constrained them since emancipation. Black Mississippians staked a claim for full freedom by subverting white control over black education and ensuring their children had a healthy start before they entered the often hostile public schools. Armed with nascent civil rights legislation and federal largesse, they were well prepared to carry on a struggle that had predated the modern civil rights movement. These freedom fighters provided their children with early childhood education, nutritious meals, and healthcare. They acquired new skills, served on governing boards, and found ways to influence local politics. In essence, they interrupted business as usual and tackled the problems brought about by their poverty.

Perhaps one of the most demonstrative examples of CDGM's value in black communities was the graduation ceremony that the Porterville CDGM center held in August 1967. Twenty-five children adorned in graduation caps and their Sunday best marched single file into a local church to celebrate their Head Start graduation. A crowd of 400 watched the youngsters receive diplomas that attested to their scholastic accomplishments and preparation for the first grade. The formality of the ceremony was in step with the premium black communities placed on education. The diplomas, which bore the names of CDGM teachers who had once been denied the opportunity to receive degrees themselves, attested to the aspiration and achievement at the center of the radical Head Start program. Commencement was both recognition of and celebration of the grassroots effort to shape the educational destiny of black youth.[145]

Even after CDGM graduations became distant memories, the Head Start program lived on, because its supporters had forced white Mississippians to seek biracial participation in community programs, institutionalizing black access to political power. It was because of CDGM and its interracial coalitions that MAP even existed. This was no small feat. While the nation was moving toward racial inclusion throughout this period, integration was not inevitable in the Magnolia State, as evidenced by the rise of private academies to evade school desegregation and Governor Williams's efforts to send an all-white delegation to the 1968 Democratic National Convention.[146]

OEO played an invaluable role in helping CDGM shake up local politics and weaken white supremacy. Dismantling Jim Crow remained a tall order even after important federal civil rights laws were in place. The antipoverty agency facilitated meaningful changes in Mississippi's racial and political status quo by circumventing state and local politicians who benefited from African Americans' second-class citizenship. In an effort to secure reauthorization from Congress, however, OEO cut ties with the embattled preschool program. The loss of such a valuable ally not only led to CDGM's end but also gave obstructionists the green light to subvert the spirit of community action.

CDGM's story, from its foundational meetings in New York and Edwards to its defunding by OEO, illustrated the fallacy of "culture of poverty"

DIPLOMA OF GRADUATION

CDGM

PORTERVILLE HEAD START CENTER

Porterville, Mississippi

THIS CERTIFIES THAT

LA REICE CAROL McCONNELL

is a graduate of the Porterville Head Start Center and
is therefore eligible for promotion to public school.

Given at Porterville, Mississippi, this Twenty-Seventh
day of August, Nineteen Hundred and Sixty-Seven.

MR. WILLIE J. JIMISON
Center Director

MRS. FANNIE L. THEDFORD
Resource Teacher

MRS. EVELYN WREN
Resource Teacher

MISS LULA M. McCONNELL
Resource Teacher

-8-

CDGM diplomas not only attested to what youngsters had accomplished but also
served as inspiration for all the other educational goals yet to be actualized.
(Presbyterian Historical Society [U.S.A.])

CDGM was a manifestation of the educational goals and aspirations that local people had for their children. They wanted to develop healthy, confident, inquisitive students who believed in themselves and their abilities. Head Start graduation was a time to celebrate all that had been achieved. (Presbyterian Historical Society [U.S.A.])

theories.[147] Throughout the sixties, leading economists and policy analysts asserted that the poor were not simply lacking resources; their behavior and lack of ambition perpetuated their poverty. For black Mississippians who had no control over the public schools, county government, or the electoral process, their issues were structural. Discrimination rather than dependency created their lack. Thus, OEO's defunding of a program that brought about systemic changes eliminated a viable avenue for meaningful improvement in the lives of poor black southerners. The agency's need for annual funding from Congress had limited its reach.

In the end, final audits vindicated CDGM's grassroots operation. OEO disallowed less than 1 percent of all CDGM funds, but the damage had already been done.[148] The charges of incompetence and economic malfeasance leveled at the Head Start program set a precedent of undermining antipoverty programs and community organizations run by the poor. We still see such tactics in play today, for example, the 2009 sabotage of the Association of Community Organizations for Reform Now (ACORN).[149]

MAP, while outlasting CDGM, encountered its own struggles.[150] In addition to wavering support from OEO and competition for students and facilities in former CDGM strongholds, MAP board members encountered backlash from segregationists who came to believe that the program too closely resembled CDGM. In 1967, former CDGM employee and African American educator Helen Bass Williams replaced Walter Smith as MAP's director. Under Williams's tenure, MAP undertook a civil rights agenda similar to CDGM's and hired many former SNCC activists, including Jimmie Travis, who had been one of the first organizers in Greenwood.[151] After several MAP centers in Brookhaven mysteriously burned to the ground in November 1967, Williams called for an economic boycott of local white businesses in retaliation.[152] Williams understood that her program pumped large sums of money into the business community, and she used the appeal of federal funds to pressure local whites to put an end to the arson. She also committed MAP to supporting the Claiborne County NAACP boycott of white merchants. The program chose to buy milk from the three black groceries in the county, although the prices were higher than those at the white stores.[153] Ironically, despite MAP's roots and its political agenda under Williams' tenure, the program attracted many more white students than CDGM ever did, which meant that a program created to placate segregationists actually promoted desegregation.

One of the earliest signs of MAP success was the seating of the integrated forty-four–person Mississippi Loyalist Democratic Party delegation at the 1968 Democratic National Convention in Chicago. Led by Aaron Henry and Hodding Carter III, the Loyalist delegation challenged the seating of the all-white regular Mississippi Democratic Party. Although delegations from six southern states filed credentials challenges based on racial discrimination, only the integrated group from Mississippi was successful in having its entire delegation seated in place of segregationists.[154] This feat was by and large the result of a multiyear effort to build a state party that, in contrast to the all-white regular party, had open and well-publicized meetings and disavowed racial discrimination. MAP brought many Loyalist Democrats together and "sped the day in which that delegation stood in Chicago."[155] Several MAP officials served as 1968 delegates to the Democratic National Convention, including Henry, Carter, Oscar Carr, and Charles Young. Patricia Derian served as National Committee Woman. Former CDGM employees and supporters were also represented in the delegation. Participants included Thelma Barnes and Fannie Lou Hamer. Unita Blackwell and Robert Miles served as alternates.[156]

The CDGM story is one of irony. Local African Americans had created a Head Start program so radical that white supremacists backed Mississippi Action for Progress (MAP), which brought black and white Mississippians together as equals on a community action board. Even in their opposition to the grassroots initiative, the white ruling class fostered change. Black participation on MAP'S board was progress in a state notorious for black disfranchisement and exclusion.

Black Mississippians translated the sense of importance and possibility cultivated by participation in CDGM into an opportunity to forever alter the state's social and political relationships with African Americans. Neither a rival Head Start program nor a federal agency that reneged on its commitment to community action destroyed black citizens' desire for quality education, civic equality, and economic opportunity. The challenge at the 1964 Democratic National Convention had prepared them for partial victories. In the years after CDGM, its supporters used the savvy they had gained from working in the Head Start program to respond to new sets of problems confronting their communities. Their actions are best explained by the words of G. O. Turner, a poor black man from Wayne County who testified during the antipoverty hearings in 1967. "CDGM built something up within them [blacks]," he explained. "It gave them desire. A lot of people haven't had a chance to even elect a deacon in a church and to elect a committee made them feel good and they had somewhere to go and something to look forward to."[157] Because they had somewhere to go and something to do, they left an indelible footprint not just on early childhood education but also on community development and political power in the state.

Epilogue
A Constant Struggle

"The federal government declared war on poverty and poverty won," said President Ronald Reagan in his 1988 State of the Union address.[1] In reality, nothing could have been further from the truth. The percentage of poor Americans decreased dramatically because of the War on Poverty. By the 1970s, the poverty rate in the United States had been cut in half.[2] CDGM was successful in improving the standard of living of a sizable number of black Mississippians. Moreover, many of these black citizens, living in the most politically repressive state in the Union, secured seats at decision-making tables. The civil rights movement–affiliated Head Start program even forced recalcitrant segregationists to concede the necessity of biracial community action boards, demonstrating how federal funds could upset the racial status quo.

Poverty did not win. Liberalism, however, conceded the fight. The federal government was unwilling to subsidize community action in a way that created lasting institutional changes. OEO director Sargent Shriver backed away from tackling the "poverty of American law, power, and spirit" when it became politically expedient to do so.[3] CDGM was a casualty of the antipoverty agency's backpedalling.

White supremacists, on the other hand, never changed their position on the radical preschool program. They opposed black control over Head Start, a more democratic Mississippi, and quality educational opportunities for black students. Rather than voice their opposition in hateful, racist language, they labeled CDGM as corrupt and called for "responsible," credentialed leadership and local (white) control. When discrediting CDGM proved unsuccessful, segregationists set up community action agencies and rival Head Start programs run by local white leaders and "acceptable" black citizens to control the antipoverty funds and subvert the "maximum feasible participation" of the poor.

Such "strategic accommodation" with changing political winds carried over into Mississippi's desegregation of its public schools.[4] Before 1964, the state had seventeen private schools, excluding Catholic schools, with approximately 1,400 white students and 900 black students. By September 1970, after the Supreme Court ordered an end to segregation in Mississippi's public schools, there were 155 private, non-Catholic schools with approximately 42,000 white students.[5] White parents abandoned the public school system rather than submitting to desegregation, subverting the spirit of the *Brown* decision. Just as white parents refused to participate in CDGM's program in the 1960s, many today choose to have nothing to do with the state's public schools. Only 46 percent of the students in Mississippi who attended public schools in 2011 were white, although the majority of the state's population was white.[6] As public schools fell out of favor with white Mississippians, resistance toward funding public education increased. Thus too many black children in Mississippi attend poor-quality educational institutions that lack the creativity, intellectual rigor, and community involvement that CDGM fostered.

Thirty-thousand children enrolled in Mississippi's Head Start centers in 2013. Many of the parents of these children serve on Head Start Policy Councils where they have a say in center operation. The councils, however, do not reflect CDGM's brand of community action. A 1970 Head Start policy mandated that half of councils' membership be reserved for parents of enrolled children, rather than community members in general. The change was part of an effort to distance Head Start from the kinds of social activism that troubled individuals such as Senator Stennis. Under present-day Policy Council rules, Winson Hudson, Unita Blackwell, and Robert Miles could not have played major roles in their local Head Start centers, because they were not parents of enrolled students. The 1970 rule made children rather than children *and* communities the focus of Head Start, a troubling reality given that Head Start's architects realized that improving the outcomes of disadvantaged children included improving the community in which the children lived.[7] Thus, CDGM did not become a lasting model for comprehensive Head Start programs that promoted institutional change.

CDGM has left its mark on Mississippi and Head Start in other ways. Two of the largest present-day Head Start programs in the state—Mississippi Action for Progress and FCM—have direct ties to CDGM. Moreover, several centers bear the names of CDGM women, including the Winson G. Hudson Head Start Center in Carthage and the Ripley Blackwell Head Start Center in Rolling Fork, named after Minnie Ripley and Unita Blackwell.

While strong Head Start programs and named buildings attest to CDGM's legacy, the program's most lasting contribution is the confidence it cultivated among women who had long been ignored and cast aside. Emboldened by the opportunity to run one of the largest Head Start programs in the nation, CDGM women tapped into latent skills and leadership abilities and continued making demands on their government. They filed school desegregation suits and sought elected office. In 1969, Sarah Johnson, a CDGM teacher from Greenville, Mississippi, and twenty-nine other black parents filed a lawsuit to desegregate the public schools in their city. Former CDGM employees made up the bulk of plaintiffs.[8] Unita Blackwell, one of CDGM's original district organizers, became mayor of Mayersville in 1976; she was the first black woman in the state to serve as a municipality's chief executive. In five terms as mayor, Blackwell brought a sewage system, paved streets, and public housing to Mayersville and served as vice chair of the Mississippi Democratic Party, the same state party that had once banned black members.[9] Mamie Chinn, a CDGM teacher in Canton, became the first African American woman to serve as a Justice Court judge of Madison County in 1993. Long after CDGM's end, Winson Hudson continued her Head Start work through FCM and used her voice to raise awareness about a host of issues plaguing African Americans in Leake County including starvation, poor healthcare options, racial profiling, and the lack of paved roads and telephone service in black communities. She testified at the 1971 annual meeting of the American Hospital Association in Chicago about the need for decent healthcare in rural communities and visited Washington, D.C. in 1978 to brief President Jimmy Carter about minority issues. Throughout the 1980s, Hudson spoke up for Edward Earl Johnson, one of CDGM's original students, just as she had advocated on behalf of six-year-old Debra Lewis in 1964. Johnson was convicted and executed by the state of Mississippi in 1987 for the 1979 murder of a police officer and the sexual assault of an elderly woman. He maintained his innocence until the very end. As Winson Hudson once remarked, "fighting is an everyday thing—don't never rest."[10] She certainly never did.

Fighting opened previously closed doors of opportunity. Many CDGM women secured professional employment. When Alean Adams of Rankin County began working for CDGM in 1965, her highest educational attainment was the eleventh grade. Her Head Start work led her to go back to school, eventually earning a master's degree in elementary education. She recalled, "for a while, two of my daughters were at Tougaloo at the same time I was. Chemistry was so hard, I told my husband that I might drop out. Then one of my daughters wrote a paper saying I was her inspiration. I couldn't drop out. I've been teaching public school for twelve years now." CDGM proved to be transformative for both mother and child. Adams's daughter, a former CDGM student, now practices dentistry in Mississippi, where she provides dental screenings to Head Start students.[11]

Like Alean Adams, Hattie Saffold became a public school teacher after CDGM. She began teaching kindergarten in 1986. Drawing on her CDGM training, Saffold helped "other kindergarten teachers to set up their centers and let the children move around and choose and do." At a faculty meeting, teachers were encouraged to share information about their background and family. "When I finished telling about where I've come up from and about each of my children," Saffold recalled, "I sat back and said 'My, I really do have some things to be proud about don't I?'" CDGM had given Hattie Saffold a head start.

The same year that Hattie Saffold became a public school teacher, Lillie Ayers became the lead plaintiff in a federal lawsuit first filed in 1975 claiming that the state of Mississippi underfunded its three public black institutions of higher education. Her husband Jake had brought the legal challenge to improve the academic programs and facilities at the historically black Jackson State, Alcorn State, and Mississippi Valley State. While the lawsuit made its way through the courts, Jake Ayers died, and Lillie became the lead plaintiff. When not in court, Lille worked as a Head Start social worker in Washington County. Her work entailed recruiting and enrolling children in the preschool program and informing their parents of the social services available to them, such as assistance with gas and water bills. As she had done in CDGM, Lillie Ayers reached out to parents in order to ensure that their children would be physically, socially, and emotionally ready for school. In 2002, the United States District Court of the Northern District of Mississippi ordered Mississippi to spend $503 million to correct past neglect at the three black institutions.[12] The Ayers's lawsuit demonstrated that African Americans' long quest for quality education in Mississippi was far from over.

Black voters face an uphill battle in ameliorating the educational landscape. Even though Mississippi has more black elected officials than any other state, conservative white lawmakers continue to hold majorities in the state houses and on many local and county boards, preventing fundamental shifts in power and priorities. In 1997, the Mississippi legislature passed the Mississippi Adequate Education Program (MAEP) to improve the education of all students by making sure public schools had adequate resources.

Legislators, however, have only fully funded MAEP twice—in election years 2003 and 2007—since it was enacted. In fiscal year 2012, public elementary-secondary school systems nationwide spent an average of $10,608 per student while Mississippi spent $8,164.[13] Mississippi governor Phil Bryant's recommended budget for fiscal year 2015 fell over $280 million short of fully funding the MAEP formula, despite significant increases in state revenues.[14] The gap in funding makes clear that Mississippi's lawmakers understand that there is political currency in supporting adequate education even when they only give lip service to the implementation of measures that actually provide adequate education.

More troubling than Mississippi's underfunding of public education are the state's harsh disciplinary measures and school-to-prison pipeline. Corporal punishment remains in effect in many school districts. Students experience arrest and incarceration because of minor infractions such as talking back to a teacher, questioning authority, or violating the dress code. In 2012, the United States Department of Justice filed suit against the City of Meridian, Lauderdale County, and other actors who colluded to arrest and incarcerate students of color at alarmingly high rates for minor school offenses. The extreme approaches to school discipline have fostered learning environments that are the antithesis of the ones that CDGM women fostered in Head Start centers.

The issues confronting Mississippi's public schools expose a hard truth about the white ruling class's ability to change course in the face of liberal social reform. The civil rights movement outlawed segregation and disfranchisement, but failed to secure quality education as a right of all children. Thus, it is politically pragmatic today for lawmakers to champion initiatives such as MAEP even if they do not have the political will or desire to invest significant funds into implementation. This co-optation of a struggle—with Reconstruction-era roots—for quality black education illuminates the limitations of hard-fought battles for civil and legal rights. Segregated schools continue to exist after court-ordered desegregation. Poor-quality public schools remain the status quo even though laws exist to improve funding. Fannie Lou Hamer and others anticipated such white recalcitrance in the face of social revolution and attempted to mitigate it through initiatives such as CDGM. While Head Start was separate from the public school system, black parents desired and sought quality education for their children in both institutions.

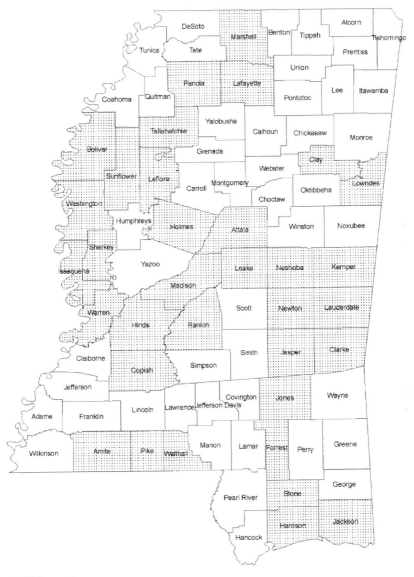

CDGM counties.

Mississippi's troubled public education system is a stark reminder that the African American freedom struggle was never simply about de jure segregation or disfranchisement. Black citizens sought freedom in all of its forms. Despite the well-founded suspicions of the federal government, the need for jobs, food, healthcare, and early childhood education led many black activists to participate in CDGM. Local people were not naïve about the limits of state-sponsored revolution. Rather, they had more confidence in their own abilities to transform their undemocratic communities with federal funds.

CDGM's brief three-year existence should not diminish the importance of its creation. The master's tools did not dismantle the master's house, but the radical Head Start program did pave the way for ordinary black people to continue their earlier quests for educational, economic, and racial justice. The program they fashioned brought dignity to local people and gave black parents a meaningful say in the education of their children. As Mississippians continue to debate the best ways to improve educational opportunities and outcomes in the state, they would do well to revisit the CDGM model that prioritized parental involvement and student self-discovery. The challenges are great, but so will be the rewards. The original spirit of CDGM, according to Unita Blackwell, was "full of faith that progress is possible."[15] Indeed it is.

Notes

Abbreviations

AHOEO • Administrative History of the Office of Economic Opportunity
Collection, Lyndon Baines Johnson Presidential Library and Archives,
University of Texas, Austin, Tex.

AM • Amzie Moore Papers, Wisconsin Historical Society, Madison, Wisc.

AY • Adam Yarmolinsky Papers, John F. Kennedy Presidential Library and
Museum, Boston, Mass.

BTV • Behind the Veil Oral History Project, John Hope Franklin Research Center,
Duke University, Durham, N.C.

CDGM • Child Development Group of Mississippi Papers, Wisconsin Historical
Society, Madison, Wisc.

COHCH • Center for Oral History and Cultural Heritage, McCain Library and
Archives, University of Southern Mississippi, Hattiesburg, Miss.

CSC • Community Studies Collection, Dickinson College, Carlisle, Pa.

DD • Doris Derby Papers, Manuscript, Archives and Rare Book Library,
Emory University, Atlanta, Ga.

DW • David Walls Collection on the Child Development Group of Mississippi,
McCain Library and Archives Special Collections, University of Southern
Mississippi, Hattiesburg, Miss.

HBC • Hodding and Betty Carter Papers, Special Collections, Mississippi State
University Library, Mississippi State, Miss.

HW • Hilda C. Wilson Papers, Mississippi Department of Archives and History,
Jackson, Miss.

JD • John Dittmer Personal Collection, New Castle, Ind.

JH • James M. Houston Papers, Wisconsin Historical Society, Madison, Wisc.

JM • James Howard Meredith Collection, Department of Archives and Special
Collections, University of Mississippi Library, Oxford, Miss.

JMR • James McRee Papers, Mississippi Department of Archives and History,
Jackson, Miss.

JS • John C. Stennis Collection, Congressional and Political Research Center,
Mississippi State University Library, Mississippi State, Miss.

LAP • Local Area Problem Files, Community Services Administration,
National Archives II, College Park, Md.

LB • Lee Bankhead Papers, Wisconsin Historical Society, Madison, Wisc.

LBJOH • Lyndon Baines Johnson Oral History Collection, Lyndon Baines
   Johnson Presidential Library and Archives, University of Texas, Austin, Tex.
LF • Lee Reiff Collection, Mississippi State University Special Collections,
   Mississippi State, Miss.
MH • Marvin Hoffman Personal Collection, Chicago, Ill.
ML • Marilyn Lowen Head Start Records, Mississippi Department of Archives and
   History, Jackson, Miss.
MSSC • Mississippi State Sovereignty Commission Digital Archives, Mississippi
   Department of Archives and History, Jackson, Miss.
MWANRC • Margaret Walker Alexander National Research Center, Jackson State
   University, Jackson, Miss.
NAACP • National Association for the Advancement of Colored People Papers,
   Library of Congress, Washington, D.C.
RBOHC • Ralph Bunche Oral History Collection, Moorland-Spingarn Research
   Center, Howard University, Washington, D.C.
RSS • Robert Sargent Shriver Papers, John F. Kennedy Presidential Library and
   Museum, Boston, Mass.
SB • Sally Belfrage Papers, Wisconsin Historical Society, Madison, Wisc.
SNCC • Student Nonviolent Coordinating Committee Papers (microfilm)
STFOEO • State Files, Office of Economic Opportunity Records of the
   Director, Community Services Administration, National Archives II,
   College Park, Md.
SUFOEO • Subject Files, Office of Economic Opportunity Records of the
   Director, Community Services Administration, National Archives II,
   College Park, Md.
TCA • Tougaloo College Archives, L. Zenobia Coleman Library, Tougaloo
   College, Tougaloo, Miss.
TL • Tom Levin Papers, Martin Luther King Center for Nonviolent Social Change,
   Atlanta, Ga.
UPC • United Presbyterian Church in the United States of America, Board of
   National Missions, Department of Mission Development Records, Presbyterian
   Historical Society, Philadelphia, Pa.
WHCFCF • White House Central Files Confidential Files, Lyndon Baines Johnson
   Presidential Library and Archives, University of Texas, Austin, Tex.

Introduction

1. Hamer, "To Praise Our Bridges," 327.
2. "Hotel Closes in Jackson," *Gazette-Virginian*, 7 July 1964; Dittmer, *Local People*, 276–77; *James* Cobb, *The Most Southern Place on Earth*, 260. In June 1966, Meredith March organizers hoped to use the event to compel federal registrars to come into a host of black-majority counties including Grenada, Tallahatchie, Bolivar, and Panola counties. See Joseph, *Stokely*, 105.

3. Historian Hassan Jeffries labeled the full benefits of freedom as "freedom rights." Jeffries asserted that African Americans wanted their "freedom rights," defined as the "fundamental civil rights and the basic human rights that whites continued to deny them, including the franchise, quality education, and the chance to earn a decent living." See Jeffries, *Bloody Lowndes*, 37.

4. Kuntz, "A Lost Legacy," 3.

5. Gillette, *Launching the War on Poverty*, esp. xviii–xix, 77.

6. *The Quiet Revolution*, 4.

7. Stossel, *Sarge*, 417; Vinovskis, *The Birth of Head Start*, 68–93.

8. Charles Cobb, *This Nonviolent Stuff'll Get You Killed*, 230.

9. Dittmer, *Local People*, 302, 320–21; Joseph, *Stokely*, 75–77.

10. Rainwater and Yancey, *The Moynihan Report*.

11. Kuntz, "A Lost Legacy," 17.

12. Payne, "Men Led, but Women Organized," 2.

13. Beginning in 1973, Head Start required its teachers to have a Child Development Associate (CDA) credential to improve teaching quality.

14. "Histories of Children, Employees, Centers and Community Support," box 1, folder 15, ML.

15. Bolton, *The Hardest Deal of All*.

16. Davis, "The Three R's—Reading, 'Riting, and Race," 5–6; Hamer, "To Praise Our Bridges," 327–28.

17. Dittmer, *Local People*, 257–60.

18. Blackwell with Morris, *Barefootin'*, 32–33.

19. "A Look at 'Head Start,'" *Jackson Daily News*, 21 May 1965, 8.

20. Historically, federal government programs had propped up white supremacy in Mississippi. During Reconstruction, many Freedmen's Bureau officials colluded with white planters to maintain control over the black labor supply and force freedmen to remain on plantations. A similar pattern prevailed when the Mississippi Delta experienced a catastrophic flood that left over half of the region under water. While white women and children were taken to higher ground, black men, women, and children were forced to remain in unsafe refugee camps under the watchful eyes and sharp bayonets of national guardsmen because planters wanted an adequate labor supply when the waters receded. For more information, see Cimbala, *Under the Guardianship of the Nation*, 50–79; Nieman, *To Set the Law in Motion*, 3–5; Foner, *Reconstruction*, 149–50; Barry, *Rising Tide*; Daniel, *Breaking the Land*, esp. 91–98; Katznelson, *When Affirmative Action was White*.

21. Hamlin, *Crossroads at Clarksdale*, 4–5.

22. See, for example, Moynihan, *Maximum Feasible Misunderstanding*; Matusow, *The Unraveling of America*; Murray, *Losing Ground*.

23. Dailey, Gilmore, and Simon, *Jumpin' Jim Crow*, 5.

24. See, for example, Orleck, *Storming Caesars Palace*; Cazenave, *Impossible Democracy*; Germany, *New Orleans After the Promises*; Ashmore, *Carry It On*; Korstad and Leloudis, *To Right These Wrongs*; Orleck and Hazirjian, *The War on Poverty*.

25. Former OEO employee and later CDGM employee Polly Greenberg first described CDGM as black Mississippians' move from protest to program. See Greenberg, *Devil Has Slippery Shoes*, inside cover.

26. Nancy Naples coined the term "activist mothering." See Naples, *Grassroots Warriors*.

Chapter One

1. Hutchinson, *Code of Mississippi*, Article 3, 16 January 1823, 526; Williams, *Self Taught*, 18–21.

2. Span, *From Cotton Field to Schoolhouse*, 32.

3. "Freedmen's Bureau Inspectors Report, 1 January 1866," *Semi-Annual Report on Schools for Freedmen*, 5.

4. Anderson, *The Education of Blacks in the South*, 4–32.

5. Du Bois, *Black Reconstruction in America*; Anderson, *The Education of Blacks in the South*; *Laws of the State of Mississippi*, 17; Bolton, *The Hardest Deal of All*, 7–8; Span, *From Cotton Field to Schoolhouse*, 126.

6. *Annual Report of the Superintendent*, 66–74.

7. Bolton, *The Hardest Deal of All*, 8.

8. Noble, *Forty Years of the Public Schools*, 28–32, 49; Bolton, *The Hardest Deal of All*, 8.

9. Noble, *Forty Years of the Public Schools*, 52–54; Bolton, *The Hardest Deal of All*, 10.

10. Bolton, *The Hardest Deal of All*, 14.

11. Loewen and Sallis, *Mississippi*, 186–88; McMillen, *Dark Journey*, 35–48; Parker, *Black Votes Count*, 26–27; U.S. Commission on Civil Rights, *Voting in Mississippi*, 4.

12. McMillen, *Dark Journey*, 41–48; Parker, *Black Votes Count*, 26–27; U.S. Commission on Civil Rights, *Voting in Mississippi*, 4; In 1954, when only 4 percent of eligible black voters in the state were registered, the Mississippi legislature passed an amendment requiring applicants to write an interpretation of a section of the state constitution given them by the registrar. See Dittmer, *Local People*, 52–53.

13. Hahn, *A Nation Under Our Feet*, 127, 445; Cresswell, *Rednecks, Redeemers, and Race*, 117–20.

14. U.S. Commission on Civil Rights, *Voting in Mississippi*, 8.

15. Noble, *Forty Years of the Public Schools*, 96.

16. McMillen, *Dark Journey*, 76–77.

17. Du Bois, *The Negro Common School*, 77.

18. *Biennial Report and Recommendations*.

19. James Cobb, *The Most Southern Place on Earth*, vii.

20. Woodruff, *American Congo*, 25.

21. McMillen, *Dark Journey*, 93.

22. *Biennial Report and Recommendations*, 64, 90.

23. Bolton, *The Hardest Deal of All*, 12; McMillen, *Dark Journey*, 229; Dittmer, *Local People*, 13.

24. Wright, *Black Boy*, 190.

25. Lillie Ayers, interview with author, 10 August 2009, Glen Allan, Miss.

26. Blackwell with Morris, *Barefootin'*, 10, 12–13.

27. McMillen, *Dark Journey*, 230–32.

28. Ibid.; Eura Bowie, interview with Paul Ortiz, 9 August 1995, tape recording, BTV.

29. Payne, *I've Got the Light of Freedom*, 281–83.

30. Hudson and Curry, *Mississippi Harmony*, 13, 24.

31. Ibid., 17–19.

32. Ibid., 6–7; McMillen, *Dark Journey*, 84; Historian James D. Anderson coined the term "double taxation" to describe African Americans' practice of making private contributions to finance public schools, since southern school boards used black tax dollars to fund white schools. See Anderson, *The Education of Blacks in the South*, 156, 170, 179; Bolton, "Mississippi's School Equalization Program," 789, see footnote 14; Franklin and Carter, *Cultural Capital and Black Education*.

33. Hudson and Curry, *Mississippi Harmony*, 20.

34. Ibid., 60.

35. Bolton, "Mississippi's School Equalization Program," 784; Katherine Mellen Charron coined the phrase "activist educator" to describe the long tradition of clandestine civil rights activism among black teachers in the South. See Charron, *Freedom's Teacher*; "Takes Lead in Teacher Pay Fight," *Chicago Defender*, 27 March 1948, 16; "Miss. Loses Pay Case Dismissal," *Philadelphia Tribune*, 12 July 1949; "Mississippi Pay Suit Killed," *Chicago Defender*, 4 March 1950, 1; Dittmer, *Local People*, 35–36; Bolton, *The Hardest Deal of All*, 46.

36. Dittmer, *Local People*, 59; Payne, *I've Got the Light of Freedom*, 34–35. For an in-depth account of the birth of the Citizens' Council movement, see McMillen, *The Citizens' Council*.

37. "Reports Economic Sanctions Being Made Against Negroes," *Atlanta Daily World*, 14 December 1955.

38. Moye, *Let the People Decide*, 33; Katagiri, *The Mississippi State Sovereignty Commission*.

39. Katagiri, *The Mississippi State Sovereignty Commission*, 167.

40. Dittmer, *Local People*, 102–3.

41. Ibid., 103–4; "Voter Registration and Direct Action in McComb, MS," Civil Rights Movement Veterans, http://www.crmvet.org/tim/timhis61.htm#1961mccomb.

42. After July 1984, the Mississippi State Board of Education appointed the State Superintendent of Public Education.

43. For more on the Citizenship Schools, see Charron, *Freedom's Teacher*.

44. Dittmer, *Local People*, 105; "Voter Registration and Direct Action in McComb, MS."

45. Dittmer, *Local People*, 105–9.

46. Parker, *Black Votes Count*, 28.

47. Payne, *I've Got the Light of Freedom*, 28–66.

48. Until 1971, the United States Postal Service was known as the United States Post Office Department.

49. Giddings, *When and Where I Enter*, 285.

50. Dittmer, *Local People*, 118–19.

51. Parker, *Black Votes Count*, 2; Dittmer, *Local People*, 200–207; Branch, *Pillar of Fire*, 158.

52. Dittmer, *Local People*, 109, 215.

53. Parker, *Black Votes Count*, 23.

54. Dittmer, *Local People*, 215–19, 244. Carson, *In Struggle*, 77–100; Payne, *I've Got the Light of Freedom*, 120–24, 297–306. For more information on the 1964 Freedom Summer, see McAdam, *Freedom Summer*.

55. Marshall, *Student Activism and Civil Rights in Mississippi*, 120; Adickes, *The Legacy of a Freedom School*, 46. For more on the Medical Committee for Human Rights, see Dittmer, *The Good Doctors*.

56. Moye, "Discovering What's Already There," 263; McAdam, *Freedom Summer*, 96; Dittmer, *Local People*.

57. Moody, *Coming of Age in Mississippi*, 132–327; Charles Cobb, "Prospectus for a Summer Freedom School Program."

58. A freedom school also existed in Prince Edward County, Virginia, where white school officials closed the schools there rather than desegregate; white children attended private academies, and black children either relocated to other areas or simply stayed home without any schooling. Subsequently, the United Federation of Teachers opened a freedom school that offered reading, writing, and arithmetic to Prince Edward's black students who had no other educational opportunities. See Payne and Strickland, *Teach Freedom*, 72; Adickes, *The Legacy of a Freedom School*, 29–30.

59. Payne and Strickland, *Teach Freedom*, 77.

60. Ibid., 73.

61. Emery, Braselmann, and Gold, "Freedom School Curriculum."

62. Zinn, *The Zinn Reader*, 531.

63. Adickes, *The Legacy of a Freedom School*, 44; Emery, Braselmann, and Gold, "Freedom School Curriculum," 18–19.

64. Belfrage, *Freedom Summer*, 91–92.

65. Emery, Braselmann, and Gold, "Freedom School Curriculum," 18.

66. Ibid., 96–97; "Resistance to Freedom Schools," Civil Rights Movement Veterans, http://www.crmvet.org/docs/640810_fs_bomb-responses.pdf; Sturkey and Hale, *To Write in the Light of Freedom*.

67. *Student Voice*, 15 July 1964, 2; "Freedom School Data," reel 1, segment 6, SB; Hudson and Curry, *Mississippi Harmony*, 82.

68. Payne and Strickland, *Teach Freedom*, 73.

69. Emery, Gold, and Braselman, *Lessons from Freedom Summer*, 288–97; Adickes, *The Legacy of a Freedom School*, 89–91.

70. Dittmer, *Local People*, 273; Hudson and Curry, *Mississippi Harmony*, 85. Hudson's name appears on the official list of delegates, but her husband served in her place.

71. "MFDP Challenge to the Democratic Convention," Civil Rights Movement Veterans, http://www.crmvet.org/info/mfdp_atlantic.pdf.

Chapter Two

1. Hudson and Curry, *Mississippi Harmony*, 47–49, 66, 88.

2. Bolton, *The Hardest Deal of All*, 102–103; "Judge Dismisses Last Miss. Suit to Mix Schools," *Pittsburgh Courier*, 6 July 1963, 17; "Orders Miss. Schools To Integrate In Fall," *Chicago Defender*, 8 July 1964.

3. Bolton, *The Hardest Deal of All*, 150; "Tiny Girl Totes a Heavy Burden," *Chicago Defender*, 3 September 1964, 5; Gail Falk, "How Debra Lewis Desegregated a School," *Southern Courier*, 11–12 February 1967, 4; Ponchitta Pierce, "The Mission of Marian Wright," *Ebony*, June 1966, 100.

4. For more on the Delta Ministry, see Newman, *Divine Agitators*.

5. Hudson and Curry, *Mississippi Harmony*, 88; Marshall, *Student Activism and Civil Rights*, 189.

6. Marvin Hoffman, a CDGM Central Staff member during the 1965 summer and again from spring 1966 until summer 1967, generously allowed the author access to his unpublished memoir on CDGM, "The Story of One Center."

7. *America's War on Poverty: Given a Chance.*

8. Lavaree Jones, Jr., Mahalia Jackson, and Quinous Johnson (children of Lavaree Jones, Sr.), interview with author, 24 March 2010, Jackson, Miss.

9. Wilson, *Education for Negroes in Mississippi*, 48.

10. Tom Levin, interview with Gordon Henderson, 1 July 1965, box 3, folder 23, TL.

11. Polly Greenberg, interview and correspondence with author, 25 March 2010, Jackson, Miss.

12. Ibid.; Adickes, *The Legacy of a Freedom School*, 34–35; Payne and Strickland, *Teach Freedom*, 71–72.

13. Friedman, "Tom Levin and Polly Greenberg's Reflections," 16–17.

14. Erika Duncan, "Encounters; Long After '65, Still Fighting to Overcome," *New York Times*, 10 September 1995.

15. Original CDGM Proposal for Community Action Program Funds, box 4, folder 25: Proposal Original, CDGM.

16. For more on the Medical Committee for Human Rights, see Dittmer, *The Good Doctors*.

17. "Matt Herron Civil Rights Movement Biography," Civil Rights Movement Veterans, http://www.crmvet.org/vet/herronm.htm; Findlay, *Church People in the Struggle*, 117; Adickes, *The Legacy of a Freedom School*, 34–35; Payne and Strickland, *Teach Freedom*, 71–72.

18. Polly Greenberg, telephone interview with author, 21 November 2006.

19. Memorandum to Sargent Shriver from Robert Cooke, box 70, folder: Head Start Papers, RSS; Greenberg, interview, 25 March 2010.

20. Polly Greenberg provided the author with a biographical statement. The statement is in the author's possession.

21. Stossel, *Sarge*, 117–29.

22. Shriver aggressively fought to have the War on Poverty exclusively under the auspices of OEO, a new federal agency, rather than assign individual antipoverty programs to existing departments (i.e., Labor, HEW). See Stossel, *Sarge*, 367–68; Gillette, *Launching the War on Poverty*, 22–23, 89.

23. Gillette, *Launching the War on Poverty*, 130.

24. Adam Yarmolinsky, Memorandum on War on Poverty, 31 July 1964, AY.

25. Sargent Shriver, address, National Association for the Advancement of Colored People, Washington, D.C., 24 June 1964, box 45, folder: Speech, RSS.

26. Sargent Shriver, address, National Committee for Community Development, Washington, D.C., 10 March 1965, box 46, folder: Speech, RSS. Other senior OEO officials shared the view that community action was a way to foster black political participation in the South. See Gillette, *Launching the War on Poverty*, 202.

27. Greenberg, *Devil Has Slippery Shoes*, 12–14.

28. Jones and Fowler, *The Head Start Program*, 7; Memorandum from Jule Sugarman to Theodore M. Berry, 21 May 1965, box 5, folder: CAP/Berry-MS, STFOEO; Greenberg, *Devil Has Slippery Shoes*, 12–14.

29. Richard Boone, telephone interview with author, 27 April 2009. Also see Gillette, *Launching the War on Poverty*, 67.

30. Carson, *In Struggle*, 128–29; Dittmer, *Local People*, 326; Stokely Carmichael, interview with Judy Richardson, 7 November 1988, Eyes on the Prize II interviews.

31. *America's War on Poverty: Given a Chance*; "History of Agency by Joan Bowman," box 3, folder 20, TL; author correspondence with Greenberg.

32. James Cobb, "Somebody Done Nailed Us on the Cross," 917.

33. Dittmer, *Local People*, 385.

34. Greenberg, *Devil Has Slippery Shoes*, 18–22.

35. "History of Agency by Joan Bowman," box 3, folder 20, TL.

36. Ibid., folder 20, TL; Alice Giles, telephone interview with author, 16 April 2009; Minnie Ripley, interview with R. Wayne Pyle, 7 November 1979, transcript, 46, COHCH.

37. Carson, *In Struggle*, 151.

38. Hollis Watkins, interview with author, 27 March 2010, Jackson, Miss.

39. Ibid.; Greenberg, *Devil Has Slippery Shoes*, 23–24. For more on Frank Smith's community organizing through the SNCC, see Dittmer, *Local People*, 135, 148.

40. Watkins, interview.

41. Ibid.

42. Proposal for Structure of Child Development Project for Mississippi Communities-Summer 1965, box 1, folder: Contracts 3, TL; CDGM Board Meeting minutes, 3 May 1965, box 5, folder 12, TL; Greenberg, *Devil Has Slippery Shoes*, 29–30. Even though black Mississippians made up two-thirds of the Delta population, only

two black citizens held elected office: the mayors of Mound Bayou and Winstonville, two all-black villages.

43. Economic Opportunity Act of 1964.

44. Dittmer, *Local People*, 87–89; information taken from keynote address by Joyce Ladner at the 50th Anniversary of the Founding of SNCC, 17 April 2010, Shaw University, Raleigh, North Carolina.

45. Barnaby Keeney Memorandums, March–April 1964, JD; Dittmer, *Local People*, 234–35.

46. Greenberg, *Devil Has Slippery Shoes*, 32.

47. Greenberg, interview, 25 March 2010.

48. Sargent Shriver, address, Joint Session of the West Virginia Legislature, Charleston, W.V., 1 March 1965, box 45, RSS.

49. "Mississippi Headstart Programs Announced," *Jackson Daily News*, 19 May 1965, 5; Stossel, *Sarge*, 403–6; "Project Head Start Local Project Approval," box 1, JMR; Jones and Fowler, *The Head Start Program*, 7.

50. List of CDGM Centers and Chairmen, box 3, folder 4, AM.

51. Memorandum to Jule Sugarman from Dudley Morris, May 1965, box 5, folder: CAP/Berry-MS, STFOEO.

52. "A Look at 'Head Start,'" *Jackson Daily News* 21 May 1965, 8; Virginia Woodward, "Action Program," *Hattiesburg American*, 6 July 1965.

53. CDGM Press Release, 18 May 1965, box 3, folder 1, AM; "Jackson Head Start Project Takes Shape," *Jackson Daily News*, 26 May 1965.

54. Ashmore, *Carry It On*, 76–77.

55. List of Central Coordinating Staff, Series 1, box 5, folder 7, JS; Greenberg, interview, 25 March 2010.

56. CDGM Original Proposal, box 4, folder 25, CDGM.

57. "Position Description: Resource Teacher," box 2, folder 17, ML.

58. "How to Recruit the Center Staff," undated, CDGM; "CDGM Fact Sheet," undated, CDGM; Polly Greenberg to Center Chairmen, 12 October 1965, CDGM.

59. Greenberg, interview, 25 March 2010.

60. Memorandum from Gordon Wilcox to Harassment File, box 3, folder 14, TL.

61. Greenberg, *Devil Has Slippery Shoes*, 72.

62. Author correspondence with Polly Greenberg.

63. Mills, *Something Better for My Children*, 132.

64. Ibid., 178–79; *The Quiet Revolution*, 33.

65. Owen Brooks, Frank Hudson, Edna Moneton, and Thelma Barnes, interview with Lavaree Jones and J. F. Jones, 28 April 1989, transcript, p. 11, MWANRC. Thelma Barnes was hired by Art Thomas to be the Delta Ministry administrative assistant in the Greenville office. Greenville had never before had black administrative assistants and several local white businessmen complained about seeing Barnes in the Delta Ministry Office. Rather than fire her as requested, Thomas purchased blinds.

66. Mississippi Action for Community Education Application, box 7, folder 15, TL.

67. U.S. Congress, *Papers Omitted*, 9 February 1965, 873–75; Reinhard, "Politics of Change," 216; "List of Center Demographics," box 1, folder 7, TL; George Slaff, "Five Seats in Congress: 'The Mississippi Challenge,'" *Nation*, May 17, 1965, 526–29.

68. David Nevin, "Struggle that Changed Glen Allan," *Life*, 29 September 1967, 109.

69. Mills, *Something Better For My Children*, 5; "Histories of Children, Employees, Centers and Community Support," box 1, folder 15, ML; "List of Center Demographics," box 1, folder 7, TL; "List of Areas and Area Codes," SCR# 6-45-4-13-13-1-1; Hudson and Curry, *Mississippi Harmony*; Payne, *I've Got the Light of Freedom*, 176.

70. Umoja, *We Will Shoot Back*, 160–61.

71. Hudson and Curry, *Mississippi Harmony*, 69.

72. Silver, *Mississippi*.

73. "List of Student Summer Job Placement Departments Contacted," 1966 Summer, reel 15, CDGM.

74. "History of Agency by Joan Bowman," box 3, folder 20, TL.

75. Harriet Feinberg, "Letter to Friends," 18 July 1965, box 1, folder 11, TL.

76. Loewen and Sallis, *Mississippi*, 22; Andrews, *Freedom Is a Constant Struggle*, 66.

77. *A Chance for Change*.

78. Greenberg, *Devil Has Slippery Shoes*, 67.

79. Ibid., 69.

80. Ritterhouse, *Growing Up Jim Crow*.

81. For more on education as a vehicle for liberation, see Fairclough, *A Class of Their Own*.

82. "Program of the First CDGM Four-Day Orientation," box 1, folder 2, DW; Greenberg, *Devil Has Slippery Shoes*, 76–77.

83. "Orientation Program," DW; Greenberg, *Devil Has Slippery Shoes*, 81, 114.

84. "CDGM Program Orientation," DW; Greenberg, *Devil Has Slippery Shoes*, 53.

85. "White Man Held in Shooting at Racial Church Center," *New York Times*, 26 June 1965; "White Man Convicted," *Clarion-Ledger*, 1 July 1965; memo from Gordon Wilcox to Robert Clempert and Ivan Scott, 25 June 1965, box 3, folder 14, TL; memo from Gordon Wilcox to Harassment File, 4 July 1965, box 3, folder 14, TL; Mills, *Something Better for My Children*, 61; Choctaw Report, box 3, folder 15, TL.

86. Greenberg, *Devil Has Slippery Shoes*, 416; Jim Dann's Valewood Report, box 3, folder 1, TL; Noel Workman, "No Report Made in Sharkey Affair," *Delta Democrat Times*, 1 August 1965; Marilyn Lowen, interview with author, 27 March 2010, Jackson, Miss.; Nevin, "Struggle that Changed Glen Allan."

87. O'Reilly, *Racial Matters*, 247; Greenberg, *Devil Has Slippery Shoes*, 106.

88. Jim Dann's Valewood Report, TL.

89. CDGM newsletter #2, box 1, folder 2, CDGM.

90. Chilcoat and Ligon, "We Talk Here."

91. "Science in our Center," p. 61, Resource Teachers Manual, box 1, folder 1, CDGM.

92. Greenberg, *Devil Has Slippery Shoes*, 3.

93. Duncan, "Encounters," *New York Times*, 10 September 1995.

94. "Art Work in CDGM Centers," p. 111, Resource Teachers Manual, box 1, folder 1, CDGM.

95. Greenberg, *Devil Has Slippery Shoes*, 156–57.

96. *Zoo Book*, 2.

97. "Oxford Workshop," 17 May 1966, box 1, folder: 1, ML.

98. "What Shall I Tell My Children Who Are Black," Teacher's Manual, box 1, folder 1, HW.

99. Letter to Tom Levin from Robert H. Fentress, 8 June 1965, reel 14, CDGM.

100. *Ebony*'s focus on material success has long made it the subject of critique. The magazine began in 1945, during a time when black media outlets were speaking out against racial discrimination and violence, yet its editors chose to focus on "the happier side of Negro life." See Green, *Selling the Race*, esp. 130–32.

101. Lowen, interview.

102. "CDGM Teachers Helpful Hints on Discipline," box 2, folder 26, ML.

103. Greenberg, *Devil Has Slippery Shoes*, 349–50.

104. "Teacher Development and Program for Children," pp. 18–19, box 3, folder 1, JMR; Studies of Economic and Nutritional Factors, 5 October 1967, box 1, folder: 9, ML; Dittmer, *Local People*, 144.

105. "The Story of One Center," MH.

106. Grace Simmons, "Basic Lesson from Program Was Confidence," *Clarion-Ledger*, 2 July 1989, 1.

107. CDGM Materials, box 6, item 12, DD.

108. Dittmer, *The Good Doctors*, 230; Robert Smith, interview with author, 15 June 2012, Jackson, Miss.

109. Dittmer, *The Good Doctors*, 1–10, 126–27.

110. Smith, interview; Mason and Smith, *Beaches, Blood, and Ballots*.

111. "Histories of Children, Employees, Centers, Community Support," box 1, folder 15, ML; Greenberg, *Devil Has Slippery Shoes*, 194.

112. "Histories of Children, Employees, Centers, Community Support," box 1, folder 15, ML.

113. Greenberg, *Devil Has Slippery Shoes*, 193–94.

114. Ibid., 181.

115. Newfield, *A Prophetic Minority*, 69–72.

116. Dittmer, *The Good Doctors*, 18–19, 44.

117. Greenberg, *Devil Has Slippery Shoes*, 189.

118. "1st District Evaluation Meeting," 29 July 1965, box 3, folder 7, TL.

119. "Newsletter from Cary Day Care Center," box 1, folder 28, TL.

120. Greenberg, *Devil Has Slippery Shoes*, 87; John Mudd, telephone interview with author, 22 October 2009.

121. "The Story of One Center," MH.

122. "Big Push in ASCS Elections," *Mississippi Freedom Democratic Party Newsletter*, 5 November 1965 and 20 December 1965; Marvin Hoffman, interview with author, 26 October 2009, Chicago, Ill.; Daniel, *Dispossession*.

123. Greenberg, *Devil Has Slippery Shoes*, 48, 52–53, 111.

Chapter Three

1. Alice Giles, telephone interview with author, 16 July 2009.

2. For more on CDGM center debates about curriculum, see, for example, "Shaw, Bolivar County Evaluation by Edna Morton," box 2, folder 30, TL.

3. Giles, interview.

4. Ibid.

5. Ransby, *Ella Baker*, 183–85; Charron, *Freedom's Teacher*, 293–99; Charron and Cline, "'I Train the People to Do Their Own Talking,'" 47–48; Hamlin, *Crossroads at Clarksdale*, 87–88.

6. List of CDGM Centers and Chairmen, box 3, folder 4, AM; list of Central Coordinating Staff, Series 1, box 5, folder 7, JS.

7. For scholarship on the lived experiences and political activity of black clubwomen, see Shaw, *What a Woman Ought to Be and Do*; White, *Too Heavy a Load*; Height, *Open Wide the Freedom Gates*.

8. Minnie Ripley, interview with R. Wayne Pyle, 7 November 1979, transcript, 8, COHCH.

9. Ibid., 46.

10. Ibid., 50–51.

11. No records remain listing every single employee, because of CDGM's decentralized structure. The author used a random sampling of employee lists from various CDGM sites to calculate the percentage of women employed. Information gathered from materials within the CDGM Papers.

12. "Shaw Evaluation by Edna Morton," box 2, folder 30, TL.

13. Rural Organizing and Cultural Center, *Minds Stayed on Freedom*, 46–54.

14. Greenberg, *Devil Has Slippery Shoes*, 127–28; Paul Murray, telephone interview with author, 29 July 2014.

15. Annie Mae King, interview with Robert Wright, 27 September 1968, transcript, 18, 21, RBOHC.

16. Ibid., 2.

17. Ibid., 20.

18. Fore more on "activist mothering," see Naples, *Grassroots Warriors*; Hamlin, *Crossroads at Clarksdale*, 60–62.

19. Statement by Mary Frances Jordan, box 1, folder 31, TL.

20. Collins, "The Meaning of Motherhood in Black Culture," 172, 174. Collins has suggested that black women's experiences as othermothers were the impetus for their social activism.

21. "Volunteers Operate Local CDG School," *Vicksburg Citizens' Appeal*, 1 November 1965, 1.

22. Rainwater and Yancey, *The Moynihan Report*.

23. Charron, *Freedom's Teacher*, 5, 336–38.

24. Blackwell with Morris, *Barefootin'*, 149.

25. Lerner, *Black Women in White America*, 401–2; Payne, *I've Got the Light of Freedom*, 318.

26. Mary Lane, interview with Robert Wright, 12 July 1969, RBOHC.

27. Ibid.

28. Rogers, *Life and Death in the Delta*, 24–26, 65; Biography/History Summary, LB; "List of Demonstrators," 30 June 1965, SCR# 6-45-1-23-4-1-1, MSSC.

29. Friedman, "Exploiting the North-South Differential"; Newman, *Divine Agitators*, 90–93.

30. Hudson and Curry, *Mississippi Harmony*, 21–25.

31. Lillie Ayers, interview with author, 10 August 2009, Glen Allan, Miss.

32. Greenberg, *Devil Has Slippery Shoes*, 87.

33. Nareatha W. Naylor to Congressmen William Colmer, 24 May 1965, box 3, folder 16, TL.

34. "Local Groups Passed Up Project Head Start," *Hattiesburg American*, 3 June 1965, 1; "Shriver to Probe Local Head Start," *Hattiesburg American*, 17 June 1965, 1; "Mostly Local Negroes Run Project Head Start," *Clarion-Ledger*, 14 July 1965.

35. "Report on Hattiesburg, MS, by Zack J. Van Landingham," 17 December 1958 (of special note are pages 26–29), SCR#1-27-0-6-1-1-1 to SCR# 1-27-0-6-37-1-1, MSSC; Branch, *Pillar of Fire*, 52–53.

36. Memo from Frankie Stein to the File Regarding Hattiesburg, 17 June 1965, box 3, folder 16, TL.

37. Mississippi Action for Community Education Application, box 7, folder 15, TL; Branch, *Pillar of Fire*, 52–53.

38. Payne, *I've Got the Light of Freedom*, 352–54.

39. Eva Tisdale, telephone interview with author, 4 February 2010.

40. Greenberg, *Devil Has Slippery Shoes*, 418.

41. "Statement by Hattie B. Saffold," in Proposal for Full Year Head Program of the Child Development Group of Mississippi, box 6, DD.

42. Sojourner with Reitan, *Thunder of Freedom*, 56, 69–70, 119.

43. Rural Organizing and Cultural Center, *Minds Stayed on Freedom*, 24, 58; Virgie Saffold, interview with Diana Vernazza, 11 September 2000. The interviewer graciously granted the author access to her recorded interviews.

44. Virgie Saffold, interview.

45. Charles Cobb, *This Nonviolent Stuff'll Get You Killed*, 187.

46. Payne, *I've Got the Light of Freedom*, 176; Meier and Rudwick, *CORE*, 272. Clarence Chinn owned a nightclub in Canton that not only brought national acts including B. B. King and the Platters to town, but it also served as a meeting place for civil

rights workers. Mamie McClendon Chinn, interview with Kim Lacy Rogers and Jerry Ward, 7 July 1997, transcript, TCA.

47. Transcript, Chinn interview.

48. Greenberg, *Devil Has Slippery Shoes*; letter to Carl Hayden from Acting Comptroller General of the United States, 17 October 1966, Series 1, Subseries OEO, box 5, folder 12, JS; "Undercover Surveillance Memo," 21 August 1965, Series 1, Subseries OEO, box 5, folder 3, JS.

49. "Histories of Children, Employees, Centers and Community Support," box 1, folder 15, ML.

50. Ibid.

51. Ibid.; Loewen and Sallis, *Mississippi*, 283.

52. David Nevin, "Struggle that Changed Glen Allan," *Life*, 29 September 1967, 109; Constance Curry, et al, *Deep in Our Hearts*, 164.

53. Lavaree Jones, Jr., Mahalia Jackson, and Quinous Johnson (children of Lavaree Jones, Sr.), interview with author, 24 March 2010, Jackson, Miss.

54. Sundquist, *On Fighting Poverty*, 113.

55. Sarah Williams and Flossie Miller, interview with Kim Lacy Rogers and Owen Brooks, 7 March 1996, transcript, 80, CSC.

56. Ibid.

57. "Histories of Children, Employees, Centers and Community Support," box 1, folder 15, ML.

58. "My Life Story" by Roxie Meredith, box 7, folder 2, JM.

59. Payne, *I've Got the Light of Freedom*, 231, 233; Memo to Sewing Project in Canton from Tom Levin, 26 July 1965, box 6, folder: Headstart/CDGM, DD. For more on the Poor People's Corporation, see Sturkey, "Crafts of Freedom."

60. Velma Bartley, interview with Kim Lacy Rogers and Owen Brooks, 9 February 1996, transcript, 51–52, CSC.

61. Blackwell with Morris, *Barefootin'*, 148.

62. "The Story of One Center," MH.

63. Greenberg, *Devil Has Slippery Shoes*, 86.

64. "CDGM: Histories of Children, Employees, Centers, Community Support," box 1, folder 1, JH.

65. Ibid.

66. Histories of Children, Employees, Centers and Community Support," box 1, folder 15, ML; Greenberg, *Devil Has Slippery Shoes*, 236.

67. For example, by October 1965, CDGM teachers Vera Liddell of Moss Point, Mississippi, and Viola Clark of Cary, Mississippi, still had not been paid for work performed during the summer. See letters to Tom Levin, box 1, folder 14, TL.

68. "The Problem of Food and Transportation," box 1, folder 26, TL.

69. "Unsigned report from Hollandale resource teacher" (author believes that the writer was Harriet Feinberg), 18 July 1965, box 1, folder 11, TL.

70. Incompetent black leadership was an old trope made famous by historian William's Dunning's interpretations of Reconstruction. Writing from the viewpoint of defeated Confederates and slave owners, Dunning argued that African American participation in government led to a carnival of graft. See Dunning, *Reconstruction*.

71. "Evaluation: Happyland Center-Walthall Precinct," box 2, folder 9, TL.

72. "Brief Program Report on the Greenwood Center at the American Legion Hut," by Polly Greenberg, 15 July 1965, box 1, folder 11, TL.

73. Letter on Itta Bena Center by Willie E. McGee, n.d., box 2, folder 14, TL; Polly Greenberg, interview with author, 25 March 2010, Jackson, Miss.

74. "Art Work in CDGM Centers," Resource Teacher's Manual, p. 111, box 1, folder 1, CDGM.

75. "Teacher Development and Program for Children," pp. 18–19, box 3, folder 1, JMR; information about the naptime at Second Pilgrim's Rest center taken from a film announcement for *A Chance for Change*, a film made in 1965 about CDGM.

76. Gilbert Moses, Doris Derby, and John O'Neal founded the Southern Free Theater in 1963 at Tougaloo College. Derby and O'Neal were active in SNCC. Through the use of plays about the struggles of blacks in America, the Southern Free Theater worked to provide blacks with theater experience and to redress poor black southerners' lack of knowledge about their heritage.

77. Holsaert et al., *Hands on the Freedom Plow*, 443.

78. Peter Titelman, telephone interview with author, 18 February 2012.

79. Bernard Dinkin, telephone interview with author, 4 November 2013.

80. Ibid.

81. Marilyn Lowen, interview with author, 27 March 2010, Jackson, Miss.; Holsaert et al., *Hands on the Freedom Plow*, 550.

82. Lowen, interview.

83. Polly Greenberg, telephone interview with author, 22 September 2009.

84. Crespino, *In Search of Another Country*, 116; Head Start: With the Child Development Group of Mississippi, *Take This Hammer*, Smithsonian Folkways Records, 1967, NR 02690-CD.

85. CDGM Head Start, *Take This Hammer*.

86. "Sound Table," Resource Teachers Manual, box 4, vol. IV, TL.

87. Greenberg, interview, 25 March 2010; Greenberg, *Devil Has Slippery Shoes*, 369–90.

88. Greenberg, *Devil Has Slippery Shoes*, 401–3; Mississippi Civil Rights Project.

89. Greenberg, *Devil Has Slippery Shoes*, 390–92, 754–55.

90. Ibid.

91. Greenberg, interview, 25 March 2010; "Centers in Area Four Newsletter," box 1, folder 2, CDGM.

92. Transcript, Bartley interview, 53, CSC.

93. "Histories of Children, Employees, Centers, Community Support," box 1, folder: 15, ML.

94. "Background of the Child Development Group of Mississippi," box 16, folder: CDGM 1966, SUFOEO.

95. Giles, interview; Gaynette Flowers, telephone interview with author, 6 May 2010; Ayers, interview; transcript, Chinn interview.

96. Greenberg, *Devil Has Slippery Shoes*, 542–43.

97. Carson, *In Struggle*, 269–72; Dittmer, *Local People*, 328–37.

98. For more on racial tensions within CDGM see "Black-White Relations in CDGM," esp. 76–82, MH.

Chapter Four

1. Letter to Head Start Grantees, 23 August 1965, box 4, folder: Head Start 1965 (2 of 6), SUFOEO; Greenberg, *Devil Has Slippery Shoes*, 254.

2. Letter from Tracey Whitaker to Tom Levin, 18 August 1965, box 1, folder 2, CDGM.

3. Letter from Winson Hudson to Tom Levin, 24 August 1965, box 2, folder 4, TL; John Mudd, telephone interview with author, 22 October 2009.

4. Gene Roberts, "Antipoverty Aid Stirs Ire In South," *New York Times*, 7 March 1966, 16.

5. Morris Cunningham, "Poor Grammar 'Uncensored' in Head Start Textbooks," *Commercial Appeal*, 10 September 1965.

6. OEO provided states with money to set up state technical assistance agencies that would help local communities design and set up community action programs. Alabama officials, though reluctant to do so because of the civil rights connection, set up a state agency to coordinate the antipoverty effort. See Ashmore, *Carry It On*, 104–5; Aiken, *The Cotton Plantation South*, 240–47.

7. CDGM and Community Action, box 6, folder 13, CDGM; Greenberg, *Devil Has Slippery Shoes*, 58.

8. Aiken, *The Cotton Plantation South*, 246–50; CDGM and Community Action, box 6, folder 13, CDGM.

9. Letter from John Stennis to Erle Johnston, 13 September 1965, Series 1, box 4, folder 7, JS; Johnston, *Mississippi's Defiant Years*, 285; Dittmer, *Local People*, 371. The Mississippi State Sovereignty Commission was the same organization that in 1964 provided law enforcement officials with the make and model of the car driven by three civil rights workers in Neshoba County. The three men—James Chaney, Michael Schwerner, and Andrew Goodman—were murdered and placed in an earthen dam. See Katagiri, *The Mississippi State Sovereignty Commission*, 164–65.

10. Memorandum from Erle Johnston to Herman Glazier, 12 July 1965, SCR# 6-45-1-14-1-1-1, MSSC; memorandum from Erle Johnston to Herman Glazier, 8 July 1965, SCR# 6-45-1-13-1-1-1, MSSC.

11. Memorandum from Tom Scarborough to Director, Sovereignty Commission, 30 September 1965, SCR# 2-153-0-12-1-1-1, MSSC; "Unionist Scores Eastland Farm; Senator Denies Poverty Charge," *New York Times*, 16 July 1965, 24; "Freedom Labor Union Strengthens Its Strike," *Vicksburg Citizens' Appeal*, 24 May 1965, 1.

12. List of Center Demographics and Committee Members, box 1, folder 7, TL.

13. C. Frazier Landrum, M.D., to John Stennis, 20 July 1965, Series 1, box 4, folder 7, JS. Segregationists had long accused Highlander of being a communist institution as a way of discrediting the work that took place there. White and black activists including Anne Braden, Martin Luther King Jr., and Rosa Parks met at Highlander to discuss ways to improve social conditions in their respective communities.

14. Letter to John Stennis from Bryce Alexander, 24 August 1965, Series 1, box 4, folder 7, JS.

15. Letter to John Stennis from Walter Sillers, 8 September 1965, Series 1, Subseries OEO, box 4, folder 7, JS.

16. Letter to John Bell Williams from Sargent Shriver, 16 September 1966, SCR# 6-45-4-16-1-1-1 to 6-45-4-16-4-1-1, MSSC.

17. Letter to John Stennis from Governor Paul B. Johnson, 8 September 1965, Series 1, Subseries OEO, box 4, folder 7, JS.

18. Crespino, *In Search of Another Country*, 116–17.

19. Fry, *Debating Vietnam*, 3–5.

20. Emily Wagster, "Five Hundred Bid Stennis Farewell," *Clarion-Ledger*, 27 April 1995, reprinted in *Memorial Tributes*, 135.

21. Fry, *Debating Vietnam*, 5.

22. Sid Salter, "Character Judged By Stennis' Measure," *New Albany Gazette*, 26 April 1995, reprinted in *Memorial Tributes*, 130–31.

23. Anthony Leviero, "6 Senators Named As A Select Panel in M'Carthy Case," *New York Times*, 6 August 1954, 1; Batten, "Why the Pentagon Pays Homage to John Cornelius Stennis," *New York Times Magazine*, 167.

24. Fry, *Debating Vietnam*, 97. Interestingly, Stennis never spoke out publicly against the influx of federal dollars into his state for military bases, levee construction, or agricultural subsidies to planters. For more on the relationship between white southerners and federal largesse, see James Cobb, *The Most Southern Place on Earth*, 253–55.

25. "Financial Assistance," box 76: OEO Subject Files, folder: Poverty Study on Mississippi, RSS.

26. "Education Problem in Mississippi," box 76: OEO Subject Files, folder: Poverty Study on Mississippi, RSS.

27. Letter to Mrs. L. P. Newsome from John Stennis, 23 August 1965, Series 1, Subseries OEO, box 4, folder 6, JS.

28. Memo to Sargent Shriver from Dr. Robert Cooke, Series 1, Subseries OEO, box 5, folder 7, JS.

29. Irons, *Reconstituting Whiteness*.

30. Ward, *Defending White Democracy*, 106.

31. Letter to Sargent Shriver from John Stennis, 19 July 1965, box 4, folder: Head Start 1965, SUFOEO.

32. List of Mississippi Head Start Projects, 17 May 1965, Series 1, box 5, folder 11, JS.

33. U.S. Congress, Senate, Appropriations Subcommittee, *Supplemental Appropriations Hearing for 1966*, 522.

34. "Report on Investigation of Child Development Group of Mississippi," by William J. Miller and Paul J. Cotter, SCR# 6-45-2-1-17-1-1 to 6-45-2-1-21-1-1, MSSC. CDGM orientation sessions were held July 3–7 and July 7–11.

35. "Report on Investigation of Child Development Group of Mississippi," SCR# 6-45-2-1-16-1-1, 6-45-2-1-28-1-1, MSSC.

36. Ibid., SCR# 6-45-2-1-21-1-1 to 6-45-2-1-22-1-1, MSSC.

37. Ibid., SCR# 6-45-2-1-32-1-1 to 6-45-2-1-33-1-1, MSSC; Greenberg, *Devil Has Slippery Shoes*, 302.

38. Asch, *The Senator and the Sharecropper*, 227.

39. "Report of Interim Audit, Biloxi Municipal Separate School District," 9 September 1966, Series 1, Subseries OEO, box 5, folder 11, JS.

40. Memo to Sargent Shriver from Gillis W. Long, 13 July 1965, box 4, folder: Head Start 1965, SUFOEO; *Supplemental Appropriations Hearing*, 589.

41. Memo to Jule Sugarman from Theodore Berry, 14 July 1965, box 4, folder: Head Start 1965, SUFOEO.

42. *Supplemental Appropriations Hearing*, 590; Gillette, *Launching the War on Poverty*, 156–57.

43. Gillette, *Launching the War on Poverty*, 285.

44. Jule Sugarman to Dr. D. I. Horn, 31 July 1965, box 1, folder 4, CDGM.

45. Minutes, CDGM Board of Directors Meeting, 1 August 1965, box 5, folder 13, TL.

46. Ibid.

47. Gillette, *Launching the War on Poverty*, 284.

48. Greenberg, *Devil Has Slippery Shoes*, 265.

49. Ashmore, *Carry It On*, 271.

50. In 1967, school superintendents lobbied Congress to move Head Start from the OEO and into the Office of Education. See Kuntz, "A Lost Legacy," 10–11; Gillette, *Launching the War on Poverty*, 201–2.

51. Gillette, *Launching the War on Poverty*, 133. "Red diaper baby" is a term describing a child raised by radical parents.

52. Gillette, *Launching the War on Poverty*, 135, 138; Stossel, *Sarge*, 384–93.

53. Greenberg, *Devil Has Slippery Shoes*, 261–67; Minutes, CDGM Board of Directors Meeting, 1 August 1965, box 5, folder 13, TL.

54. Jule Sugarman to Dr. D. I. Horn, 31 July 1965, box 1, folder 4, CDGM.

55. Memo to Julius Richmond from Director of Audits, 1 November 1965, box 4, folder: Head Start 1965, SUFOEO.

56. Greenberg, *Devil Has Slippery Shoes*, 272.

57. Ibid., 272–75.

58. Minutes, CDGM Board Meeting, 7 August 1965, box 5, folder 13, TL.

59. Greenberg, *Devil Has Slippery Shoes*, 264, 283–84.

60. Minutes, CDGM Board Meeting, 7 August 1965, box 5, folder 13, TL; Greenberg, *Devil Has Slippery Shoes*, 284–85.

61. When testifying before Congress in October 1965, Sargent Shriver admitted that his office recommended that Tom Levin be terminated. See *Supplemental Appropriations Hearing*, 611; Joseph A. Loftus, "Poverty Center Is Reorganized," *New York Times*, 11 August 1965, 21; Greenberg, *Devil Has Slippery Shoes*, 283–84.

62. Hollis Watkins, interview with author, 27 March 2010, Jackson, Miss.

63. Hudson and Curry, *Mississippi Harmony*, 91; Marilyn Lowen, interview with author, 27 March 2010, Jackson, Miss.

64. Watkins, interview.

65. Martha Woodall, "Marriage-Counseling Pioneer Dies at 99," *Philadelphia Inquirer*, 4 May 1998; "Negro Housing Progress Reviewed at U.L. Confab, *Philadelphia Tribune*, 1 July 1958, 1.

66. John Mudd, interview; Greenberg, *Devil Has Slippery Shoes*, 332–34.

67. John Mudd, interview.

68. Letter to Head Start Grantee, 23 August 1966, box 4, folder: Head Start 1965 (2 of 6), SUFOEO.

69. Jule Sugarman, interview with Stephen Goodell, 14 March 1969, transcript, 8, Lyndon B. Johnson Presidential Library, Austin, Tex.; Ashmore, *Carry It On*, 71–73; Gillette, *Launching the War on Poverty*, 160–61, 199–200.

70. Memo ATG Workshop: Future CDGM and CAP, box 1, folder 7, CDGM.

71. In becoming involved in the antipoverty program to control the purse strings, CDGM opponents practiced "strategic accommodation." They preserved the priorities of the white ruling class while appearing to support programs for the poor. See Crespino, *In Search of Another Country*, 3, 11–12, 135–136.

72. Gordon Brown, "Shriver Admits Some 'Fiscal Weaknesses,'" *Hattiesburg American*, 16 August 1965, 1.

73. John Mudd, interview.

74. *Supplemental Appropriations Hearing*, 514–16. Because CDGM applied for a Head Start grant through an institution of higher education, the program was not subject to a governor's veto.

75. Ibid., 579–80.

76. Ibid.

77. Letter to Tom Levin from Jule Sugarman, 29 June 1965, box 1, folder 11, TL.

78. *Supplemental Appropriations Hearing*, 594–95; "Report on Investigation of Child Development Group of Mississippi," SCR# 6-45-2-1-21-1-1, MSSC.

79. "Statement of Sargent Shriver Before the Senate Appropriations Committee," 14 October 1965, box 1, folder 5, CDGM.

80. *Supplemental Appropriations Hearing*, 603.

81. "Arrests of Beulah Pair Is Uncovered," *Jackson Daily News*, 11 October 1965, 1.

82. *Supplemental Appropriations Hearing*, 604.

83. Ibid., 605.

84. Hubert Humphrey (D-Minn.), the majority whip charged with overseeing the legislation, chose Pastore as "captain" of the act's Title VI, which banned federal funding to racially discriminatory programs. See Graham, *Civil Rights and the Presidency*, 57; Loevy, *The Civil Rights Act of 1964*, 183.

85. *Civil Rights Act of 1963* (the bill originally had the date 1963 when it first went to committee).

86. "Phew Political Carton," *Jackson Daily News*, 15 October 1965, 8.

87. Blackwell with Morris, *Barefootin'*, 61; Dittmer, *Local People*, 366–68.

88. "Why We Are Here At the Greenville Air Force Base," 31 January 1966, box 52, folder: Notes Concerning the Delta Ministry 1964–1966, HBC.

89. Sue Thrasher, "Air Force Evicts Poor," *New South Student* 2 (February 1966): 11–12.

90. "Demonstrators Escorted From Base By Air Police; One Woman Jailed," *Delta Democrat Times*, 1 February 1966, 1.

91. Hilton, *The Delta Ministry*, 98–99; "Call to Chaos," *Delta Democrat Times*, 2 February 1966.

92. "Press Release," box 1, folder 5, CDGM.

93. Ibid.; Greenberg, *Devil Has Slippery Shoes*, 440.

94. "The Child Development Group of Mississippi," October 1966, box 1, folder 9, CDGM; CDGM Newsletter #6, box 1, folder 2, CDGM.

95. Velma Bartley, interview with Kim Lacy Rogers and Owen Brooks, 9 February 1996, transcript, 53, CSC.

96. *America's War on Poverty: Given a Chance*, part 2.

97. Vernazza, "Who Killed the Child Development Group of Mississippi," 52.

98. Letter to President Johnson from Roberta Lewis et al., 16 August 1965, box 1, folder 2, CDGM; Greenberg, *Devil Has Slippery Shoes*, 317.

99. Greenberg, *Devil Has Slippery Shoes*, 348.

100. Alean Adams, interview with author, 5 August 2009, Brandon, Miss.

101. Ibid.

102. Ibid.

103. James Cobb, *The Most Southern Place on Earth*, 270–71.

104. Copies of Telegram Texts, box 1, folder 2, CDGM.

105. "CDGM Press Release," 11 February 1966, box 16, folder: CDGM 1966, SUFOEO; Greenberg, *Devil Has Slippery Shoes*, 444.

106. Author conversation with Raylawni Branch, 21 October 2010, Hattiesburg, Mississippi.

107. "CDGM Press Release," 11 February 1966, box 16, folder: CDGM 1966, SUFEOE; Joseph A. Loftus, "Youthful Lobby Asks School Fund," *New York Times*, 12 February 1966, 56; Eve Edstrom, "Mississippi Children Hold Show 'n Tell To Ask for Head Start School," *Washington Post*, 12 February 1966, 1; "Tots Charm Solons Into Renewed Funds for CDGM Program," *Delta Democrat Times*, 13 February 1966, 3.

108. "Notice to the Press," 11 February 1966, box 16, folder: CDGM 1966, SUFOEO; Adam Fairclough defined "street theater" as acts of political drama geared toward the news media. See Fairclough, *Race and Democracy*, 386.

109. David Nevin, "Struggle that Changed Glen Allan," *Life*, 29 September 1967, 112.

110. Ibid.

111. Letter to Sargent Shriver from Mary Luckett, 24 August 1965, box 1, folder 28, TL; "Why Senator Stennis Attacks Us," box 1, folder 36, TL.

112. Lee Bandy, "Stennis, Williams Probe Large Grant," *Jackson Daily News*, 23 February 1966, 1; "The Nonsense in Farm Subsidies," *Chicago Tribune*, 26 June 1967; "Strengthening of Administration of Mississippi Head Start Program OEO Press Release," 23 February 1966, box 98, WE 8-1 Project Head Start, Confidential Files WE/MC, WHCFCF.

113. Inflation calculator, http://www.coinnews.net/tools/cpi-inflation-calculator/.

114. "Child Development Group of Mississippi," 89th Cong., 1st sess., *Congressional Record* (23 February 1966), 3837, 3896.

115. Bandy, "Stennis, Williams Probe Large Grant," *Jackson Daily News*, 2.

116. Telegram to the president from Paul B. Johnson, 23 February 1966, box 41, folder: Staff: White House Correspondence Jan.–June 1966, RSS.

117. John Childs, "Stennis Attacks OEO for Big Grant," 24 February 1966, *Delta Democrat Times*, 1.

118. See "Mid-Delta Group Receives $441,000 from OEO," *Delta Democrat Times*, 25 March 1966, 1.

119. Historian Joseph Crespino defined "practical segregationists" as those who shared the sentiments, but not the actions, of hardline segregationists who used emotional pledges of defiance to defend racial segregation into the 1960s. In response to civil rights, "practical segregationists" advocated realistic approaches that tried to maintain the appearance of good relations with African Americans and minimize federal interference. See Crespino, *In Search of Another Country*, 19.

120. On "outside agitators," see Crespino, *In Search of Another Country*, 71; Dittmer, *Local People*, 97.

121. Bolton, *The Hardest Deal of All*, 88; "A Report on School Integration in Issaquena and Sharkey Counties," fall 1965, reel 740, SNCC.

122. Barnes Carr, "Bolivar Committee to Study Poverty," *Delta Democrat-Times*, 27 June 1965; Letter to John Mudd from Theodore Berry, 28 April 1966, box 16, folder: CDGM Audit Files, STFOEO; Aiken, *The Cotton Plantation South*, 248.

123. Statement of Lee Bankhead, box 2, folder 8, AM; letter to Sargent Shriver from Mary Wince et al., 24 September 1965, box 3, folder 1, CDGM.

124. Greenberg, *Devil Has Slippery Shoes*, 523.

125. Letter to Eph Criswell from Colbert Crowe, 9 February 1968, Series 29, box 7, folder 2, JS.

126. Greenberg, *Devil Has Slippery Shoes*, 588.

127. Mike Smith, "War on Poverty Big Business in Mississippi," *Jackson Daily News*, 22 October 1966.

128. Transcript, Jule Sugarman interview, 8; Ashmore, *Carry It On*, 71–73; Gillette, *Launching the War on Poverty*, 160–61.

129. Christine Cox, "Anti-Poverty Headed by Alexander," *Delta Democrat Times*, 6 March 1966, 1.

130. Moye, *Let the People Decide*, 141–42.

131. Bryce Alexander to John Stennis, 24 August 1965, Series 1, box 4, folder 7, JS.

132. Jan Robertson, "Outgoing Anti-Poverty Chief Feels His Group Has Been Fair," *Delta Democrat Times*, 24 April 1966, 1.

133. Mills, *This Little Light of Mine*, 207; Charles McLaurin, interview with author, 11 August 2009, Indianola, Miss.

134. Fannie Lou Hamer quoted in Dittmer, *Local People*, 376; "Negroes Ask Apologies of Officials," *Delta Democrat Times*, 22 April 1966, 1. Many southern whites, in an attempt to display their superiority, refused to use the courtesy titles "Mr." or "Mrs." when addressing blacks. See James Cobb, *The Most Southern Place on Earth*, 163.

135. Testimony of Lee Bankhead, box 2, folder 8, AM.

136. Report on Bolivar County, 13 August 1965, SCR# 2-61-2-9-4-1-1, MSSC.

137. Petition to Sargent Shriver, Association of Communities of Bolivar County, n.d., box 2, folder 10, AM.

138. "The CAP Board of Bolivar County," by Sammie Rash, box 2, folder 8, AM.

139. Testimony of Lee Bankhead, box 2, folder 8, AM.

140. "Chronological History," box 3, folder 1, AM.

141. Andrews, "Social Movements," 88.

142. Greenberg, *Devil Has Slippery Shoes*, 523; Andrews, "Social Movements," 88–89; Mills, *This Little Light of Mine*, 210. For a more in-depth account of the battles between Sunflower County Progress and the ACSC, see Mills, 203–15.

Chapter Five

1. Dittmer, *Local People*, 391; Greenberg, *Devil Has Slippery Shoes*, 422; "Fire Destroys House Used for Headstart Classes," *Jackson Daily News*, 16 May 1966.

2. Gail Falk, "Judge Permits March—About A Year Later," *Southern Courier*, 7–9 July 1967, 1; Greenberg, *Devil Has Slippery Shoes*, 95.

3. "Shubuta Head-Start Committee Demands to the Board of Alderman," SCR# 2-100-0-54-3-1-1, MSSC; memo from Director of Sovereignty Commission, 1 September 1966, SCR# 2-100-0-46-1-1-1, MSSC.

4. Letter to Selective Service Local Board No. 13 from Mayor of Quitman, 16 September 1966, SCR# 2-100-0-56-1-1-1, MSSC; John Otis Sumrall, Appellant, v. United States of America, Appellee, 397 F.2d 924 (5th Cir. 1968); Sumrall, "Freedom at Home," 87–91. After losing an appeal on charges that he refused induction into the armed forces,

Sumrall became a fugitive, before the FBI finally arrested him in California. He served time in federal prison. For more information on Sumrall, see Jason Morgan Ward, "Caught Between Two Wars: Poverty Politics, Draft Resistance, and a Mississippi Family's Freedom Struggle," unpublished conference paper in author's possession.

5. "Administrative History of OEO, Volume 1, Part 1," 86–91, quote on 88, box 1, AHOEO.

6. Gillette, *Launching the War on Poverty*, 327.

7. Alfred Friendly, "Militant 'Poor' Decry Role in Poverty War," *Washington Post*, 17 January 1966, A2; Eve Edstrom, "Shriver Is Booed Out of Meeting," *Washington Post*, 15 April 1966, A1; George Ladner Jr. "Poverty War Just a Sham Battle, GOP Claims in Urging Changes," *Washington Post*, 8 July 1966, A2.

8. Greenberg, *Devil Has Slippery Shoes*, 471, 475.

9. Fry, *Debating Vietnam*, 97.

10. Mike Smith, "War on Poverty Big Business in Mississippi," *Jackson Daily News*, 22 October 1966.

11. "Stennis Asks Checks on CDG Operation," *Commercial Appeal*, 23 March 1966.

12. Community Action Memorandum No. 23-A, 26 August 1966, box 34 A, folder: CAP Memos 23 and 24, LAF.

13. CDGM Accusations and Answers Press Release, box 3, folder 2, AM.

14. Dittmer, *Local People*, 396–97.

15. "Stennis Would Halt Funds to CDGM," *Clarion-Ledger*, 23 August 1966; "State CDG Gave Food to Marchers," *Clarion-Ledger*, 24 August 1966; untitled report, 24 June 1966, SCR# 9-31-5-48-1-1-1, MSSC; telephone report, 24 June 1966, SCR# 9-31-5-48-1-1-1, MSSC.

16. CDGM Accusations and Answers, box 3, folder 2, AM.

17. Letter to D. I. Horn from Frank Sloan, 22 July 1966, box 3, folder 51, CDGM.

18. Kuntz, "A Lost Legacy," 14.

19. Records of the Director, reel 15, CDGM; Greenberg, *Devil Has Slippery Shoes*, 633–34.

20. Records of the Director, reel 15, CDGM, WHS; Greenberg, *Devil Has Slippery Shoes*, 633–34.

21. Records of the Director, reel 15, CDGM; "The Report," box 6, folder 6, CDGM.

22. Paul Murray, telephone interview with author, 29 July 2014.

23. Newman, "Hazel Brannon Smith."

24. Crespino, *In Search of Another Country*, 120–22.

25. Robert Walters, "OEO Charged with Spying on Poverty Project in South," *Washington Evening Star*, 4 October 1966, 1; William R. MacKaye, "Politics Behind OEO's Fund Cutoff, Head Start Project in Miss. Charges," *Washington Post*, 5 October 1966.

26. OEO Findings, box 38, folder: OEO Correspondence CDGM (1 of 3), RSS.

27. Carl Rowan, "Compromise May Save Mississippi Poverty Plan," *Washington Evening Star*, 9 November 1966.

28. "Statewide Meeting Flyer," box 6, DD; "CDGM State-Wide Public Hearing" photo, box 17, folder 5, STFOEO; Greenberg, *Devil Has Slippery Shoes*, 574, 584–85.

29. John Beckler, "8 in House GOP Charge Poverty War 'Scandals,'" *New York Times*, 29 May 1966.

30. Korstad and Leloudis, *To Right These Wrongs*, 297, 306.

31. Stossel, *Sarge*, 465.

32. Memo from KD, 7 September 1966, box 1, folder 7, CDGM; "CDGM Episode Discussed in Address by Aaron Henry," *Vicksburg Citizens' Appeal*, 23 November 1966, 1.

33. Aaron Henry, interview with Neil McMillen and George Burson, 1 May 1972, COHCH.

34. Dittmer, *Local People*, 341–43.

35. Payne, *I've Got the Light of Freedom*, 340; Asch, *The Senator and the Sharecropper*, 213; Hamlin, *Crossroads at Clarksdale*, 146.

36. Memorandum for the Director from Samuel Yette, 6 January 1967, box 38, folder 3, RSS; memo from KD, 7 September 1966, box 1, folder 7, CDGM Papers.

37. See Ashmore, *Carry It On*, 227.

38. Meeting with Marion Wright, Aaron Henry, Rev. McRee, 10 September 1966, box 1, folder 7, CDGM.

39. Payne, *I've Got the Light of Freedom*, 87, 340; Dittmer, *Local People*, 381–82.

40. Gail Falk, "OEO Decides: No Money For CDGM," *Southern Courier*, 8–9 October 1996, 2.

41. The federal government commissioned the Westinghouse Learning Corporation and Ohio University to conduct the first national evaluation of Head Start's quality and efficacy in 1969. The study found that the test scores of children who attended Head Start in its first fours years were not much different from the test scores of children who had not attended Head Start. Many elected officials and OEO employees promptly discredited the study. See Robert B. Semple Jr. "Head Start Pupils Found No Better Off Than Others," *New York Times*, 14 April 1969; John Herbers, "Director Defends Head Start's Work; Says It Aids Pupils," *New York Times*, 15 April 1969; "Finch Criticizes Head Start Study," *New York Times*, 25 April 1969.

42. Hodding Carter III, interview with author, 31 August 2009, Chapel Hill, N.C.

43. Editorial, *Delta Democrat Times*, 24 June 1964.

44. "Justice Must Prevail," *Delta Democrat Times*, 9 August 1964.

45. Carter, interview. Carter could not recall who phoned him, but it was most likely Douglass Wynn, a Greenville lawyer who was close to President Johnson and a leading Democrat in Mississippi. In July 1966, Wynn became the lawyer for the Mississippi Young Democrats, an organization run by Carter.

46. *Delta Democrat Times*, 6 March 1965; Newman, *Divine Agitators*, 37.

47. Newman, *Divine Agitators*, 85.

48. Carter, interview; Crespino, *In Search of Another Country*, 102–3.

49. Crespino, *In Search of Another Country*, 103–5.

50. Many white Mississippi Democrats felt betrayed by the national party in Atlantic City and began to not just support Republican candidates but to switch their party affiliation. Charles W. Pickering, a Laurel, Mississippi, lawyer and future federal judge, switched from the Democratic to the Republican Party in 1964. See Crespino, *In Search of Another Country*, 103.

51. Draper, *Conflicts of Interests*, 150–53; Crespino, *In Search of Another Country*, 209–10.

52. Crespino, *In Search of Another Country*, 210.

53. Carter, interview.

54. Dittmer, *Local People*, 378. According to historian Joseph Crespino, the MDC went to great lengths to "avoid the stigma of being a civil rights organization." See Crespino, *In Search of Another Country*, 209.

55. McPherson, *A Political Education*, 353.

56. "Charter of Incorporation of Mississippi Action for Progress, Inc.," 13 September 1966, SCR# 6-45-3-71-1-1-1, MSSC.

57. "Information on Mississippi Action for Progress: Who Are Their Board Members and What Are Their Ties?," box 5, folder 1, AM.

58. List of Mississippi Businessmen, November 1962, SCR# 1-67-3-26-1-1-1, MSSC.

59. "Charter of Incorporation of Mississippi Action for Progress, Inc.," 13 September 1966, SCR# 6-45-3-71-3-1-1, MSSC.

60. Bill Rainey, "12 Man Board Replaces CDGM," *Jackson Daily News*, 30 September 1966, 1; Tougaloo president George Owens agreed to serve as a MAP board member until pressure from CDGM supporters caused him to resign. See Falk, "OEO Decides."

61. Rainey, "12 Man Board"; W. C. Shoemaker, "State Leaders Say Changes Are Coming," *Clarion-Ledger*, 21 February 1965; Crespino, *In Search of Another Country*, 32.

62. "MFDP Challenge to the Democratic Convention," Civil Rights Movement Veterans, http://www.crmvet.org/info/mfdp_atlantic.pdf. Lawrence Guyot, the chairman of the Mississippi Freedom Democratic Party, was in a Mississippi jail cell during the convention, making Fannie Lou Hamer the most senior ranking party official in Atlantic City.

63. Hamlin, *Crossroads at Clarksdale*, 87–89; Payne, *I've Got the Light of Freedom*, 266.

64. Chronology of CDGM Events, box 3, folder 21, CDGM.

65. Rainey, "12 Man Board."

66. Richard Lyons, "House Passes Poverty Bill, 210 to 156," *Washington Post*, 30 September 1966, A1; "OEO Confirms Cutoff of Miss. Preschool Cash," *Washington Post*, 4 October 1966, A2.

67. "OEO Builds Community Action in Mississippi" press releases, 11 October 1966, box 16, SUFOEO; "Stennis Raps OEO for Grant to Rust," *Jackson Daily News*, 13 October 1966; Nicholas von Hoffman, "Manna From OEO Falls on Mississippi," *Washington Post*, 13 October 1966, 1; Chronology of CDGM Events, box 3, folder 21, CDGM; Southwest Mississippi Opportunity Press Release, 11 October 1966, box 38, folder: CDGM, RSS.

68. Von Hoffman, "Manna from OEO."

69. "Items of interest in the MAP application," box 1, folder 10, CDGM.

70. "Mississippi Action for Progress Receives $3 Million Head Start Grant," 11 October 1966, box 16, SUFOEO.

71. "Gov. Johnson Likes Shift From CDGM to MAP," *Clarion-Ledger*, 11 October 1966; Memo to Martin Fraley from Sovereignty Commission Director, 7 October 1966, SCR# 6-45-3-64-1-1-1, MSSC.

72. Memorandum to Jule Sugarman and Ted Berry from Edgar May, 19 November 1966, box 5, folder: CAP/Berry-MS, STFOEO.

73. "Meeting with Marian Wright, Aaron Henry, Rev. McRee," 10 September 1966, box 1, folder 7, CDGM; "Henry Asks Continuance of CDGM," *Clarion-Ledger*, 3 October 1966; telegram to Sargent Shriver from Aaron Henry, 31 October 1966, box 5, folder: CAP/Berry-MS, STFOEO; "Henry Asks for Continuance of CDGM," *Clarion-Ledger*, 3 October 1966; transcript, Henry interview, 57.

74. "Resolutions," 8 October 1966, box 1, folder 8, CDGM; "CDGM Leaders Lash Fund Cuts," *Vicksburg Evening Post*, 10 October 1966. Owen Cooper fought against a minimum wage in Mississippi and prohibited labor unions at Mississippi Chemical Corporation.

75. *American Idealist.*

76. "CDGM Leaders Lash Fund Cuts," *Vicksburg Evening Post*, 10 October 1966.

77. Dittmer, *Local People*, 378.

78. Ibid., 338–43; Meier and Rudwick, *CORE*, 340.

79. Letter to Center Chairman from Dr. Aaron Henry and Charles Evers, October 1966, box 1, folder 9, CDGM.

80. "Cooks, Maids Become Teachers to Keep Project Alive," *Jet*, 2 February 1967, 26.

81. "Why Are We Here?," box 5, folder 17, TL.

82. Memorandum for Sargent Shriver from W. Marvin Watson, 30 November 1966, box 38, folder 3, RSS. Mamie Phipps was also a member of the husband-wife psychologist team whose doll experiment helped to desegregate public schools. Telegram to Ted Berry from Mamie Phipps Clark, 6 October 1966, box 16, SUFOEO; telegram to Sargent Shriver from Jacob Javits, 12 October 1966, box 1, folder 8, CDGM.

83. Letter to Adam Clayton Powell from Sargent Shriver, 11 October 1966, and letter to Sargent Shriver from Ben Neufeld, 12 October 1966, box 16, SUFOEO.

84. "Shriver Denies Pressure On Mississippi Action," *Washington Evening Star*, 19 October 1966.

85. Dick Boone, telephone interview with author, 27 April 2009; William C. Selover, "Shriver Turnabout on Poverty Project Criticized," *Christian Science Monitor*, 19 October 1966, 3.

86. Memorandum to all OEO regional directors and public affairs officers from Herb Kramer, 12 October 1966, box 38, CDGM folder 2 of 3, RSS.

87. Minutes of OEO meeting with CDGM Board, Atlanta, GA, 13 October 1966, box 1, folder 8, CDGM.

88. Ibid.

89. Ibid.

90. Ibid.

91. William R. MacKaye, "3 Churches Threaten to Leave Poverty War," *Washington Post*, 16 October 1966; Greenberg, *Devil Has Slippery Shoes*, 642; Findlay, "The Mainline Churches and Head Start in Mississippi," 237–50.

92. "Say It Isn't So, Sargent Shriver," *New York Times*, 19 October 1966, 35; Boone, interview.

93. "Say It Isn't So," *New York Times*.

94. Jule Sugarman, interview with Stephen Goodell, 14 March 1969, transcript, 34, Lyndon B. Johnson Presidential Library, Austin, Tex.

95. Letter to the *New York Times* editor from Sargent Shriver, 19 October 1966, box 38, RSS (the op-ed ran on 26 October 1966).

96. Eve Edstrom, "Two Top Shriver Aides Quitting; Poor Lost in CDGM Case, One Says," *Washington Post*, 27 November 1966, A6.

97. "OEO Aide on Rights Has Quit," *Washington Post*, 18 February 1967.

98. Transcript of CDGM/OEO meeting in Atlanta, Georgia, 24 October 1966, box 1, folder 9, CDGM.

99. Ibid.; "CDGM Postpones Washington March," *Jackson Daily News*, 5 November 1966.

100. Kotz, *Judgment Days*, 92–93.

101. For more on the gendered division of labor among black educators, see Charron, *Freedom's Teacher*, 63.

102. "CDGM Reports More Than 50 Centers Reopen," *Clarion-Ledger*, 1 November 1966; "CDGM Bulletin Number 4," 14 December 1965, SCR# 6-45-4-91-5-1-1, MSSC.

103. Chester Higgins, "Head Start Agency Takes Toys from Miss. Kids," *Jet*, 2 February 1967, 18–29.

104. Mittelstadt, "Philanthropy, Feminism, and Left Liberalism," 106–8, 114–15.

105. "CDGM Bulletin Number 4," 14 December 1955, SCR# 6-45-4-91-6-1-1, MSSC.

106. "Field Report on Volunteer Centers: Jones County," 20 December 1966, box 1, folder 4, ML.

107. Ibid.

108. Chester Higgins, "Head Start Agency Takes Toys," *Jet*, 2 February 1967, 18–29; "Field Report on Volunteer Centers: Jones County," 20 December 1966, box 1, folder 4, ML.

109. Harwell, "Wednesdays in Mississippi," 652.

110. James Saggus, "Smith Named New Director of MAP," *Clarion-Ledger*, 20 October 1966; letter to Jule Sugarman from Mary Emmons, 16 December 1966, box 1, folder 11, CDGM; memo from Sargent Shriver to Julius Richmond and Jule Sugarman, 11 February 1966, box 40, folder: Staff, Poverty, and Staff Memos, 1966, RSS.

111. Letter to Jule Sugarman from Mary Emmons, 16 December 1966, box 1, folder 11, CDGM.

112. Gillette, *Launching the War on Poverty*, 290.

113. "Mississippi Action for Progress Immediate Openings Advertisement," box 31, folder: Gov.'t., National OEO, CDGM, Aug–Oct 66, Group IV, NAACP; Rowland Evans and Robert Novak, "Inside Report," *Washington Post*, 30 January 1967, 17.

114. Memorandum to Jule Sugarman and Ted Berry from Edgar May, 19 November 1966, box 5, folder: CAP/Berry-MS, STFOEO; "MAP Opens Two Centers," *Clarion-Ledger*, 22 November 1966; James Saggus, "Smith Named New Director of MAP," *Clarion-Ledger*, 20 October 1966.

115. Letter to the Reverend Bryant George from Jule Sugarman, 9 November 1966, box 38, folder: CDGM, RSS; Joseph Loftus, "Head Start Talks Resume In Capital," *New York Times*, 15 December 1966, 40; Eve Edstrom, "Dispute Over New CDGM Funding Appears Near Compromise Solution," *Washington Post*, 17 December 1966, 2.

116. Transcript, Sugarman interview, 38, LBJOH; "Humphrey Would Aid Mississippi Poverty Dispute," *New York Times*, 9 December 1966, 29; Greenberg, *Devil Has Slippery Shoes*, 655.

117. "CDGM to Continue Head Start in Mississippi Press Release," 16 December 1966, box 5, folder: CAP/Berry-MS, STFOEO; Joseph Loftus, "Mississippi Unit Gets Poverty Aid, *New York Times*, 18 December 1966, 63; Loftus, "Mississippi Unit Gets Federal Aid," *New Times*, 31 January 1967, 18.

118. "CDGM to Continue Head Start in Mississippi Press Release," 16 December 1966, box 5, folder: CAP/Berry-MS, STFOEO; letter to President Lyndon B. Johnson from United States senator John Stennis, 5 April 1967, box 42, Gen WE 9, WHCFCF.

119. "U.S. Seeks Grand Jury Action in Mississippi Rights Slayings," *New York Times*, 13 January 1967, 12.

120. Mike Smith, "Johnson Calls OEO Decision 'Incredible,'" *Jackson Daily News*, 23 December 1966.

121. Memo to Theodore Berry from John Dean, 13 January 1967, box 5, folder: CAP/Berry-MS, STFOEO. MAP's original counties were Adams, Claiborne, Jefferson, Warren, Leflore, Yalobusha, Lauderdale, Neshoba, Clarke, Greene, George, Humphreys, and Wayne. See "Friends of the Children of Mississippi," SCR# 6-45-4-88-1-1-1, MSSC.

122. "CDGM Bulletin Number 5," 1 January 1967, SCR# 6-45-4-93-2-1-1, MSSC; report to Governor Paul Johnson from Erle Johnston, 13 July 1967, SCR# 6-45-5-44-1-1-1, MSSC. For an example of how local politics undermined community action outside of Mississippi, see Ashmore, *Carry It On*, 69–70, 257–67.

123. Payne, *I've Got the Light of Freedom*, 36–38, 132–79.

124. "FCM Proposal for Head Start Funds, 1969–1970," box 2, folder 1, HW; Greenberg, *Devil Has Slippery Shoes*, 667.

125. "History of Friends of the Children of Mississippi," box 6, DD.

126. "FCM Proposal for Head Start Funds, 1969–1970," box 2, folder 1, HW; "History of Friends of the Children of Mississippi," box 6, DD.

127. U.S. Congress, Senate, Subcommittee on Employment, Manpower, and Poverty, *Examination of the War on Poverty*, 522–34.

128. Ibid., 584–85.

129. The Leflore County Board of Supervisors voted to end its food commodities program after SNCC began voter registration drives in the area. See Dittmer, *Local People*, 143–45.

130. Ibid., 383–84.

131. *Examination of the War on Poverty*, 595.

132. Joseph Loftus, "Inquiry Told of Relatively Minor Spending Gap by Mississippi," *New York Times*, 11 April 1967, 18.

133. Greenberg, *Devil Has Slippery Shoes*, 658.

134. "NAACP Activity," 12 May 1961, SCR# 2-55-2-59-4-1-1, MSSC; "Letter to the Editor," *Southern Courier*, 11–12 September 1965; Greenberg, *Devil Has Slippery Shoes*, 658–62.

135. John Mudd, telephone interview with author, 22 October 2009.

136. "Negro Heads CDGM, Says OEO Office," *Clarion-Ledger*, 8 September 1967; Hoffman, "Black-White Relations in CDGM," MH.

137. Minutes, CDGM Board Meeting, 23 September 1967, box 1, folder: Bd. Min., LR; Hoffman, "Black-White Relations in CDGM," MH. George Raymond was a civil rights activist who set up the CORE office in Canton in 1963, which conducted most of the voter registration drives in Madison County. See Meier and Rudwick, *CORE*, 271–72.

138. Hoffman, "Ambivalence Toward Authority," MH; memo to File from Erle Johnston, 2 October 1967, SCR# 6-45-5-82-1-1-1, MSSC.

139. "Poverty: The Program Has Friends in Congress," *New York Times*, 13 August 1967, 151; Korstad and Leloudis, *To Right These Wrongs*, 297–300.

140. Gillette, *Launching the War on Poverty*, 189–90. The Green Amendment signaled politicians' disillusionment not only with community action but with the entire War on Poverty. In 1968, amendments to the Economic Opportunity Act prohibited Legal Services, an antipoverty program, from defending anyone indicted for criminal activities. See Naples, *Grassroots Warriors*, 210–11.

141. Gillette, *Launching the War on Poverty*, 329. Congressman James Gardner (R-N.C.) also crafted amendments to the antipoverty bill that limited the political nature of antipoverty programs. His proposal, which was ultimately subsumed in the Green Amendment, "prohibited poverty agencies and its employees from engaging in any partisan or nonpartisan political activity." See Greene, *Our Separate Ways*, 133–34.

142. Joseph A. Loftus, "Senate Votes $1.9-Billion Poverty Bill: Many Private Agencies," *New York Times*, 9 December 1967, 51.

143. Citizens Crusade Against Poverty, "The War on Poverty—Do We Care?," SCR# 6-45-6-50-1-1-1 to SCR# 6-45-6-50-7-1-1, MSSC; "Children Picketing White House to Bar Cuts in Head Start," *New York Times*, 22 April 1968, 33.

144. Elizabeth Shelton Washington, "No Pickets Fence Her Out," *Washington Post*, 22 April 1968, D3; "Start Group Stopped," *Washington Post*, 26 April 1968.

145. CDGM scrapbook, box 45, folder 28, UPC.

146. Johnston, *Mississippi's Defiant Years*, 371–75; Moye, *Let the People Decide*, 177–78; Mills, *This Little Light of Mine*, 226–27.

147. For more on the "culture of poverty," see Patterson, *America's Struggle against Poverty*, 12–14, 114–20.

148. Transcript, Sugarman interview, 29, LBJOH.

149. Orleck and Hazirjian, *War on Poverty*, 453–55.

150. MAP continues to exist in Mississippi. At the time of this writing, MAP operated sixty-one Head Start centers in Mississippi and employed 1,200 people.

151. On 28 February 1963 Travis was shot in the neck and shoulder as he attempted to leave Greenwood, Mississippi. He was with fellow SNCC worker Bob Moses and Voter Education Project field director Randolph Blackwell at the time of the shooting. See Payne, *I've Got the Light of Freedom*, 162–63.

152. Memorandum to File from Erle Johnston, 30 November 1967, SCR# 6-45-6-17-1-1-1, MSSC.

153. Memorandum to Erle Johnston from Lee Cole, 29 December 1967, SCR# 6-45-6-27-1-1-1, MSSC. For more on the Claiborne County boycott, see Crosby, *A Little Taste of Freedom*, esp. 112–68, 199–206.

154. Schmidt and Whalen, "Credentials Contests," 1451.

155. Carter, interview.

156. "Loyal Democrats of Mississippi Press Release," SCR# 3-17A-2-49-1-1-1 to 3-17A-2-49-4-1-1, MSSC; Dittmer, *Local People*, 421.

157. *Examination of the War on Poverty*, 587.

Epilogue

1. Ronald Reagan, "Address Before a Joint Session of Congress on the State of the Union," 25 January 1988.

2. Orleck and Hazirjian, *The War on Poverty*, 6.

3. Sargent Shriver, address, National Association for the Advancement of Colored People, Washington, D.C., 24 June 1964, box 45, folder: Speech, RSS.

4. "Strategic accommodation" was a segregationist practice of measured compliance with civil rights laws. See Crespino, *In Search of Another Country*, 11.

5. Ibid., 240.

6. National Center for Education Statistics.

7. Kuntz, "A Lost Legacy," 28–29; Zigler and Muenchow, *Head Start: The Inside Story*, 109–12.

8. Sarah H. Johnson, interview by Thomas Healy, 10 September 1968, transcript, 14–15, COHCH.

9. Blackwell with Morris, *Barefootin'*, 208–14.

10. Hudson and Curry, *Mississippi Harmony*, 108–10, 126–27

11. Greenberg, *Devil Has Slippery Shoes*, 723–24.

12. Reed Branson, "Judge OK's Ayers vs. Miss. Judgment," *Commercial Appeal,* 16 February 2002.

13. U.S. Census Bureau, 2012 Census of Governments: Survey of School System Finances.

14. "Governor Bryant Recommends Underfunding MAEP," http://msparentscam paign.org/education-funding?id=139.

15. Blackwell with Morris, *Barefootin',* 156.

Bibliography

Primary Sources

MANUSCRIPT COLLECTIONS

Atlanta, Georgia
  Emory University
    Manuscript, Archives, and Rare Book Library
      Doris Derby Papers
    Martin Luther King Jr. Center for Nonviolent Social Change
      Student Nonviolent Coordinating Committee Records, 1959–1972
      Tom Levin Papers
Austin, Texas
  Lyndon Baines Johnson Presidential Library
    Oral History Collection
    Task Force Reports
    White House Central Files
Boston, Massachusetts
  John Fitzgerald Kennedy Presidential Library
    Robert Sargent Shriver Papers
    Adam Yarmolinsky Papers
Carlisle, Pennsylvania
  Community Studies Center, Dickinson College
    Delta Oral History Project
Chicago, Illinois
  Marvin Hoffman Personal Papers
College Park, Maryland
  National Archives II
    Community Services Administration Record Group 381 (OEO),
      1965–1969
Durham, North Carolina
  Duke University
    Behind the Veil: Documenting African American Life in the
      Jim Crow South
    Eura Bowie
Green Castle, Indiana
  John Dittmer Personal Collection

Hattiesburg, Mississippi
   University of Southern Mississippi
      McCain Library and Archives
         David Walls Collection
         Oral History Digital Collection
            Aaron Henry
            Sarah H. Johnson
            Amzie Moore
            Minnie Ripley
            Hollis Watkins
Jackson, Mississippi
   Jackson State University
      Margaret Walker Alexander National Research Center
         Owen Brooks, Frank Hudson, Edna Moneton, and Thelma Barnes
            group interview
      Mississippi Department of Archives and History
         Mississippi State Sovereignty Commission Papers
         Marilyn Lowen Papers
         James McRee Papers
         Hilda Wilson Papers
Madison, Wisconsin
   Wisconsin Historical Society
      Child Development Group of Mississippi Papers, 1964–1969
      Sally Belfrage Papers
      James Houston Papers
      Amzie Moore Papers
Oxford, Mississippi
   University of Mississippi
      James O. Eastland Collection
      James Howard Meredith Collection
Philadelphia, Pennsylvania
   Presbyterian Historical Society
      United Presbyterian Church in the United States of America,
         Board of National Missions
Starkville, Mississippi
   Mississippi State University
      Hodding and Betty Weirlein Carter Papers
      Pat Derian Papers
      Lee Reiff Collection
      John C. Stennis Collection
Tougaloo, Mississippi
   Tougaloo College Archives Oral History Collection

    Mamie McClendon Chinn
    Annie Seaton Smith
Washington, D.C.
  Howard University
    Ralph J. Bunche Oral History Collection
      Unita Blackwell
      Annie Mae King
      Mary Lane
  Library of Congress
    National Association for the Advancement of Colored People Papers

ORAL INTERVIEWS WITH AUTHOR

Alean Adams	5 August 2009, Brandon, Miss.
Lillie Ayers	10 August 2009, Glen Allan, Miss.
Thelma Barnes	10 August 2009, Greenville, Miss.
Valentine Blue	26 September 2009, by telephone
Dick Boone	27 April 2009, by telephone
Hodding Carter III	31 August 2009, Chapel Hill, N.C.
Clarice Coney	6 October 2009, by telephone
Bernard Dinkin	4 November 2013, by telephone
Gaynette Flowers	6 May, 2010, by telephone
Lenore Gensburg	16 April 2010, by telephone
Alice Giles	16 April 2009, by telephone
Polly Greenberg	21 November 2006, by telephone,
	22 September 2009, by telephone,
	25 March 2010, Jackson, Miss.
Jesse Harris	26 March 2010, Jackson, Miss.
Marvin Hoffman	26 October 2009, Chicago, Ill.
Lavaree Jones, Jr., Mahalia Jackson,	
and Quinous Johnson (children	
of Lavaree Jones, Sr.)	24 March 2010, Jackson, Miss.
Marilyn Lowen	27 March 2010, Jackson, Miss.
Charles McLaurin	11 August 2009, Indianola, Miss.
Jim Monsonis	23 April 2009, by telephone
John Mudd	22 October 2009, by telephone
Lucia Mudd	23 June 2010, by telephone
Paul Murray	29 July 2014, by telephone
Robert Smith	15 June 2012, Jackson, Miss.
Eva Tisdale	4 February 2010, by telephone
Peter Titelman	18 February 2012, by telephone
Hollis Watkins	27 March 2010, Jackson, Miss.

NEWSPAPERS AND PERIODICALS

Atlanta Daily World
Chicago Defender
Christian Science Monitor
Clarion-Ledger
Commercial Appeal
Congressional Record
Delta Democrat Times
Ebony
Gazette-Virginian
Hattiesburg American
Jackson Daily News
Jet
Life
*Mississippi Freedom Democratic
    Party Newsletter*
Mississippi Free Press

Nation
New South Student
New York Times
New York Times Magazine
Northeast Mississippi Daily Journal
Opportunity
Philadelphia Inquirer
Philadelphia Tribune
Pittsburgh Courier
Southern Courier
Student Voice
Vicksburg Citizens' Appeal
Vicksburg Evening Post
Washington Evening Star
Washington Post

UNPUBLISHED WORKS

Friedman, Ilana. "Tom Levin and Polly Greenberg's Reflections on the Rise and
    Demise of the Child Development Group of Mississippi." Undergraduate honors
    thesis, Brown University, 2004.
Vernazza, Diana. "Who Killed the Child Development Group of Mississippi? The
    Local Politics of the War on Poverty." Undergraduate honors thesis, Dartmouth
    College, 2001.
Ward, Jason Morgan. "Caught Between Two Wars: Poverty Politics, Draft Resis-
    tance, and a Mississippi Family's Freedom Struggle." Conference paper,
    University of Southern Mississippi, 2010.

GOVERNMENT DOCUMENTS

*Annual Report of the Superintendent of Public Education of the State of Mississippi for
    the Year Ending December 31, 1871.* Jackson, Miss.: Kimball, Raymond and Co.,
    State Printers, 1872.
*Biennial Report and Recommendations of the State Superintendent of Public Education to
    the Legislature of Mississippi for the Scholastic Years 1913–1914 and 1914–1915, 1943–1944
    and 1944–1945.* Jackson, Miss.: State of Mississippi, Department of Public Education.
Economic Opportunity Act of 1964, Pub. L. 88-452, 78 Stat. 508, 1964.
Eighth Semi-Annual Report on Schools for Freedmen, 1 July 1869. Washington, D.C.:
    Government Printing Office, 1869.
Hutchinson, A., comp. *Code of Mississippi: Being an Analytical Compilation of the
    Public and General Statutes of the Territory and State, with Tabular References to the
    Local and Private Acts, from 1798–1848.* Jackson, Miss., 1848.

Jones, Jean Yavis and Jan Fowler. *The Head Start Program—History, Legislation, Issues, and Funding—1964–1982, Report No. 82–93.* Congressional Research Service, Washington, D.C., 1982.

Journal of the Proceedings in the Constitutional Convention of the State of Mississippi, 1868. Jackson, Miss.: E. Stafford, 1871.

Laws of the State of Mississippi Passed at a Regular Session of the Mississippi Legislature. Jackson, Miss.: Kimball, Raymond, and Co., State Printers, 1870.

Memorial Tributes Delivered in Congress: John Cornelius Stennis, 1901–1995, Late a Senator from Mississippi. Washington, D.C.: Government Printing Office, 1996.

The Quiet Revolution: Office of Economic Opportunity 2nd Annual Report. Washington, D.C.: Government Printing Office, 1967.

Reports of Cases Decided by the Supreme Court of Mississippi at the October Term, 1892 and March Term, 1893, vol. 70. Nashville, Tenn.: Marshall and Bruce Co., Law Publishers, 1893.

Semi-Annual Report on Schools for Freedmen. Washington, D.C.: Government Printing Office, 1866.

U.S. Commission on Civil Rights. *Voting in Mississippi.* Washington, D.C., 1965.

U.S. Congress. *Congressional Record.* 89th Cong., 1st sess., 1966.

U.S. Congress. House. Committee on House Administration. *Papers Omitted in Printing Pursuant to Provisions of the Statutes Involving the Five Congressional Districts in the State of Mississippi.* 89th Cong., 1st sess., 1965. Washington, D.C.: Government Printing Office, 1965.

U.S. Congress. House. Committee on the Judiciary. *Civil Rights Act of 1963* (the bill originally had the date 1963 when it first went to committee). 88th Cong., 1st sess., 1963, H.Rep.

U.S. Congress. Senate. Appropriations Subcommittee. *Supplemental Appropriations Hearing for 1966.* 89th Cong., 1st sess., 14 October 1965. Washington, D.C.: Government Printing Office, 1967.

U.S. Congress. Senate. Subcommittee on Employment, Manpower, and Poverty. *Examination of the War on Poverty. Part 2: Jackson Mississippi.* 90th Cong., 1st sess., 10 April 1967. Washington, D.C.: Government Printing Office, 1967.

VIDEO AND SOUND RECORDINGS

American Idealist: The Story of Sargent Shriver. Produced by Bruce Orenstein. Chicago Video Project, 2006. DVD.

America's War on Poverty: Given A Chance. Produced by Henry Hampton. Alexandria, Va.: Blackside, Incorporated, 1995. Videocassette.

A Chance for Change. Produced by Tom Levin, Adam Gifford, Ellen Gifford, and Science Film Services, 1965. Videocassette.

Head Start: With the Child Development Group of Mississippi. Washington, D.C.: Smithsonian Folkways Records, 1967. Compact disc.

WEBSITES

Civil Rights Movement Veterans. http://www.crmvet.org. 15 August 2013.
Emery, Kathy, Sylvia Braselmann, and Linda Gold, eds. "Freedom School
    Curriculum: Mississippi Freedom Summer, 1964." http://www
    .educationanddemocracy.org/FSCpdf/CurrTextOnlyAll.pdf. 12 July 2014.
Eyes on the Prize II Interviews, Washington University Digital Gateway Texts,
    http://digital.wustl.edu/e/eii/. 18 August 2014.
Inflation Calculator. http://www.coinnews.net/tools/cpi-inflation-calculator/.
Mississippi Civil Rights Project. http://mscivilrightsproject.org. 6 June 2015.
National Center for Education Statistics. http://nces.ed.gov/programs/digest/d13
    /tables/dt13_203.70.asp. 20 July 2014.
U.S. Census Bureau. http://www2.census.gov/govs/school/current_spending.pdf.
    19 July 2014.

Secondary Sources

Adickes, Sandra E. *The Legacy of a Freedom School*. New York: Palgrave Macmillan,
    2005.
Aiken, Charles S. *The Cotton Plantation South Since the Civil War*. Baltimore: Johns
    Hopkins University Press, 1998.
Anderson, James D. *The Education of Blacks in the South, 1860–1935*. Chapel Hill:
    University of North Carolina Press, 1988.
Andrews, Kenneth. *Freedom Is a Constant Struggle: The Mississippi Civil Rights
    Movement and Its Legacy*. Chicago: University of Chicago Press, 2004.
———. "Social Movements and Policy Implementation: The Mississippi Civil Rights
    Movement and the War on Poverty, 1965 to 1971." *American Sociological Review* 66
    (February 2001): 71–95.
Asch, Christopher Myers. *The Senator and the Sharecropper: The Freedom Struggles of
    James O. Eastland and Fannie Lou Hamer*. New York: The New Press, 2008.
Ashmore, Susan Youngblood. *Carry It On: The War on Poverty and the Civil Rights
    Movement in Alabama, 1964–1972*. Athens: University of Georgia Press, 2008.
Barry, John M. *Rising Tide: The Great Mississippi Flood of 1927 and How It Changed
    America*. New York: Simon and Schuster, 1998.
Belfrage, Sally. *Freedom Summer*. Charlottesville: University of Virginia Press, 1990.
Blackwell, Unita, with JoAnne Prichard Morris. *Barefootin': Life Lessons from the
    Road to Freedom*. New York: Crown Publishers, 2006.
Bolton, Charles C. *The Hardest Deal of All: The Battle Over School Integration in
    Mississippi, 1870–1980*. Jackson: University Press of Mississippi, 2007.
———. "Mississippi's School Equalization Program, 1945–1954: A Last Gasp to Try
    to Maintain a Segregated Educational System." *Journal of Southern History* 66
    (November 2000): 781–814.

Branch, Taylor. *Pillar of Fire: America in the King Years, 1963–1965.* New York: Simon and Schuster, 1998.

Carson, Clayborne. *In Struggle: SNCC and the Black Awakening of the 1960s.* Cambridge, Mass.: Harvard University Press, 1995.

Carter, David C. *The Music Has Gone Out of the Movement: Civil Rights and the Johnson Administration, 1965–1968.* Chapel Hill: University of North Carolina Press, 2009.

Cazenave, Noel. *Impossible Democracy: The Unlikely Success of the War on Poverty Community Action Programs.* Albany: State University of New York Press, 2007.

Charron, Katherine Mellen. *Freedom's Teacher: The Life of Septima Clark.* Chapel Hill: University of North Carolina Press, 2009.

Charron, Katherine Mellen, and David P. Cline. "'I Train the People to Do Their Own Talking': Septima Clark and Women in the Civil Rights Movement." *Southern Cultures* (June 2010): 31–52.

Chilcoat, George, and Jerry A. Ligon, "'We Talk Here. This Is a School for Talking.' Participatory Democracy from the Classroom to the Community: How Discussion Was Used in the Mississippi Freedom Schools." *Curriculum Inquiry* 28, no. 2 (Summer 1998): 165–93.

Cimbala, Paul. *Under the Guardianship of the Nation: The Freedmen's Bureau and the Reconstruction of Georgia, 1865–1870.* Athens: University of Georgia Press, 1997.

Cobb, Charles E., Jr. "Prospectus for a Summer Freedom School Program in Mississippi." *Racial Teacher* 40 (Fall 1991): 36.

———. *This Nonviolent Stuff'll Get You Killed: How Guns Made the Civil Rights Movement Possible.* New York: Basic Books, 2014.

Cobb, James C. *The Most Southern Place on Earth: The Mississippi Delta and the Roots of Regional Identity.* New York: Oxford University Press, 1992.

———. "Somebody Done Nailed Us on the Cross: Federal Farm and Welfare Policy and the Civil Rights Movement in the Mississippi Delta." *Journal of American History* (December 1990): 912–36.

Collins, Patricia Hill. "The Meaning of Motherhood in Black Culture." In *The Black Family: Essays and Studies,* edited by Robert Staples, 157–66. Belmont, Calif.: Wadsworth Publishing Company, 1998.

Crespino, Joseph. *In Search of Another Country: Mississippi and the Conservative Counterrevolution.* Princeton: Princeton University Press, 2007.

Cresswell, Stephen. *Rednecks, Redeemers, and Race: Mississippi after Reconstruction.* Jackson: University Press of Mississippi, 2006.

Crosby, Emilye. *A Little Taste of Freedom: The Black Freedom Struggle in Claiborne County, Mississippi.* Chapel Hill: University of North Carolina Press, 2005.

Curry, Constance, et al. *Deep in Our Hearts: Nine White Women in the Freedom Movement.* Athens: University of Georgia Press, 2002.

Dailey, Jane, Glenda Gilmore, and Bryson Simon. *Jumpin' Jim Crow: Southern Politics from Civil War to Civil Rights.* Princeton: Princeton University Press, 2000.

Daniel, Pete. *Breaking the Land: The Transformation of Cotton, Tobacco, and Rice Cultures Since 1800*. Urbana: University of Illinois Press, 1985.

———. *Dispossession: Discrimination against African American Farmers in the Age of Civil Rights*. Chapel Hill: University of North Carolina Press, 2013.

Davis, Rebecca Miller. "The Three R's—Reading, 'Riting, and Race: The Evolution of Race in Mississippi History Textbooks, 1900–1995." *Journal of Mississippi History* 72, no. 1 (Spring 2010): 1–45.

Dittmer, John. *The Good Doctors: The Medical Committee for Human Rights and the Struggle for Social Justice in Health Care*. New York: Bloomsbury Press, 2009.

———. *Local People: The Struggle for Civil Rights in Mississippi*. Urbana: University of Illinois, 1994.

Draper, Alan. *Conflicts of Interests: Organized Labor and the Civil Rights Movement in the South, 1954–1968*. Ithaca, N.Y.: ILR Press, 1994.

Du Bois, W. E. B. *Black Reconstruction: An Essay toward a History of the Part Which Black Folk Played in the Attempt to Reconstruct Democracy in America, 1860–1880*. New York: Russell and Russell, 1935.

———. *The Negro Common School: Report of a Social Study Made under the Direction of Atlanta University by the Sixth Atlanta Conference*. Atlanta: Atlanta University Press, 1901.

Dunning, William. *Reconstruction: Political and Economic, 1865–1877*. New York, Harper and Row, 1907.

Eagles, Charles. *The Price of Defiance: James Meredith and the Integration of Ole Miss*. Chapel Hill: University of North Carolina Press, 2009.

Emery, Kathy, Linda Reid Gold, and Sylvia Braselmann. *Lessons from Freedom Summer: Ordinary People Building Extraordinary Movements*. Monroe, Maine: Common Courage Press, 2008.

Fairclough, Adam. *A Class of Their Own: Black Teachers in the Segregated South*. Cambridge, Mass.: Belknap Press of Harvard University Press, 2007.

———. *Race and Democracy: The Civil Rights Struggle in Louisiana, 1915–1972*. Athens: University of Georgia Press, 1995.

Findlay, James F. *Church People in the Struggle: The National Council of Churches and the Black Freedom Movement, 1950–1970*. New York: Oxford University Press, 1993.

———. "The Mainline Churches and the Head Start in Mississippi: Religious Activism in the Sixties." *Church History* 64 (June 1995): 237–50.

Foner, Eric. *Reconstruction: America's Unfinished Revolution 1863–1877*. New York: Harper and Row Publishers, 1988.

Franklin, V. P., and Julian Savage Carter, eds. *Cultural Capital and Black Education: African American Communities and the Funding of Black Schooling, 1865 to the Present*. Greenwich, Conn.: Information Age Publishing, 2004.

Friedman, Tami J. "Exploiting the North-South Differential: Corporate Power, Southern Politics, and the Decline of Organized Labor after World War II." *Journal of American History* 95 (September 2008): 323–48.

Fry, Joseph A. *Debating Vietnam: Fulbright, Stennis, and Their Senate Hearings*. New York: Rowman and Littlefield Publishers, 2006.

Germany, Kent B. *New Orleans After the Promises: Poverty, Citizenship, and the Search for the Great Society*. Athens: University of Georgia Press, 2007.

Giddings, Paula. *When and Where I Enter: The Impact of Black Women on Race and Sex in America*. New York: William Morrow and Company, 1984.

Gillette, Michael L. *Launching the War on Poverty: An Oral History*. New York: Twayne Publishers, 1996.

Graham, Hugh Davis. *Civil Rights and the Presidency: Race and Gender in American Politics, 1960–1972*. New York: Oxford University Press, 1992.

Green, Adam. *Selling the Race: Culture, Community and Black Chicago, 1940–1955*. Chicago: University of Chicago Press, 2007.

Greenberg, Polly. *The Devil Has Slippery Shoes*. New York: MacMillan, 1969.

Greene, Christina. *Our Separate Ways: Women and the Black Freedom Movement in Durham, North Carolina*. Chapel Hill: University of North Carolina Press, 2005.

Hahn, Steven. *A Nation Under Our Feet: Black Political Struggles in the Rural South from Slavery to the Great Migration*. Cambridge, Mass.: Belknap Press of Harvard University Press, 2003.

Hamer, Fannie Lou. "To Praise Our Bridges." In *Mississippi Writers: Reflection of Childhood and Youth, Volume II: Nonfiction*, edited by Dorothy Abbott, 321–30. Jackson: University Press of Mississippi, 1986.

Hamlin, Francoise N. *Crossroads at Clarksdale: The Black Freedom Struggle in the Mississippi Delta after World War II*. Chapel Hill: University of North Carolina Press, 2012.

Harwell, Debbie Z. "Wednesdays in Mississippi: United Women Across Regional and Racial Lines, Summer 1964." *The Journal of Southern History* 76 (August 2010): 617–54.

Height, Dorothy. *Open Wide the Freedom Gates: A Memoir*. New York: Public Affairs, 2003.

Henry, Aaron with Constance Curry. *Aaron Henry: The Fire Ever Burning*. Jackson: University Press of Mississippi, 2000.

Hilton, Bruce. *The Delta Ministry*. New York: Collier Macmillan, 1969.

Holsaert, Faith S., et al., eds. *Hands on the Freedom Plow: Personal Accounts by Women in SNCC*. Urbana: University of Illinois Press, 2010.

Hudson, Winson, and Constance Curry. *Mississippi Harmony: Memoirs of a Freedom Fighter*. New York: Palgrave MacMillan, 2002.

Jeffries, Hassan. *Bloody Lowndes: Civil Rights and Black Power in Alabama's Black Belt*. New York: New York University Press, 2009.

Johnston, Erle. *Mississippi's Defiant Years, 1953–1973: An Interpretive Documentary with Personal Experiences*. Forest, Miss.: Lake Harbor Publishers, 1990.

Joseph, Peniel. *Stokely: A Life*. New York: Basic Civitas, 2014.

Irons, Jenny. *Reconstituting Whiteness: The Mississippi State Sovereignty Commission.* Nashville, Tenn.: Vanderbilt University Press, 2010.

Katagiri, Yasuhiro. *The Mississippi State Sovereignty Commission: Civil Rights and States' Rights.* Jackson: University Press of Mississippi, 2001.

Katznelson, Ira. *When Affirmative Action was White: An Untold History of Racial Inequality in Twentieth-Century America.* New York: W.W. Norton and Company, 2006.

Korstad, Robert Rodgers, and James Leloudis. *To Right These Wrongs: The North Carolina Fund and the Battle to End Poverty and Inequality in 1960s America.* Chapel Hill: University of North Carolina Press, 2010.

Kotz, Nick. *Judgment Days: Lyndon Baines Johnson, Martin Luther King, Jr., and the Laws that Changed America.* New York: Houghton Mifflin, 2005.

Kuntz, Kathryn R. "A Lost Legacy: Head Start's Origins in Community Action." In *Critical Perspectives on Project Head Start: Revisioning the Hope and Challenge,* edited by Jeanne Ellsworth and Lynda J. Ames, 1–48. Albany: State University of New York Press, 1998.

Lerner, Gerda, ed. *Black Women in White America: A Documentary History.* New York: Vintage Books, 1992.

Loevy, Robert D. *The Civil Rights Act of 1964: The Passage of the Law that Ended Segregation.* Albany: State University of New York, 1997.

Loewen, James, and Charles Sallis. *Mississippi: Conflict and Change.* New York: Pantheon Books, 1974.

Marshall, James P. *Student Activism and Civil Rights in Mississippi: Protest Politics and the Struggle for Racial Justice, 1960–1965.* Baton Rouge: Louisiana State University Press, 2013.

Mason, Gilbert and James Patterson Smith. *Beaches, Blood, and Ballots: A Black Doctor's Civil Rights Struggles.* Jackson: University Press of Mississippi, 2007.

Matusow, Allen. *The Unraveling of America: A History of Liberalism in the 1960s.* New York: Harper and Row, 1984.

McAdam, Doug. *Freedom Summer.* New York: Oxford University Press, 1988.

McMillen, Neil R. *The Citizens' Council: Organized Resistance to the Second Reconstruction.* Urbana: University of Illinois Press, 1971.

———. *Dark Journey: Black Mississippians in the Age of Jim Crow.* Urbana: University of Illinois, 1989.

McPherson, Harry. *A Political Education.* Boston: Little Press, 1992.

Meier, August, and Elliot Rudwick. *CORE: A Study in the Civil Rights Movement.* Urbana: University of Illinois Press, 1973.

Mills, Kay. *Something Better for My Children: The History and People of Head Start.* New York: Dutton, 1998.

———. *This Little Light of Mine: The Life of Fannie Lou Hamer.* Lexington: University of Kentucky Press, 2007.

Mittelstadt, Jennifer. "Philanthropy, Feminism, and Left Liberalism, 1960–1985." *Journal of Women's History* 20, no. 4 (Winter 2008): 105–31.

Moody, Anne. *Coming of Age in Mississippi: The Classic Autobiography of Growing Up Poor and Black in the Rural South*. New York: Dell, 1968.

Moye, J. Todd. "Discovering What's Already There: Mississippi Women and the Civil Rights Movement." In *Mississippi Women: Their Histories, Their Lives*, vol. 2, edited by Martha H. Swain, Marjorie Julian Spruill, and Brenda M. Eagles, 263. Athens: University of Georgia Press, 2010.

———. *Let the People Decide: Black Freedom and White Resistance Movements in Sunflower County, Mississippi, 1945–1986*. Chapel Hill: University of North Carolina Press, 2004.

Moynihan, Daniel P. *Maximum Feasible Misunderstanding: Community Action in the War on Poverty*. New York: Free Press, 1969.

Murray, Charles. *Losing Ground: American Social Policy 1950–1980*. New York: Basic Books, 1984.

Naples, Nancy. *Grassroots Warriors: Activist Mothering, Community Work, and the War on Poverty*. New York: Routledge, 1998.

Newfield, Jack. *A Prophetic Minority*. New York: New American Library, 1966.

Newman, Mark. *Divine Agitators: The Delta Ministry and Civil Rights in Mississippi*. Athens: University of Georgia Press, 2004.

———. "Hazel Brannon Smith: Journalist Under Siege." In *Mississippi Women: Their Histories, Their Lives*, vol. 1, edited by Martha H. Swain, Elizabeth Anne Payne, and Marjorie Julian Spruill, 220–34. Athens: University of Georgia Press, 2003.

Nieman, Donald. *To Set the Law in Motion: the Freedmen's Bureau and the Legal Rights of Blacks, 1865–1868*. Millwood, N.Y.: KTO Press, 1979.

Noble, Stuart Grayson. *Forty Years of the Public Schools in Mississippi, with Special Reference to the Education of the Negro*. New York: Teachers College, Columbia University, 1918.

O'Reilly, Kenneth. *"Racial Matters": The FBI's Secret File on Black America, 1960–1972*. New York: Free Press, 1992.

Orleck, Annelise. *Storming Caesars Palace: How Black Mothers Fought Their Own War on Poverty*. Boston: Beacon Press, 2005.

Orleck, Annelise, and Lisa Gayle Hazirjian, eds. *The War on Poverty: A New Grassroots History, 1964–1980*. Athens: University of Georgia Press, 2011.

Parker, Frank R. *Black Votes Count: Political Empowerment in Mississippi after 1965*. Chapel Hill: University of North Carolina Press, 1990.

Patterson, James T. *America's Struggle against Poverty in the Twentieth Century*. Cambridge, Mass.: Harvard University Press, 2000.

Payne, Charles M. *I've Got the Light of Freedom: The Organizing Tradition and the Mississippi Freedom Struggle*. Berkeley: University of California Press, 1995.

———. "Men Led, but Women Organized: Movement Participation of Women in the Mississippi Delta." In *Women in the Civil Rights Movement: Trailblazers and Torchbearers, 1941–1965,* edited by Vickie L. Crawford, Jacqueline Rouse, and Barbara Woods. 1–11, Bloomington: Indiana University Press, 1993.

Payne, Charles M., and Carol Sills Strickland. *Teach Freedom: Education for Liberation in the African American Tradition.* New York: Teachers College Press, 2008.

Rainwater, Lee, and William L. Yancey. *The Moynihan Report and the Politics of Controversy.* Cambridge, Mass.: MIT Press, 1967.

Ransby, Barbara. *Ella Baker and the Black Freedom Movement: A Radically Democratic Vision.* Chapel Hill: University of North Carolina Press, 2003.

Reinhard, Rachel B. "Politics of Change: The Mississippi Freedom Democratic Party and the Emergence of a Black Political Voice in Mississippi." Ph.D. diss., University of California, Berkeley, 2005.

Ritterhouse, Jennifer. *Growing Up Jim Crow: How Black and White Southern Children Learned Race.* Chapel Hill: University of North Carolina Press, 2006.

Rogers, Kim Lacy. *Life and Death in the Delta: African American Narratives of Violence, Resilience, and Social Change.* New York: Palgrave Macmillan, 2006.

Rural Organizing and Cultural Center. *Minds Stayed on Freedom: The Civil Rights Struggle in the Rural South: An Oral History.* Boulder: Westview Press, 1991.

Schmidt, John R., and Wayne W. Whalen. "Credentials Contests at the 1968— and 1972—Democratic National Conventions." *Harvard Law Review* 82 (May 1969): 1438–70.

Shaw, Stephanie J. *What a Woman Ought to Be and Do: Black Professional Women during the Jim Crow Era.* Chicago: University of Chicago Press, 1996.

Silver, James W. *Mississippi: The Closed Society.* New York: Harcourt, 1964.

Sojourner, Sue [Lorenzi], with Cheryl Reitan. *Thunder of Freedom: Black Leadership and the Transformation of 1960s Mississippi.* Lexington: University of Kentucky Press, 2012.

Span, Christopher. *From Cotton Field to Schoolhouse: African American Education in Mississippi, 1862–1875.* Chapel Hill: University of North Carolina Press, 2009.

Stossel, Scott. *Sarge: The Life and Times of Sargent Shriver.* Washington, D.C.: Smithsonian Books, 2004.

Sturkey, William. "'Crafts of Freedom': The Poor People's Corporation and Working-Class African American Women's Activism for Black Power." *Journal of Mississippi History* 74, no. 1 (Spring 2012): 25–60.

Sturkey, William and John N. Hale, eds. *To Write in the Light of Freedom: The Newspapers of the 1964 Mississippi Freedom Schools.* Jackson: University Press of Mississippi, 2015.

Sumrall, John Otis. "Freedom at Home." In *We Won't Go: Personal Accounts of War Objectors,* edited by Alice Lynd, 87–91. Boston: Beacon Press, 1968.

Sundquist, James L., ed. *On Fighting Poverty: Perspectives from Experiences.* New York: Basic Books, 1969.

Umoja, Akinyele K. *We Will Shoot Back: Armed Resistance in the Mississippi Freedom Movement.* New York: New York University Press, 2013.

Vinovskis, Maris. *The Birth of Head Start: Preschool Education Policies in the Kennedy and Johnson Administrations.* Chicago: University of Chicago Press, 2005.

Ward, Jason Morgan. *Defending White Democracy: The Making of a Segregationist Movement and the Remaking of Racial Politics, 1936–1965.* Chapel Hill: University of North Carolina Press, 2011.

White, Deborah Gray. *Too Heavy a Load: Black Women in Defense of Themselves, 1894–1994.* New York: W. W. Norton, 1999.

Williams, Heather Andrea. *Self-Taught: African American Education in Slavery and Freedom.* Chapel Hill: University of North Carolina Press, 2005.

Wilson, Charles H. *Education for Negroes in Mississippi Since 1910.* Boston: Meador Publishing Company, 1947.

Woodruff, Nan Elizabeth. *American Congo: The African American Freedom Struggle in the Delta.* Cambridge, Mass.: Harvard University Press, 2003.

Wright, Richard. *Black Boy: A Record of Childhood and Youth.* New York: Harper and Row, 1945.

Zigler, Edward, and Susan Muenchow. *Head Start: The Inside Story of America's Most Successful Educational Experiment.* New York: Basic Books, 1992.

Zinn, Howard. *The Zinn Reader: Writings on Disobedience and Democracy.* New York: Seven Stories Press, 1997.

Zoo Book. Jackson, MS: Child Development Group of Mississippi, 1966.

Index